Language development and social interaction in blind children

Miguel Pérez-Pereira
University of Santiago de Compostela, Spain

Gina Conti-Ramsden
University of Manchester, UK

Psychology Press
a member of the Taylor & Francis group

Psychology Press Ltd
27 Church Road
Hove
East Sussex, BN3 2FA
UK

British Library Cataloguing in Publication Data

A catalogue record for this book is available from the British Library

Library of Congress Cataloging-in-Publication Data are available

ISBN 0-86377-795-3
ISSN 0959-3977

Typeset by Facing Pages, Southwick, West Sussex
Printed and bound in the United Kingdom by Biddles Ltd, Guildford and King's Lynn.

Para nuestras familias.
Para John y Magoya,
para Pedro, Michael, Frances y Filipito,
que tuvieron que soportar largas horas de ausencia.

Contents

About the authors

Miguel Pérez-Pereira is Professor of Developmental Psychology at the University of Santiago de Compostela, Spain. He is the author of several books on child development and language acquisition.

Gina Conti-Ramsden is Professor of Child Language and Learning at the University of Manchester, UK. She is the author of several books on language disorders in children.

Preface

This books aims not only to interest developmental psychologists, but also to engage students and scientists in other disciplines such as speech-language pathology, linguistics, cognitive science, and education in the debates surrounding blind children's linguistic and social development. We also hope, however, that the book will help establish the study of atypical populations as a serious theoretical science capable of contributing to the discussion of how language is learned, and not as merely an interesting applied sideline of normal development mostly relevant to clinicians.

A book such as this one can only be produced with much support from a number of sources. In our case, we gratefully acknowledge the generous support of the University of Santiago de Compostela and the University of Manchester. In particular we want to thank the Centre for Educational Needs and its Director, Mel Ainscow, for much needed collegiate and financial support. During the writing of the book Miguel Pérez-Pereira was supported by an academic leave from the University of Santiago de Compostela and Gina Conti-Ramsden was also supported by an academic leave from the University of Manchester. Miguel Pérez Pereira's research has been supported by a number of grants from the Ministerio de Educación y Ciencia (CICYT) of the Spanish Government and the Consellería de Educación of the Galician Autonomic Government. Gina Conti-Ramsden's research on parent–child interaction has been supported by the University of Manchester Research Support Grant and a March of Dimes Grant (12-FY91-0835).

Support from our colleagues has been extremely generous as well. Most importantly, a number of colleagues read portions of the manuscript and provided useful and insightful suggestions. We thank those who read selected chapters and in some cases the whole manuscript. Thank you Alison Garton, Jana Iverson, Chris

Kiernan, Ann Peters, Danny Povinelli, and Bob Stillman. We also want to thank those colleagues with whom we have had many fruitful discussions and who without a doubt influenced our thinking: Martyn Barrett, Nicola Botting, Juan Carlos Gómez and Mike Tomasello. Thank you all. We of course hold none of them responsible for the particular focus we have chosen for the book nor for any errors or omissions that may remain.

Finally, we also want to thank another set of silent partners who contributed to this book. We are grateful to the editors and production staff of Psychology Press, to the anonymous reviewers, and to Hilda Procter, Gina Conti-Ramsden's secretary.

Miguel Pérez-Pereira
Gina Conti-Ramsden
Montecelo, Vigo, Spain, December 1998

CHAPTER ONE

Introduction: The study of blind children's development

BLIND CHILDREN AND DEVELOPMENTAL PSYCHOLOGY

The study of children with visual disabilities is an interesting realm of research for two reasons. On the one hand, there are practical reasons. Knowledge about how blind children develop can help us design new techniques of intervention and offer blind children better services to improve their quality of life. In this connection, the study of blind children is particularly important in providing information for the development of educational programmes for blind children and for the implementation of intervention programmes. In addition, intervention programmes may be able to help us better understand how educational and environmental changes affect blind children's development. It is important that we allow intervention studies to have a more central role in theoretical discussions about the importance of environment in development. At present such studies have been valued mostly for their immediate practical interest without regard to the possible contribution that well-designed and well-controlled intervention studies can provide to theory.

On the other hand, the study of blind children's development constitutes a unique opportunity to study the effect of vision on development. Thus, congenitally blind children without added handicaps allow us to study how lack of vision affects human development. In this regard, congenitally blind children provide us with what can be called a natural experiment. For this reason, the study of blind children's development will help us to get a better understanding of more general issues surrounding developmental processes. Lewis and Collis (1997b) have suggested a number of areas which can be illuminated by the findings of the studies of children with disabilities. These may help scholars to elucidate whether certain achievements are a prerequisite for later achievements, as well as interdependencies between developmental processes. For example, the issue of the cognitive underpinnings of a first language may be tested with data from research with blind children, who, in general, show a delay in their early cognitive development (see Chapter 2). As Lewis and Collis (1997b) point out, the fact that two different behaviours emerge at the same time in normally developing children does not imply that there exists a relationship of dependency between them. The results of the studies of children with disabilities may help us to view things from a different perspective. These results may also be useful to readjust the importance given to certain aspects of psychological functioning. Traditionally, normal children have been seen as a benchmark of achievement and as exemplars of what areas may be of interest in development. This approach disregards or overlooks important phenomena which may arise more clearly in children with disabilities. Concerning vision in particular, Developmental Psychology has traditionally given visual information an important role in development to the detriment of other aspects of development, such as language and the information it provides to human beings. The study of blind children's development may contribute to these issues being reconsidered. We need to have bi-directional influences in our understanding of development from research with normal, sighted children and from research with children with disability/impairments such as blindness.

From a theoretical point of view, the study of blind children's development has been approached from different perspectives. Roughly, two approaches to the study of blind children may be discerned. The first perspective, which was predominant in the field for many years, views blind children's development in terms of the normal developmental milestones achieved by other non-impaired children. Discrepancies between blind children and sighted children are attributed to visual impairment. As Webster and Roe (1998) have indicated, this approach assumes a "visual impairment as deficit" model and tends to locate the causes of delay inside the child. Furthermore, this deficit stance adopts a homogeneous view of development, according to which all the children follow a similar pattern of development. Individual differences are not seriously taken into account, and there is no room for considering different routes or patterns of development.

In contrast, the second perspective contemplates the possibility that children may show different routes and styles of development. Blind children may use different strategies and learning styles through which they can compensate for the absence of visual information by paying more attention to other sources of information. This may result in blind children following different routes in development. The consideration of differences in developmental patterns is even more pertinent if we take into consideration that the population of blind people is highly heterogeneous. Blind children vary in their aetiologies or causes of blindness, which produces important individual differences, they also vary in their degree of vision, even within the category of legal blindness, in the existence or not of additional handicaps, in the time when visual loss took place, and so on. Moreover, environmental variables, such as parental styles of rearing, educational practices, available social services, etc., may vary greatly around the world, and the development of blind children can be affected by these circumstances. All these reasons should make researchers who are interested in blind children less reluctant to adopt an individual differences approach (Warren, 1994). In Chapter 4 we will return to this issue.

THE CHILDREN IN QUESTION

It is difficult to know with certainty how many people are blind because registers are not always reliable (Webster & Roe, 1998). It is even more difficult to know the incidence of blindness in childhood, and specially congenital blindness. Figures vary depending on the institution which offers the data. Discrepancies between the criteria used to define blindness in different countries adds complexity to the task. In general, the prevalence of visual impairment under the age of 16 as estimated by the Royal National Institute for the Blind in Great Britain reaches 1 in 1000 children (Walker, Tobin, & McKennell, 1992). In Spain, the estimate of visual impairment prevalence reaches 1.63 per 1000. According to the data of the ONCE (Organización Nacional de Ciegos de España, "Spanish National Organisation for the Blind"), 44% of the population of blind people were born blind, and 24% of the total population of blind people lost vision from 1 to 15 years of age (Alvira, 1988; Rosa, 1993). Therefore, 68% of the total population of blind people were blind under 16 years of age, which makes a prevalence of blindness under 16 years of age of 1.1 in 1000. This figure is very similar to the estimates for Great Britain. Estimates of the population of children born blind in Spain are predicted to reach 0.7 in 1000. Guralnick and Bennett (1987) discuss a prevalence of 0.4 per 1000 of developmental disability due to visual impairment in the early years in the USA.

As already pointed out, there are differences among countries in how legal blindness or visual impairment are defined. For example, a person is considered blind if he or she has a visual acuity after correction which is equal or less than 3/60 in UK, 20/200 in EEUU, or 1/20 (80% of visual loss) in Spain. Partial sight is defined as visual acuity between 3/60 and 6/60 in UK, and 20/200 and 20/80 in USA. None the less, many legally blind children may have some degree of vision, and individual differences exist among children who are considered blind. Children may become blind as a consequence of different aetiologies, which may bring about differences in their degree of vision, and the existence or not of additional disabilities (see Webster & Roe, 1998 for a clear summary). Even though two children have identical visual acuity, they may show important differences, depending on their styles of learning, developments of other areas, everyday experiences, etc. This means that researchers must look at individual differences and diversity all along. Individual differences have been observed among typically developing children also. Notwithstanding, the individual differences that sighted children show are magnified in the blind population.

Our hypothesis is that the environment may play a more critical role in the development of blind children than in other handicaps or in non-impaired children. Or to put it in other words, blind children may be able to exploit a conducive, supportive environment in order for them to learn. This is in sharp contrast to what is evident in children with autism in that such children lack the ability to "make use" of the information and support provided by the environment (Davidson & Harrison, 1997; Dawson & Osterling, 1997). This contrast between children with autism and blind children illustrates the different effects that the environment has depending on the nature of children's disabilities. For example, blind children are able to make use of routines used by their parents to promote their cognitive, social, and linguistic development (Pérez-Pereira & Castro, 1997; Peters, 1994). Nevertheless, children with autism are not able to go beyond replicating "pure" routines. In a similar vein, it is known that intervention programmes seem to have a more effective result with blind children than with children with autism. It is our assumption that the effect of intervention programmes will differ depending on the characteristics of the children. Intervention programmes may be able to help us understand how education/environmental changes affect blind children's development, and to compare the effects of these programmes in blind children and other children such as children with autism. As for the effect of environmental circumstances in blind and sighted children, the developmental distance between blind children who live in impoverished circumstances and those who live in stimulating familial environments is probably higher than that existing between sighted children in those environments, suggesting that blind children may be more prone to the effects of the environment than sighted children are.

METHODOLOGICAL CONSIDERATIONS

In spite of its potential value, the research with blind children has suffered from a lack of methodological rigour. This may be the case for a number of reasons. Most studies have been carried out from a comparative, cross-sectional perspective. In this type of studies, mean comparisons predominate, which hide individual differences. These studies also adhere to a normative view which has been often linked to cross-sectional methodology in general. Cross-sectional studies provide general information, in other words a group view. Moreover, cross-sectional studies can not inform us about possible patterns of change, nor about differences in patterns of change. Developmental processes are derived from data from subjects who may vary greatly. Such an approach also assumes that subgroups of different ages follow the same developmental pattern, and that the results obtained by older subjects in a particular study would be the same to those obtained by the youngest subgroup if such subgroup were to be examined a few years later. That is to say, this position suggests that all children develop in the same way, following the same route. However, if we take into consideration the great variability observed in particular behaviours in blind children, which is in accordance with the wide variation of the population of blind children, it is difficult to make general statements from the data obtained in cross-sectional studies. It is particularly difficult to ascertain whether a particular behaviour in blind children is typical of blind children's behaviours or atypical of blind children's behaviours. We can not apply the same notions of normal distributions to populations of blind children. We simply do not have enough information to be able to make informed judgements. The comparative approach has resulted in many small scale, cross-sectional, comparative studies. As a consequence, there has been a dearth of in-depth, longitudinal studies of blind children.

Longitudinal studies have advantages over cross-sectional studies in a number of fronts. They allow us to observe changes across time, to document the course of development, to evaluate the impact of blindness at different stages of development, and so on. Other advantages include being able to obtain an actual picture of the development of blindness and different routes that children may follow, and thus, open up the opportunity for the researcher to appreciate individual differences in development. In addition, such studies allow us to observe how children's difficulties change across time. Longitudinal methods do not hide individual differences but highlight them by providing opportunities for the researcher to observe patterns of development.

However, longitudinal studies are labour intensive and expensive; inevitably, the few longitudinal studies carried out with blind children have usually been small in scale. In addition, the population of blind children is small, and it is difficult to find blind children with the appropriate characteristics. This state of affairs has created difficulties in being able to make general statements about blind children's development. It is problematic to generalize to the whole population of blind children from the study of five subjects, especially given the high variation which is known to exist in this population. This may account for some of the discrepant findings of different longitudinal studies perhaps due to the heterogeneity of the subjects used in the investigations.

In the same vein, there has been a lack of rigour in the methodological approach to the study of children with disability, especially blind children. The fact that little status has been given to the importance of disability in our understanding of development has worked as a disadvantage to the field as the same rigorous principles of study have not been applied to the "applied" area of the study of disability and blindness in particular. In addition to these, there are other methodological pitfalls that affect cross-sectional studies as much as longitudinal studies. These pitfalls diminish the value of a number of studies. The first deals with the use of instruments used (tasks, tests, techniques) in research investigating blind children's development. It is not unusual to read studies on blind children's development where the authors used tests and techniques that were designed for non-impaired children, but that are not well suited for blind children (Tobin, 1994). We will offer two examples. The first one is the study of Brown, Hobson, Lee, and Stevenson (1997) where the authors applied the WIPPSI or the WISC, two intelligence tests for sighted children, to blind and sighted children in order to assign the children into two groups with different IQs. It is clear that the scores obtained by the blind subjects are not comparable to those gained by the sighted children, since both tests require the processing and handling of visual material. The use of such material therefore introduces a bias into the design of the study that makes comparisons across subject groups difficult. Furthermore, these authors made partial use of these tests (such as the verbal subtests of the WISC) only, complicating further the measure of IQ they obtained in the study (see also Dekker, Drenth, & Zaal, 1991; Groenveld & Jan, 1992).

The second example is Dunlea's sorting tasks to study the generalization of concepts (Dunlea, 1989). The tasks developed in this study were not well adapted to blind children's characteristics, and, consequently, may again introduce bias which may result in the task underestimating blind children's capacities (see also Chapter 4). In cases like these, the tests and techniques used do not allow for blind children to demonstrate a given skill. This points to the need to develop new methodologies, tasks, and techniques that allow blind children an equal chance to demonstrate a given ability (Lewis & Collis, 1997b).

A second methodological issue in research with blind children deals with the comparability of the behaviours observed in blind and sighted children. In some occasions, there is a problem of narrowness of interpretation by assuming that a behaviour has a similar function by the mere fact that it is outwardly identical to behaviours observed in normal sighted children. Two apparently identical behaviours may serve different functions and can be the result of different underlying processes, and vice versa, two different behaviours may fulfil a similar function. The problem of the meaning and the function of a given behaviour has arisen not only in doing comparisons between blind and sighted children, but also in doing comparisons between blind children and other disabled children, namely children with autism. In the case of the comparisons between sighted and blind children, the absence of a given behaviour in blind children has been considered as an indication of the non-existence of the function that this behaviour fulfils in sighted children, without considering that alternative behaviours may exist in blind children that perform the desired function. For example, it has been considered that the absence of typical early communicative behaviours, such as pointing or offering, indicates that blind children are unable to communicate until they begin to use language. However, a number of researchers (Preisler, 1991; Urwin, 1984a) have shown that blind children may use alternative behaviours to communicate with their mothers. The identification of these behaviours, which use not the visual channel, but touch, movement, and sound, calls for sensitivity on the part of the researchers to be able to appreciate the meaning of such non-conventional behaviours. Now taking it the other way round, we also need to realize that similar behaviours may have different meanings for blind and sighted children. In this connection, Burlingham (1964) was the first who pointed to the different meaning that quieting behaviours have for sighted and blind children. For the latter this behaviour is exhibited not because blind children are uninterested in social stimuli, but because in being quiet blind children can appreciate such stimuli better, they can attend. All this means that, sometimes, the behaviour subjected to scrutiny and investigation may be inappropriate in that it falsely highlights what cannot be done by blind children. This state of affairs is not only inaccurate but makes it quite difficult to recognize alternative routes for development.

In the case of the comparisons between blind children and children with autism, we are suspicious of comparisons of blind children with autism and of descriptions of blind children as autistic-like. It is our opinion that the term "autistic-like" is vacuous and does not provide an explanation of why the behaviour may be occurring and for what purposes. Such use of terminology as explanation glosses over the complexity of the context within which behaviours occur and it wrongly assumes that superficial similarities translate into functional and developmental similarities. It needs to be made clear that we are not against comparisons. But, such comparisons across populations need to be carefully designed and examined so that they are informative to the conditions in question. In addition, explanations need to include how and why similarities are found across different disability groups and whether or not they serve similar functions. For example, the use of stereotypic speech seems to have different functions in blind children than in children with autism (see Chapter 4 for a more detailed discussion). Thus, to call blind children "autistic-like" does little for our understanding of the use of stereotypic speech in this population.

There are other methodological pitfalls in a number of studies involving blind children. The conditions under which the subjects are tested is important if we want to make sure that sighted and blind children have similar opportunities to demonstrate their abilities. Nevertheless, in studies which compare blind children to a control group of sighted children in certain tasks, the amount and type of information used to succeed in the task is not always clear or controlled for. For example, in some studies there is a lack of use of blindfolded sighted controls[1] in the performance of false belief tasks in which visual information is important (McAlpine & Moore, 1995; Minter, Hobson, & Bishop, 1998). The use of reliability measures in observational studies is considered a guarantee of objectivity and accuracy of the observations reported. Nevertheless there are still some studies with blind children where this procedure is not put into practice (Brown et al., 1997; Dunlea, 1989). These pitfalls result in comparisons that are not suitable, or well grounded, and that affect the validity of the conclusions reached.

Regarding the study of language development in blind children, there is a dearth of rigorous studies that offer clear quantitative and qualitative data. Unfortunately, most of the studies of blind children's language development offer anecdotal observations or personal impressions supported by a few examples of the behaviour under consideration, with little quantitative information to support their conclusions (Andersen, Dunlea, & Kekelis, 1984, 1993; Fraiberg & Adelson, 1973). It is important that this state of affairs changes with future research.

The former points should not be interpreted as a dismissal of previous research. Research in a field is always carried out under difficult conditions and with scarce knowledge of the topic. The findings obtained by first researchers in a field are of great value for later studies, and this is also the case with the study of blind children. Our claim is that, at the present time, the study of blind children's psychological development should meet higher standards of methodological rigour in accordance with what is taking place in the study of non-impaired children's development.

ABOUT THIS BOOK

In this book we deal mainly with communication and language development in blind children. In our opinion, this is a topic of the highest relevance for blind children, since whether blind children engage in such activities appears to have important consequences for their development. Probably, social isolation is one of the major dangers to blind children. Generally speaking, two different developmental patterns may be differentiated in blind children. On the one hand, there are those blind children who progress well in development, who attain the most important psychological functions without noticeable problems, and who will be able to lead a productive life in their adulthood. On the other hand, there are those blind children who present serious delays in their development, and do not attain basic psychological functions such as communication or language, or do so in a limited way and with major delays. The impression that these children's developmental achievements give us is that early communicative and language development have an important role in blind children's development. Language seems to have an important compensatory function, allowing the children access to the external world and social information that they could not obtain by other means. Moreover, the capacity to communicate and speak promotes the development of other domains, such as cognitive and social development. Thus, language and its acquisition, as well as its developmental functions, becomes a central point of our interest in blind children.

At the same time, we are concerned with the investigation of the development of blind children, a particular case of children with disabilities, not as a peripheral branch of Developmental Psychology, but as an important area of research that has major implications for the construction of theories of development. Disability has not been the preferred daughter of Developmental Psychology. Only recently has disability taken a more centre-stage in theoretical debates (Baron-Cohen, 1995; Leonard, 1998). There is a need to recognize the complexity that different disabilities present to the problem of development. It is important that we understand children with different disabilities within their own contexts and characteristics before comparisons are made across disability groups. As discussed earlier, this has not been the case and studies have compared the behaviour of different disability groups with the implicit assumption that such behaviours have similar functions. In the same vein, there has been lack of rigour in the approach to the study of children with disability, especially in the case of blind children. It has been considered enough to treat single, clinical anecdotes in development as illustrative and interesting without any concerted effort to attempt to understand the underlying processes and mechanisms that may be at play in order to have a fuller picture of the impact of disability in development. The fact that little status has been given to the importance of disability in our understanding of development has worked as a disadvantage to the field as the same rigorous principles of study have not been applied to the "applied" area of the study of disability and blindness in particular. It is our view that the same scientific rigour has to apply to the study of blind children as well as the same in-depth consideration of multiple possible explanations. We would go further and argue that at least some of those possible explanations should emanate from the context of blindness itself, that is, understanding blind children in and of themselves, prior to comparative attempts and we follow this stand wherever possible throughout the book.

Furthermore, the study of children with disabilities, and blindness in particular, may be considered an area of research that highlights the relevance of individual differences in development. Because of their handicap, blind children emphasize human diversity. The old ideas of Developmental Psychology, which stated that there was a pattern of development common to all children and which deemed delays in development as the only source of variation are coming to an end. Human beings may follow different patterns in their development. However, it is not an easy task to develop models of development that integrate the issue of individual differences as a central point. The study of blind children is a realm that may shed light onto these problems, and help to investigate the existence of different routes in development. We approach the study of blind children with this hope. There is a need to take a serious and comprehensive stand in research with children with disabilities that informs development in general, not as an ancillary "interesting" side consideration in terms of examples and clinical cases, but as a discipline of study in its own right. It is our thought that only when such recognition is evident will there be useful contributions of the study of disability and blind children in particular to our understanding of development. The result will be a richer Developmental Psychology that informs, predicts, and explains the range of behaviours in young children in general. Nevertheless, this task requires to overcome many limitations that the research of blind children's development has traditionally had. Studying blind children requires much sensitivity in the interpretation of behaviours. In this sense, we have to consciously escape the temptation to make interpretations centred on sighted children, and to adopt a functional viewpoint that tries to analyse the meaning of children's behaviours in their context of occurrence. Overtly similar behaviours in blind and sighted children do not always have the same meaning and furthermore, what apparently are different behaviours are not always unrelated. As previously discussed, superficial similarities do not mean similarity of the function of the behaviours in development. In this book, we hope to illustrate these points when comprehensively reviewing the available research on blind children's social and language development.

CHAPTER TWO

Motor and cognitive development

INTRODUCTION

In this chapter we will review the findings gathered by researchers interested in motor and cognitive development. On doing this, we will not make an outline of motor and cognitive development in sighted children as a reference for systematic comparison; instead we will report what is known on the development of these domains in blind children. In order to keep the chapter to a manageable length, comparisons with sighted children will be presented only when necessary. As a matter of fact, our aim is to use this chapter to present a general picture of blind children's development to help the reader better understand the main topic of the book: the development of social interaction and language in blind children. This is so because, as we will try to demonstrate, the development of blind children is not homogeneous, and important differences exist between different domains of development. This makes the concept of asynchrony of development of special interest to our understanding of blind children's development, since not every domain follows a similar pattern of development and, furthermore, an imbalance between different domains may exist. This concept was first proposed by Zazzó (1969) in relation to the development of children with mental handicap to indicate that these children develop at different rates in different domains of development as compared to non-impaired children. Probably, the most striking contrast in blind children is that which exists between motor and language development. Whereas language development follows a reasonably normal rate of development, motor development may be seriously delayed in the majority of blind children.

Concerning cognitive development, blind children seem to be delayed during the period of sensorimotor development, and later on during the periods of preoperational and operational thought, but, as soon as they reach propositional thought, the use of language appears to have a compensatory function, and they no longer show a delay in their reasoning abilities.

MOTOR DEVELOPMENT

We will review the findings on motor development of blind children in three separate subsections. In the first we will present the development of gross motor skills, in the second we will present the development of fine motor skills, and finally we will address the issue of blind children's individual differences in motor development.

Gross motor skills

To what extent does the lack of vision affect motor development? Does blindness affect all motor abilities to the same extent? Adelson and Fraiberg (1974; see also Fraiberg, 1977) tried to answer these questions by doing a longitudinal study of 10 congenitally blind children without any additional handicap. They compared the ages of achievement of different motor abilities in this group of blind children with the norms obtained by Bayley (1969) with sighted children. They found that although the blind children did not show delay in those aspects concerning postural control, they showed an important delay in those motor abilities requiring self-initiated mobility. Compared to sighted children, blind children showed reasonably normal rates of development in the following postural achievements: sitting down momentarily (6.75 months: +1.45),[2] rolling from back to stomach (7.25 months: +0.85), sitting steadily (8.00 months: +1.40), walking supported by hands (10.75 months: +1.95), standing alone (11.00 months: +2.00), and supporting themselves on hands and knees (9.25 months: +0.25). In addition, head control seems to be acquired approximately at the same time as with sighted children, although Adelson and Fraiberg could not directly observe all the children achieving head control.

In contrast, the blind children in the study showed important delays in those motor abilities requiring self-initiated movement. These included: elevating themselves using their arms, prone (8.75 months: +6.65), raising themselves to sitting position (11.00 months: +2.70), pulling themselves up to stand up by furniture (13.00 months: +4,40), walking alone 3 steps (15.25 months: +3.55), walking alone across a room (19.25 months: +7.15), and crawling (13.25 months: +4.25).

Wyatt and Ng (1997) related the delay that blind children show in the skills of raising themselves using the arms in prone position, and crawling during infancy, with the weaker strength of knee and hip extensors that blind children show as compared to normally sighted children at 6 to 12 years of age. Wyatt and Ng suggested that the reported weakness was due to blind children's resistance to activities in the prone position and their lack of self-initiated movements, such as crawling and standing from the crawl position, in infancy and early childhood. Activities in prone position strengthen the hip extensors as well as knee extensors.

Interestingly, Adelson and Fraiberg (1974) also observed that whereas the time span between leaning on their hand and knees and crawling was much as 8 months in the blind children, in the sighted children these behaviours appeared one after the other. According to these authors, the former type of behaviour is static, whereas the latter requires mobility. In a similar vein, there was an 8–9 month gap between blind children being able to walk supported by hands and walking alone, whereas for the sighted children this gap was only of 3 months. Therefore, in Adelson and Fraiberg's opinion, lack of vision does not equally affect all aspects of motor development. Whereas those behaviours requiring postural control are hardly affected by lack of vision, those motor abilities that need initiative and mobility on the part of the children are seriously delayed in blind children. However, the question still remains as to why this may be the case. Adelson and Fraiberg suggest that auditory clues do not have the same motivational effect as visual clues. Sighted infants move to reach those objects and toys that are seen by them (they raise their arms to see them, try to reach them, crawl or walk to fetch the target, and so on). Nevertheless, blind children do not have a similar motivation to reach objects and toys because sound cues are only permanently associated to an object much later in development. In fact, the capacity to associate a sound cue to an invisible object presupposes object permanence, that is to say, that the object is a permanent entity with a number of features. Thus, the motivation for initiating movement in blind children seems to be related to the search of objects with sound cues that are heard by the children, and this, in turn, is related to the achievement of the notion of object permanence.

Previously, Wilson and Halverson (1947) had already observed an important delay in the motor development of one blind child they studied. This delay was particularly remarkable in those behaviours requiring locomotion, such as crawling, standing, walking alone, and climbing steps. Thus, Wilson and Halverson were the first researchers who called attention to the difficulties of blind children in initiating movements spontaneously.

Fine motor skills

Wilson and Halverson (1947) also observed a delay in behaviours related to searching and grasping. The differences found between the blind child and the norms for sighted children given by Gesell and Amatruda (1946) were even greater than those differences found by Adelson and Fraiberg (1974) between the 10 blind children they studied and the norms for sighted children provided by Bayley. This, probably, is due to the beneficial effect of the intervention programme that the blind subjects studied by Adelson and Fraiberg followed. Interestingly, and in contrast, Wilson and Halverson did not find a delay in the linguistic and personal-social (autonomy) development of the blind child they studied as compared to sighted children norms.

In addition to the problems for representing permanent objects, Warren (1984) has suggested that a delay in the development of spatial concepts may be responsible for the late appearance of those motor behaviours that require self-initiated mobility. These spatial concepts imply a given capacity of orientation in the external environment, which may be problematic in blind children.

In their study, Adelson and Fraiberg (1974) also compared the results they found in their sample with the results obtained by Norris, Spaulding, and Brodie (1957) in a sample of 66 blind children. They found that, although the blind children studied by Norris et al. showed a slight delay of approximately 2 months as compared with the children studied by Adelson and Fraiberg during the first months of the study, the delay increased to 7–13 months as the children were older. According to Adelson and Fraiberg the increasing delay was the cumulative effect of the intervention programme that their subjects followed, which was not available to the children in the Norris et al. study.

Even though Norris et al. (1957) pointed out that the blind children in their study showed a similar pattern of development to the sighted children in their capacity for supporting head and chest, as well as using fingers to handle objects, they found that the blind children showed delays in some areas such as prehension with one hand, grasping objects, and fine-grained motricity, such as pincer grasping, scrawling, fitting pieces in holes, etc. It is interesting to note that Fraiberg (1977) carried out an in-depth study of the evolution of grasping behaviour in 10 blind subjects without additional handicaps. She observed that at 3 months of age, as many blind children as sighted children had their hands opened; however, at 5 months of age the blind children did not grasp their own hands, neither did they play with their fingers, as the sighted children were doing at this stage. At this same age the blind children were also unable to hold two cubes, one in each hand, nor could they switch a cube from one hand to the other, as sighted children normally do. The blind children also did not use pincer grasping at 9 months, which corresponds to sighted children's norms, but intead they used palmar grasping. Pincer grasping, characterized by the opposition of thumb and index when grasping a small object, did not appear in the blind children until they were 10 months old, and, in any case, pincer grasping was scarcely used (Fraiberg, 1968). It also needs to be noted that the results of Fraiberg's study suggest a much earlier point in development at which blind children are able to do pincer grasping than that reported by Norris et al. (1957) for their subjects.

Regarding ear–hand coordination, that is to say, grasping an object that makes a sound within reach, this appears not to be achieved by the blind children until they were 8.27 months old, approximately (range 6.18–11.1). In contrast, sighted children achieved eye–hand coordination, that is to say grasping an object that is seen, at 4.15 months of age. Nevertheless, sighted children are not able to reach a hidden object which makes noise (ear–hand coordination) until they are 8 or 9 months old, more or less. Fraiberg (1977) suggests that the later achievement of ear–hand coordination in relation to eye–hand coordination is due to the fact that ear–hand coordination requires a certain degree of permanence, which corresponds to Stage 4 of the sensori-motor period and thus is not available to young children around 4 months of age.

Interestingly, blind children can reach a sound-making object earlier (around 6–8 months) provided that a previous contact with the object had been made. If the blind children held or touched a sound-making object before, they could reach it again, but if there was no previous tactile contact they were not able to reach the object (Fraiberg, 1968, 1977). This achievement indicates that touching and hearing schemes begin to be coordinated at 6 or 8 months of age. However, searching for a sound-making object that was recently held by the child requires a less-developed ability than that needed to search a sound-making object without previous tactile experience. When blind children try to search for a noisy object that has fallen down from their hands or was removed by somebody else, the children are only extending their movements of accommodation. In other words it seems to be as if the object was at the disposal of the children. This level corresponds to Stage 3 of sensorimotor intelligence, and, thus, must be achieved earlier than those behaviours corresponding to Stage 4.

In summary, Fraiberg's account indicates that blind children have important difficulties in those motor behaviours related to orientation towards the external environment as well as self-initiated mobility, such as reaching and grasping objects, seating down by themselves, crawling, walking, and so on.

Individual differences

As suggested by the somewhat different results obtained in some of the studies of motor development reported before, blind children do not seem to follow a unique developmental pattern. On the contrary, individual differences seem to be usual. One study (Pérez-Pereira & Castro, 1994) is particularly pertinent to illustrate the important variation that may exist among visually impaired children regarding their motor development.

Pérez-Pereira and Castro (1994) carried out a longitudinal study of the motor development of four blind children and one visually impaired child. Subject 1, a totally blind child with important delays in development including social isolation, absence of communicative behaviours, and so on, was studied from the age of 9 months until he was 36 months old. Subject 2, a visually impaired child, was studied from 9 months of age to 23 months of age. Subject 3, a blind girl with minimal perception of light, was studied from 24 to 35 months of age. Subjects 4 and 5, two children with minimal perception of light, were studied from the age of 29 months to 41 months of age. All the blind subjects suffered from retinopathy of prematurity, and the visually impaired child suffered from chorioretinian degeneration. Subject 1 showed an important delay in his motor development, which was extremely slow. Compared with the norms for sighted children, Subject 1 progressed at nearly one-third of the normal rate of development. For example, Subject 1 grasped a cube with his hand at 21 months of age, whereas most sighted children achieve this at 8 months of age; similarly, this blind child stood up alone at 30 months of age, whereas sighted children usually attain that behaviour at 10 months of age. In Table 2.1 a comparison of the motor development of Subject 1 with that of sighted children (Gassier, 1983; Helbrügge, Lajosi, Menara, Schanberger, & Rautenstrauch, 1980; Secadas, 1988) and the blind children studied by Fraiberg (1977) and by Norris et al. (1957) is presented.

Compared with the results obtained by Norris et al. (1957), the pattern of motor development shown by Subject 1, is very delayed. The most delayed motor behaviours are those which call for keeping balance, such as to sit alone or stand alone. Even more delayed are those behaviours that, in addition to balance, require dynamic coordination, or dynamic balance, such as to walk supported by the hands

TABLE 2.1

Comparison of the motor development of Subject 1 (multiple deficient), with that of the blind children studied by Fraiberg and Norris et al., and with the norms for sighted children*

Skills	Subject 1	Fraiberg	Norris	Sighted
Supports head 5" sit	9	**	–	2
Supports head 30" sit	11	–	–	3
Rolls from back to stomach	15	7.25	12	7
Sits alone momentarily	18	6.75	12	8
Sits alone steadily	21	8.00	12	9
Stands alone	30	11.00	23	10
Supports him/herself on hands and knees	30	9.25	–	10
Stepping movements (walks on hands held)	36	10.75	18	11
Stepping movements (leaning on furniture)	–	–	18	12
Elevates self by arms, prone	14	8.75	–	4
Raises self to sitting position	24	11.00	–	10
Stands up by furniture (pulls up stand)	36	13.00	17	11
Crawls	–	13.25	–	11
Walks alone, three steps	***	15.25	30	13
Walks alone, across room	–	19.25	36	15
Shifts a cube from one hand to the other	15	9	–	6
Palmar grasping	15	9	–	6
Takes a cube in each hand	21	–	–	8
Searches for an object touched before	9	7	–	–
Searches for an object on sound cue	20	9	–	–

* The mean age (in months) of achievement is given for the subjects studied by Adelson and Fraiberg (1974) and Fraiberg (1968, 1977), with prematurity correction; the age of 75% of subjects' success is given for the study of Norris et al. (1957), without prematurity correction; and the age established in the norms for sighted children by Helbrügge et al. (1980), until the age of 12 months, and by Gassier (1983) and Secadas (1988), after 12 months of age, is given.
  ** Not observed.
  *** Had not been acquired by 36 months.

of someone else, or pulling themselves up to the standing position leaning on a piece of furniture. In contrast, those skills that do not need balance, such as palmar grasping, or switching a cube from one hand to another, or rolling from back to stomach, are not so seriously delayed.

In contrast, the visually impaired Subject 2 showed excellent motor development, similar to sighted children's norms, and in certain aspects even better. For example, this child began to walk alone at 9 months of age, which is early even for sighted children. In general, all aspects of motor development (grasping, sitting, crawling, standing, walking) followed a similar pattern to that of sighted children. For example, Subject 2 could climb a chair, climb a staircase, run, sit on his heels, bend down to take an object from the floor, or throw a ball when he was 23 months old. This indicates that the existence of residual vision in visually impaired children has beneficial consequences on their motor development, which shows a similar pattern to that of sighted children, as other authors have also indicated (Fraiberg, 1968, 1977; Warren, 1984, 1994). This conclusion is supported by the longitudinal study carried out by Hatton, Bailey, Burchinal, and Ferrell (1997) with a large sample of 186 visually impaired children aged between 12 and 73 months of age. These authors found that scores on motor skills measured through the Battelle Developmental Inventory were significantly lower for those children with a visual function of 20/800 or less than for the group of children with a visual function of 20/500 or more.

Regarding Subjects 3, 4, and 5, their motor development kept pace with other descriptions of blind children's motor development, in contrast to Subjects 1 or 2. All these children were totally blind or only had minimal light perception. One of the children, Subject 3 had slightly better motor development than the others, except in crawling skills and the skills preceding crawling. She never used crawling (which also happens to some sighted children), and even had difficulties in standing in a crawling position, supporting herself on her hands and knees. At 24 months of age, Subject 3 could raise an arm when she was supported under both arms, and at 35 months of age she showed seal crawling. Thus, with the former exception of crawling-related skills, her motor development in other areas was between the norms given by Norris et al. (1957) and those given by Adelson and Fraiberg (1974) for blind children, although closer to Norris et al.'s norms. She could walk with support at 24 months of age, and at 26 months of age she could walk alone. She had attained the skills of pincer grasping and raising herself to the sitting position before 24 months of age, which was the time of the first observation. At the time of the last observation, when she was 35 months old, Subject 3 was able to climb a sofa or a chair, go down steps with help, throw a ball, take a spoon to her mouth and eat some food on her own.

Subjects 4 and 5 followed similar patterns of development. In general, they attained the milestones of motor development at similar ages to the subjects studied by Norris et al. (1957). Both Subjects 4 and 5 were unable to walk without support at 29 months of age. Independent walking appeared in both of them at 30 months of age, in line with norms given by Norris et al. (1957) for blind children (see Table 2.1).[3] At 29 months of age, the time of the first observation, both children already crawled with ease. At the end of the study, when both Subjects 4 and 5 were 41 months old, they could go up stairs by crawling or walking with support, bend down to take an object from the floor while maintaining balance, throw a ball, or jump on their feet. In general, their motor skills, although seriously delayed in relation to sighted norms, were not developing in an asynchronous way. In the period of time studied, these children's various motor skills appeared to be developing at the same pace.

To summarize, large individual differences may exist among blind children's motor development. In general, those children who show delays in other areas of their development also present dramatically slow motor development. Those children who have a relatively good pattern of development in other areas do not show such a deficient pattern of development in their motor skills. However, in comparison with sighted children, blind children who do not have a general delay still show remarkable delays in various aspects of their motor development, particularly in the acquisition of gross motor skills related to dynamic balance and self-initiated movements. On the other hand, the existence of residual vision appears to be crucial for the motor development of visually impaired children, who appear to take good advantage of the visual input they have.

In conclusion, research indicates that blindness negatively affects motor development. Motor skills of blind children are seriously delayed not only in the areas of gross motor development (sitting down, walking, and crawling skills), but also in the areas of fine motor development (reaching, grasping, and handling objects skills). A converging observation is that independent walking skills are seriously delayed in all blind children, who usually do not walk independently before 24 months of age. In general, dynamic skills, which seem to be related to self-initiated activity, are specially affected by lack of vision. None the less, it is important to note that individual differences are extremely large amongst the population of blind children, thus, it is not possible to offer a common pattern of development for all blind children (Warren, 1994). It also seems clear that the existence of residual vision enhances the motor development of visually impaired children. Consequently, the motor development of visually impaired children with residual vision is very similar to that of sighted children (Fraiberg, 1968; Hatton et al., 1997; Pérez-Pereira & Castro, 1994; Warren, 1984, 1994).

It also needs to be noted that early intervention with blind children appears to enhance their motor development. Thus, the subjects in the study by Adelson and Fraiberg (1974) who participated in an intervention programme had better motor development than was expected. In connection to this, Warren (1994) has suggested that delays in motor development are probably due to the restriction of opportunity for physical exercise of blind children, and not necessarily to blindness.

COGNITIVE DEVELOPMENT

For the sake of clarity, we will present the results of the research on blind children's development under five separate subheadings. The first subsection deals with sensorimotor development in general, and, more precisely, with the development of the notion of object permanence, which has been studied in depth. In the second subsection, cognitive development research on the use of standardized tests (specially the Reynell–Zinkin scales) is reported. In the third subsection, we discuss research carried out on symbolic play, which has been a controversial topic since Fraiberg's report of blind children's difficulties in pretend play. The fourth subsection deals with investigations on the development of operational thinking in blind children. The last subsection delves into a topic which has aroused an important amount of research, namely, space representation and space orientation in blind children.

Object permanence

Fraiberg, once again, was the first author to investigate the cognitive development of blind children, from a Piagetian frame of reference. This author studied the development of the notion of object permanence (Fraiberg, 1968, 1977), that is to say, the understanding that an object continues to exist even if it is not currently perceived. She differentiated two stages. In the first stage, around 6 or 8 months of age, blind children could find a sound-making object if the children had handled or touched the object immediately before. This corresponds to Stage 3 behaviours. Shortly after, the blind children Fraiberg studied could search a sound-making object following a sound cue only. The blind children did not need previous tactile experience with the object. However, the object needed to be placed in front of the children. Otherwise, if the object was placed at the left or the right side, the children had more difficulties in reaching for the object. This behaviour appeared in the 10 blind children studied by Fraiberg (1968, 1977) between 0;6.11 and 0;11.1 months of age (mean age: 0;8.27).[4] This behaviour corresponds to stage 4. What she called a "directional search of an object on sound cue alone" appears shortly later (Fraiberg, 1977). Now, the blind children show the intent to reach the object independent of its placement. This behaviour is typical of Stage 5.

The developmental pattern suggested by Fraiberg indicates that blind children acquire the coordination between ear and hand later than sighted children acquire the coordination between eye and hand. Fraiberg has pointed out that ear–hand coordination in blind children has a greater complexity than eye–hand coordination in sighted children. Several studies have also pointed out that ear–hand coordination is established in sighted children several months later than eye–hand coordination (Bigelow, 1983; Clifton, Rochat, Litovsky, & Perris, 1991; Freedman, Fox-Colenda, Margileth, & Miller, 1969; Perris & Clifton, 1988). According to Fraiberg, searching for a noisy object needs a degree of development of the notion of object permanence equivalent to Stage 4, as we have already discussed. Giving support to the idea that reaching in the dark implies some kind of mental representation of the object, Clifton and colleagues observed that six and a half month-old infants adapted their reach (hand and arm preparation) according to the object's size depending on which sounds they heard in the dark (Clifton et al., 1991). Bigelow (1983) observed that the searching for an object by using only sound cues does not appear in sighted children until they achieve Stage 4 of the sensorimotor period, that is to say, later than the searching of a hidden object, which needs eye–hand coordination. In addition, Bigelow observed that sighted children use sound as a cue that indicates location of an object in space, first, and later they use sound as a cue that indicates movement in space.

Following Fraiberg's observations, there have been two important studies to test her hypothesis. The two studies employed specially designed tasks that attempted to clarify the sequence that blind children follow in acquiring the notion of object permanence. The first one was carried out by Bigelow. Bigelow (1986) prepared 11 tasks to assess the level achieved by blind children in their development of object permanence. Following Fraiberg's opinion, these tasks were based on the importance of sound, as well as touch, as clues used by the children to reach objects. Task 1 was typical of Stage 3, tasks 2 to 8 were typical of Stage 4, and tasks 9 to 11 were characteristic of stage 5. As mentioned before, blind children who are in Stage 3 can find a sound-making object if the children have handled or touched the object inmediately before. Those blind children who are in Stage 4 can search an object following a sound cue alone, provided the object is located in a fixed position. Those who are in Stage 5 reach an object independent of its placement, or if the object has moved from one place to another. Bigelow applied tasks of this type to five totally blind children (some with minimal light perception) who were 11, 13, 15, 17, and 32 months old at the beginning of her longitudinal study. The children were studied every month at home for a period of 5, 13, 6, 5, and 13 months, respectively. The results indicate that there is a progressive sequence in the mastering of the tasks. The sequence observed by Bigelow coincides with that observed by Fraiberg in that the children search earlier for a sound object that was removed from their hands than an object with which the children had had no previous contact. However, Bigelow (1986) did not find that objects located at the right or the left side of the children at chest level were more difficult to reach than objects located in front of the children at the same height. However, this author found that whenever an object was located further up or down chest height, the children had more difficulties in finding them than when the objects were placed at chest height. Therefore, it seems that directional search implies a higher level of development. The fact that directional search is more difficult than the search for objects placed in front of children was also observed in sighted children (Wishart, Bower, & Dunkeld, 1978; but see Perris & Clifton, 1988 for contrary results). Bigelow found that four of the children she studied could search for an object placed in front of them by using sound cue alone when they were between

15 and 32 months of age (mean age, 20.73 months) (the fifth subject had not yet achieved this at 21 months of age, when he left the study). Fraiberg (1977) found the same behaviours at an earlier age. Nevertheless, this 11-month delay may be due, in part, to the more stringent criteria used by Bigelow for the achievement of front reaching.

Therefore, it seems that blind children start by using tactile information to locate an object, and later they can use acoustic information. When blind children have at their disposal converging touch and acoustic information on the placement of an object, the task of searching for an object is easier than when blind children can only use tactile information. According to Bigelow (1986), this means that sound gives information on the location or direction of objects to blind children. In those circumstances in which blind children have to process sound and touch cues that give them contradictory information, the blind children studied by Bigelow (1986) seemed to prefer touch information. For example, when the children perceived by touch that an object disappeared in a given point, but they heard the sound of that object coming from a different point in space because the experimenter had moved the object, the blind children searched the object in the area where they had lost contact with the object. This happened to children who already knew how to search by sound alone, which indicates that in a situation with contradictory cues, the blind children adopted a more primitive strategy of searching by touch.

As Bigelow (1986) stated, the blind children's order of task mastery suggests that the tasks tap the development of object permanence from Stage 3 to Stage 5. "Thus both blind and sighted children may develop object permanence through a cognitively similar process, i.e. the sequence with which they understand the concept of object may be parallel, although the modalities used to organise information into higher-order functioning are necessary different" (Bigelow, 1986, p. 365).

The results of Bigelow were interpreted by Landau (1991) as suggesting that sound information is a kind of impoverished information in relation to visual information for the children to reach and explore objects (see also Bower, 1977 for a similar position). Sound information only offers limited data about the relative position of objects, but gives no cues on their form, size, trajectory, or substance, in contrast with visual information. Although blind children are delayed in their ability to search sound objects to explore them, their touch exploratory patterns are intact. Touch exploration of form and texture is similar in blind and sighted children who are 2 years of age. This exploration allows both of them to apprehend the qualities of objects. However, blind children may have limitations in their capacity to get qualities from objects which are too big or cannot be rotated.

In addition, Bigelow (1992b) compared the results obtained by three of the children studied previously (Bigelow, 1986) in the object permanence tasks and the children's locomotion development (crawling and walking alone). She observed that the blind children's emergence of locomotive skills appeared to be related to their development of object permanence despite considerable age differences among the children. Stage 4 occurred approximately at the same time as crawling, whereas all the children began walking alone during the transition to Stage 5 or subsequent to entry to Stage 5. These results indicate that, for blind children, the development of object permanence mediates attainments in locomotion, since understanding of objects and their location in space motivates blind children's locomotion and exploration (see also Fraiberg, 1977). However, the reverse may also be true. That is to say, the attainments in locomotion may drive developmental changes in object permanent behaviours (see Ross & Tobin, 1997 for a criticism of this cognitive theory of motor development).

The second study on the development of object permanence was carried out by Rogers and Puchalski (1988). These researchers used a series of six tasks ranging in difficulty from Stage 3 to Stage 5. Nevertheless, Rogers and Puchalski excluded sound from the cues that blind children could process, since in their opinion those tasks in which the children need to coordinate touch and sound information imply additional complexity, because of cross-modal transfer.[5] Rogers and Puchalski applied the tasks to 11 blind children and 9 visually impaired children between 4 and 25 months of age. The visually impaired children could use visually guided search. Ten of the children were premature, and six showed additional handicaps, mainly cerebral palsy. The children were followed over a period of time, which, regrettably, the authors do not specify. In addition to the object permanence tasks, Rogers and Puchalski also applied the Reynell–Zinkin scales to assess the children's cognitive development in three different occasions every 2 months, as well as the Bayley scales. In addition, the authors observed if the children used symbolic play, and if the children showed reactions to strangers or discomfort reactions to mother's separation in a strange situation.

The results of Rogers and Puchalski's study seem to indicate that the tasks show a progressive level of complexity, and that there is no difference between blind and visually impaired children regarding the age at which object permanence is achieved. The 16 children who solved any task (4 of the subjects left the study before they could solve any task) did it at the following mean ages: tasks 1 and 2, corresponding to Stage 3, were solved around 16 or 17 months of age; tasks 3 and 4, corresponding to Stage 4, were solved around 19 months of age; and tasks 5 and 6, corresponding to Stage 5, were solved around 20 to 22 months of age. However, large variations between subjects was found (see Rogers & Puchalski, 1988, p. 138). Taken together, these results showed that the blind children show a delay of 8–12 months in the acquisition of object permanence as compared to the sighted children studied by Piaget. Nevertheless, the period of time elapsed between the point at which the blind children studied by Rogers and Puchalski solved the simplest task (16.27 months of age) and the most complex task (21.80) was five and a half months, which is comparable to that of sighted children.

In addition, Rogers and Puchalski (1988) found no A–B errors in the blind children, unlike sighted children. As is well known, the A–B error consists in children searching a target object in the first place in which it was hidden (A), without taking into account the last displacement of the object to B. This difference in the performance of blind children is not easily interpretable as it is not clear that the tasks used by Rogers and Puchalski were equivalent to those used with sighted children, and which lead to the A–B error in sighted children. Furthermore, Rogers and Puchalski did not apply the task to a group of sighted children in order to compare the results with the group of blind children. Therefore Rogers and Puchalski's findings are tentative with regard to this particular point, and we must be cautious in their interpretation.

Another surprising result of Rogers and Puchalski's research is that there was no difference between blind and visually impaired children in relation to the ages at which permanence tasks were solved. Nevertheless, this finding is in disagreement with that of Bigelow (1990), who compared two totally blind children and one visually impaired child, and found that the latter achieved the notion of object permanence 10 or 23 months in advance in relation to the two totally blind children. The idea that residual vision has a facilitating factor for cognitive development in general, and the notion of object permanence in particular, has also been suggested by Warren (1994) in his review of the studies done on the topic. This variable may account for some of the discrepant results obtained in this area.

In addition to the results obtained with the object permanence tasks, Rogers and Puchalski obtained a significant positive correlation between their subjects' scorings in these tasks and the sensorimotor understanding scale of the Reynell–Zinkin scales (.72, $P < .05$). Finally, the authors did not find any relationship between the development of object permanence and blind and visually impaired children's anxiety reactions to strangers and to mother's disappearance. Nor did they find any relationship between the attainment of object permanence and symbolic play abilities, such as pretending to eat, by using cups and spoons. However, Rogers and Puchalski (1988) point out that the first uses of symbolic play are more closely related to other aspects of the capacity of representation, such as language, than with sensorimotor development. An interesting result is that seven of the subjects studied by Rogers and Puchalski used symbolic play between the ages of 21 and 37 months, whereas another seven children who were at an age to use symbolic play (that is to say, between 18 and 32 months old) did not engage in it. This result seems to contradict Fraiberg's suggestion that blind children show difficulties in attaining symbolic play across the board. Her 10 blind children did not play with dolls or participate in role playing by the end of the second year (Fraiberg, 1977). According to Fraiberg, this delay in the development of symbolic play is linked to their delay in the development of self representation.

In Table 2.2, a summary of the results of the studies on object permanence of blind children is presented. As it can be observed, important differences exist among the results found by different researchers. It is remarkable that Fraiberg (1977) found that the blind children she studied achieved the different stages of object permanence earlier than the blind children studied by Bigelow (1986) and Rogers and Puchalski (1988), who obtained similar developmental results. Probably, the

TABLE 2.2

Mean ages (in months) of achievement of the different stages of the acquisition of object permanence in different studies in relation to Piaget's norms

	Piaget	*Fraiberg*	*Bigelow*	*Rogers & Puchalski*
No. of children	3	10	5	20
Stage 3	4–8	6-8	20.5	16–17
Stage 4	8–12	9	20.75	19
Stage 5	12–18	>10	22.6	20–22

differences found are a consequence of the different methods used in the studies. Whereas Fraiberg credited the attainment of a given stage from the observation of an instance of the critical behaviour in natural settings, Bigelow used more stringent criteria in her tasks. In Bigelow's study, the children were credited mastery of a given behaviour if they passed two trials out of three. In addition, the subjects studied by Fraiberg benefited from an intervention programme, and this probably promoted their development.

In summary, it appears that blind children have a slower development of the notion of object permanence than sighted children, unless they benefit from environmental circumstances which promote their development including significant amounts of residual vision.

Standardized tests

Pérez-Pereira and Castro (1994), administered the Reynell–Zinkin scales (Reynell, 1979) to a visually impaired child and to the four blind children described earlier. They applied these scales at two different moments in the children's development (with the exception of Child 5). The Reynell–Zinkin scales assess five areas of development: social adaptation, sensorimotor understanding, exploration of the environment, response to sound and verbal comprehension (receptive understanding), expressive language: content, and expressive language: structure. Therefore, the Reynell–Zinkin scales are considered to measure mental development, in a loose sense (Reynell, 1979; Tobin, 1994). As suggested by the results of other investigations (Rogers & Puchalski, 1988), the attainment of the notion of object permanence correlates with the results in the Reynell–Zinkin scale of sensorimotor understanding. Thus, this scale seems to measure abilities very closely related to sensorimotor intelligence in a Piagetian sense. Our main interest in this subsection is to appreciate possible imbalances in children's development in different areas, such as imbalance between language and cognitive development. Figures 1 to 6 show the results obtained by these five subjects in the Reynell–Zinkin scales, as well as the mean results for the group of blind children studied by Reynell (1978).

These results show that Subject 1 had an important delay in all the scales, and particularly in the scale of expressive language: content (Fig. 6), since the child

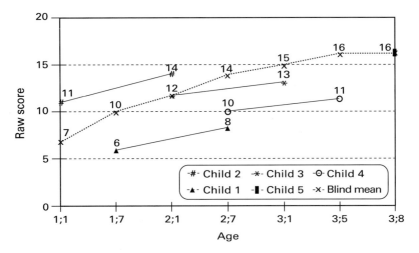

FIG. 1   Social adaptation.

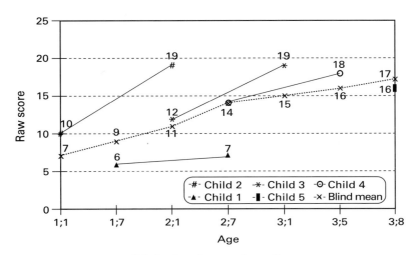

FIG. 2   Sensorimotor understanding.

did not use any communicative gestures. This child had an overall delay, which was also noted in his motor development. His rate of development was approximately half of what would be expected of an average blind child. In contrast, Child 2, who had partial vision, showed remarkably good development in the scales of social adaptation, exploration of environment, and, particularly at 25 months of age, sensorimotor understanding. In addition, his development in the other scales related to language was also quite good. In general his cognitive development was as good as that of a sighted child. This pattern of development was probably due to the excellent use of his residual vision, his good motor

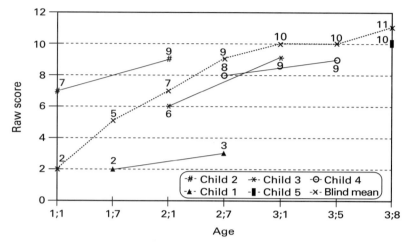

FIG. 3   Exploration of environment.

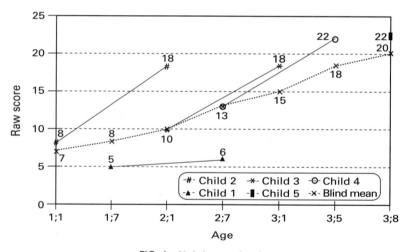

FIG. 4   Verbal comprehension.

development, and the educational attitude of his mother, which was very effective in promoting her child's development.

As for the other three blind children, those areas less developed were exploration of environment, and social adaptation in Subject 3, and also, although to a lesser extent, in Subject 4. However, Subjects 3 and 4 showed relatively good development in verbal comprehension, and expressive language, content and structure, specially Child 3. Child 5 showed average development in all the scales, except in expressive language: content, where she attained very good scores. This area (expressive language) is likely to be particularly affected

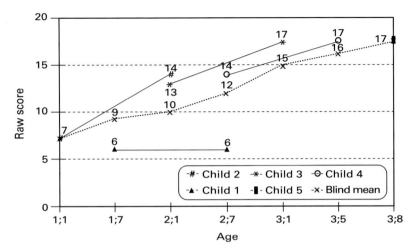

FIG. 5   Expressive language: structure.

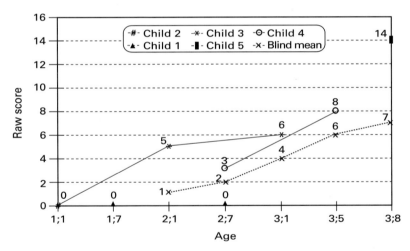

FIG. 6   Expressive language: content.

by the quality of early educational intervention in sensorimotor understanding, which in turn is related to the knowledge of objects' characteristics and the relationships between objects. Those children, such as Subject 3, who benefited from stimulating experiences of exploration of objects, had better scores in this scale, than children (such as Child 4) who did not have as much access to these experiences.

Coinciding with McConachie's findings (McConachie, 1990), young blind children showed slower development in the verbal comprehension scale than in expressive language: structure. However, this discrepancy between comprehension and production of language appeared to be stage dependent and disappeared by 3;5.

In general, Pérez-Pereira and Castro's (Pérez-Pereira & Castro, 1994) results do not agree with those studies (e.g. McConachie, 1990) that do not find differences between blind and partially sighted children. Our visually impaired child had clearly better results than Child 3 (blind, and with a good developmental pattern) at comparable ages in every scale, except in expressive language: structure and content. The differences were more remarkable in the scales of sensorimotor understanding, exploration of environment, and verbal comprehension. In these areas, the relevance of a certain degree of vision seems to be evident.[6] The importance of residual vision for cognitive development has also been confirmed by Hatton and colleagues (Hatton et al., 1997). These authors have found in a large longitudinal study of 186 visually impaired children (aged 12 to 73 months), that the cognitive development of those children whose visual function was 20/800 or less was significantly lower than that of children whose vision was 20/500 or more, as measured through the Battelle Developmental Inventory (BDI).[7]

To summarize, those aspects measured by the Reynell–Zinkin scales that appear to be more vulnerable in totally blind children are: exploration of environment, social adaptation (autonomy), and, to a lesser extent, sensorimotor understanding. Nevertheless, those aspects related to the use of language (expressive language: structure and content) seem to have a relatively good pattern of development in blind children. This is in agreement with additional data gathered on language development on the same five subjects discussed here (see Chapters 4 and 5), and with data presented by Hatton et al. (1997) using the Communication development dimension of the BDI with 186 visually impaired children. In part, the differences found among the blind children seem to indicate the importance of educational intervention, as Pérez-Pereira and Castro (1994) have suggested.

Symbolic play

Another important topic for researchers interested in blind children's development is symbolic play, also referred to as pretend play. This kind of play was investigated in depth in non-impaired children by Piaget (1959), who suggested there was a relationship between symbolic play and the development of representation. In symbolic play, the child uses an object as if it were another different object, for instance a box is used as if it were a car. Leslie (1987) has suggested that pretend play requires a metarepresentational capacity, although this idea has been questioned by other authors (Perner, 1991). Fraiberg (1977) has stated that blind children cannot participate in symbolic play before 3 years of age. However, other authors (Parsons, 1986a, 1986b; Pérez-Pereira & Castro, 1994; Peters, 1994; Rogers & Puchalski, 1984, 1988; Urwin, 1983; Webster & Roe, 1998) have reported instances of symbolic play (such as feeding dolls, cooking meals, going shopping, talking on the telephone, and so on) in blind children younger than 3 years. Those studies that offered quantitative results on the use of different types of play behaviour in blind children (Ferguson & Buultjens, 1995) have found that blind children are able to use symbolic play from very early in development.

Rogers and Puchalski (1984) studied the capacity to participate in symbolic play in 16 blind children between 18 and 37 months of age in three different settings. These authors observed symbolic play in nine of the children before they were 26 months old. However, blind children participate in symbolic play less frequently than sighted children (Tröster & Brambring, 1994), which is probably related, in part, to the inadequacy of play settings for blind children (Webster & Roe, 1998). Furthermore, there are data which suggest that symbolic play may be associated with good levels of language development: For example, Ferguson and Buultjens (1995) reported that fantasy play and role play occurred more often in children with good verbal comprehension, and good receptive and expressive language levels, respectively. Rogers and Puchalski (1988) also suggested that a relationship between symbolic play and language development exists.

Thus, a number of reports put into question Fraiberg's claim that blind children are delayed in symbolic play. It also needs to be noted that there have been reported examples of complex symbolic play in 5-year-old blind children. For example Pérez-Pereira and Castro (1994) described an instance of pretend play between one blind girl and her sighted twin sister in which the children pretended to be swimming in the sea. Suddenly, a shark appeared and they had to swim as fast as possible and go up to a boat (a sofa) to be safe. This is an example of how blind children are able to create situations of play from non-existing real experiences, or even from situations about which they have very limited information.

Operational thinking

Other studies have also been carried out on later cognitive development of blind children. Those studies that used Piagetian tasks of conservation and classification have found that blind children have slower cognitive development than sighted children (Gottesman, 1976; Hatwell, 1966; Ochaita, Rosa, Pozo, & Fernández, 1985; Rosa, 1980, 1981; Tobin, 1972). Nevertheless, when researchers used conservation tasks that required haptic perception, blind and sighted children showed similar patterns of results (Cromer, 1973; Gottesman, 1971, 1973). In addition, researchers who used verbal reasoning tasks that did not require touch to process the material observed that blind children did not show delay as compared to sighted children (Hatwell, 1966). Similarly, blind children obtained results that were closer to those of sighted children in verbal classification tasks than in figurative classification tasks (Dimcovic & Tobin, 1995). Visually impaired children 7;5 years old were found to recognize and resolve the incongruity of riddles better than a comparable group of sighted children (Rogow, 1981b), which, according to the author, was evidence that blind and visually impaired children's ability to perform on a concrete operational level on language-based tasks did not lag behind that of their sighted peers. There is evidence that as blind children grew older they performed relatively better in verbal tasks, up to the point that blind children's results in tasks that require formal propositional thought were similar to sighted children's results after 13 years of age (Pozo, Carretero, Rosa, & Ochaita, 1985). These data suggest that touch processing requires slower processing speed and higher attentional demand than visual processing, and that language seems to have a compensatory role in blind children's cognitive development (Rosa & Ochaita, 1988).

Other pieces of information on later cognitive development include the attainment of conservation of substance and weight, which appears around 8 to 11 years, and the attainment of conservation of volume which appears around 12 to 14 years (Warren, 1994). Warren has also pointed out, when reviewing the studies on the conservation of substance, weight, and volume in blind and visually impaired children, that the severity of visual loss was an important factor that led to important individual differences. Again, the existence of a residual vision seems to have a positive effect on the development of conservation concepts.

Space knowledge

How do blind children develop a representation of space without visual information? How are they able to orient themselves in a space without visual references? In Warren's opinion (Warren, 1984), the development of space representation in blind children is seriously delayed. This delay may be due to blind children's inability to react to events through the sounds they produce. Kephart, Kephart, and Schwartz's (1974) results agree with this suggestion, as these authors found that blind children between 5 and 7 years of age had a much poorer representation of the environment (house structure, neighbourhood), and of their own bodies, than those of their sighted peers.

However, Landau, Spelke, and Gleitman (1984) have carried out a series of experiments to investigate the space knowledge of a blind girl between 31 and 53 months old, which offered totally different results. These authors observed that their subjects had representations of the location of objects or people in a room, that she could orient herself in the space correctly, and that she was able to locate the objects even though they were placed in different locations. The authors verified that the blind girl could infer the placement of one object in relation to another object by representing angles and distances, and was also able to find and follow an appropriate path to go from a given place to another place, in spite of the fact that she has never followed the path before. Therefore, Landau et al. conclude that vision is not a necessary condition to obtain knowledge of space, and that this knowledge comes from Euclidean geometry. This geometry has the features of being generative (the girl could generate new paths), abstract (that is to say, independent from the input), and has metric characteristics (system of geometric rules and principles which can be applied to the information on the space and derive new space knowledge). Thus, space knowledge arises in a natural way in human beings, with hardly any training, and without the need of visual experience. Moreover, they argue that this knowledge is more complex than what Piaget had thought (topological space).

After this study, Landau (1991) indicated that the same blind girl at 4 years of age had difficulties in solving a rotation task. In this task the blind girl had to locate two people who were on her right and on her left at a table, when the experimenter was in front of her. Later, the experimenter asked the girl to sit down beside him and, in that location (180° rotation), the girl had again to locate the two people, who now were in interchanged placements. The child could not locate the two people correctly after the 180° rotation placement, until she was 5 years old.[8] In Landau's opinion (Landau, 1991), the child failed this task because, in contrast to path-finding tasks, the information at her disposal to establish space marks was not appropriate, since the human voice is not usually a reliable point of reference. On the other hand, as the child had no other points of reference in space, she could not orient herself again after the perspective shift. Landau states that, provided adequate cues are provided, blind children are able to have appropriate space representation, and to orient themselves in space by using a metric geometry.

Nevertheless, Landau's conclusions (Landau et al., 1984) have been criticized by Millar (1988). This author points out that Landau and colleagues did not take into account the effect of the experience that the blind girl obtained during the unfolding of the tasks, nor did they consider that, in addition to vision, other senses may have led the child to obtain knowledge of space. According to Millar (1994), touch and movement play an important role in understanding and representing space in blind children. In the absence of vision, touch and movement offer converging and complementary information on space layout. The processing of spatial and object information is favoured by the existence of redundant information coming from different sensorial sources (Millar, 1994). Moreover, Millar (1988) doubts that a blind child's behaviour can be only explained through principles of metric or Euclidean geometry, as Landau suggests.

Other studies with older blind children point to important developments in space knowledge along time, which seem to be in disagreement with Landau's claim of the early existence of metric geometry in blind children (Landau, 1991; Landau et al., 1984). Ochaita (1984) studied the behaviour of a group of blind children between 7 and 15 years of age using three space tasks, in which the children could explore the space and handle the materials (scale models) with their hands. Ochaita found that the blind children went through the developmental path indicated by Piaget and Inhelder (1948). That is to say, the children first achieved the topological relationships, and later the projective and Euclidean relationships.[9] Moreover, she found that the blind children showed a delay in their development of space understanding as compared to sighted children, and, to a lesser extent, to sighted blindfolded children. However, this delay was surmounted when blind children were

12–15 years old. Therefore, Ochaita's findings seem to contradict Landau's claim that blind children have Euclidean geometry shortly after they are 2 years of age.

Bigelow (1991b) also obtained results which do not concord with Landau's point of view. This author found that two totally blind children between 6 and 8 years of age had difficulties in inferring whether a person could see an object or not, if the distance between this person and the object was over one metre, and if there were objects interposed. These results seem to indicate that blind children have difficulties in representing Euclidean space. Bigelow (1991a) tested two totally blind children, two visually impaired children, and eight sighted children. The children, between 6 and 8 years of age, were longitudinally studied every 2 months for 15 months (or until they solved the tasks). They had to point to locations in their houses on the same level, in their houses but on a different floor, in the surrounding garden, and in the neighbourhood. The blind children performed much worse than the partially blind and the sighted children. At the end of the study, only one of the blind children could point to familiar locations on the same floor and in the garden. None the less, these results may have been affected by the need to use pointing to identify a location. In fact, most of the errors were produced because the children pointed to the direction of the correct route, not to the final location. Consequently, Bigelow (1991a) suggested that blind children's spatial knowledge was based on routes between places (their own travel routes) rather than on an Euclidean (objective) understanding of locations.

In another study, Bigelow (1996) explored the ability of children in judging (1) the routes necessary to get to familiar locations on the same floor of their houses, on a different floor, or in the garden; and (2) in judging by straight-line distances to the locations. As in the previous study, there were three groups of children who varied in their degree of vision. One group of two blind children, another group of two visually impaired children, and a third group of twenty sighted children. All of them were between 10 and 12 years of age, approximately. The results indicated that the blind children were delayed in mastery of the task, particularly the straight-line distance estimation between familiar locations, as compared to the other children. These results suggest that the blind children had a knowledge of space based on their routes between places rather than on their knowledge of the overall, structured, layout of the environment.

Miletic (1995) reported that 8-year-old blind children had more difficulties than visually impaired and sighted children of the same age in a perspective-taking task. The blind children were unable to represent how a geometric figure would be seen by a doll from a different perspective than their own perspective. The visually impaired group could represent the doll's perspective if the doll was placed in their same location, or in a 180° location (opposite perspective), but not if the doll was in a different angle (for instance 225°). In contrast, the sighted children could represent the perspective seen by the doll from any angle of orientation. These results show that blind children have difficulties in understanding projective representational space.

On their part, Ungar, Blades, and Spencer (1995) observed that visually impaired children from 6 to 13 years of age reconstructed a tactile map less accurately than sighted children of the same age, and that most of the children with visual impairments used learning strategies that were inappropriate for the task. Moreover, the authors did not find any age differences. None the less, in a subsequent study, Ungar, Blades, and Spencer (1997) observed that visually impaired children from 5 to 11 years of age performed less well than a comparison group of sighted children in a task in which they had to estimate the position of a third object on an actual path in which two objects were present by using the information given in a map in which the symbols of the three objects were present. However, it is interesting to note that in a second experiment, the blind children improved their performance after a brief training session on how to calculate distances from a map.

In contrast with the difficulties in locating an object in relation to other objects that visually impaired children seem to have, Ungar, Blades, and Spencer (1996) observed that visually impaired children from 6 to 11 years of age were good at locating themselves (self-location and route tracing) in a tactile map from a layout in which they followed different routes and occupied different positions. As the authors indicate, to perform correctly in this type of task, the children only needed to locate the correct sequence of landmarks without necessarily realizing that other points on the map also referred to other places in the layout (Ungar et al., 1996, p. 534).

The results of Ungar's investigations seem to indicate that visually impaired children under 11 years of age do not have problems in understanding location concerning their own movements and sequence of movements (self-centred or topological space), but that they do have problems in representing an objective spatial frame of reference (allocentric or Euclidean space).

The idea that blind children show difficulties in surmounting the initial use of self-centred strategies to encode spatial information (topological space) has also been pointed out by Warren (1994) in his review of the literature. According to this author, the transition from an egocentric spatial frame of reference to an external or allocentric frame of reference (Euclidean space and projective space) takes a longer time in blind children than in those children who can use visual information (see also Bigelow, 1996 for a similar consideration). Millar (1994) has suggested that this is so because self-centred reference, which is related to own body and own movements, is more reliable for blind children than external reference.

Ochaita, Huertas, and Espinosa (1991) have also studied older blind children's ability for space representation of two unknown environments with different size, in which the children had to orientate themselves. The subjects were 38 blind children between 9 and 17 years of age. Two techniques were used for the children to externalize their space representations: scale models, which allowed representation of the spaces, and distance estimation. The results indicated that there was a developmental progression through these ages, and an important jump at around 13 years of age. Ochaita et al. relate this remarkable progression after 13 years of age with the appearance of verbal-propositional thinking, which allows the blind children to compensate for their figurative deficits. The authors did not find any effect of the size of the space or previous visual experience of the subjects (but note that not all the children in this study were born blind), but could observe a positive effect of experience with the environment, as the subjects improved their representations and reduced the need for help in consecutive tests of the route.

Huertas and Ochaita (1992) studied a group of 40 blind people, distributed in four age levels of 9, 11, 14, and 17 years, who had to learn a route with seven landmarks in an unknown urban square. After four consecutive learning sessions, the subjects had to represent the space through estimation of distance and the construction of a scale model. Moreover, Huertas and Ochaita also analysed the subjects' spatial behaviours by using three measures: quantification of the instances in which the subjects required assistance (graded in five levels), measurement of success, and the time the subjects took to walk around the route. Huertas and Ochaita found a high correlation between the scores in the two representational measures and between those and the spatial behaviour as measured through the required level of assistance and success, but not the time to follow the route. The results indicate that blind subjects after 14 years of age (probably in the formal operational stage) are able to form a global, structured, configuration of a space by successive and fragmentary recognition thanks to the use of a propositional, abstract, format of representation.

Using a similar design, Ochaita and Huertas (1993) also analysed the possible effect of previous visual experience, size of the area to be learned, subjects' developmental level, and experience with the environment. In addition to the learning of a large-scale space (the urban square previously referred to), the blind children had also to learn the layout of a small space (the grounds of the blind children's school). Moreover, half of the subjects (which were the same as those of the study of Huertas & Ochaita) were born blind whereas half had acquired blindness. Ochaita and Huertas did not find any difference between the two groups of blind children. They also did not find that size of space was an important factor in the subjects' representations. The authors considered that this was the case because previous visual experience seems to assist in spatial representation of complex and configurational environments, but not of simple routes. Besides, as both the small and the large space were relatively simple, there was no effect of size. However, the authors found that the older subjects (the two age groups of 14 and 17 years) made more accurate and adjusted representations than did the younger subjects (the groups of children who were 9 and 11 years of age), although there were also differences between the group of children who were 14 years of age and the group who were 17 years of age. This points to the developmental level needed in space tasks performance. Subjects' level of representation changed from the first to the fourth session, indicating the effect of experience and familiarity. Thus, the results seem to suggest that at the beginning of adolescence blind people show an important advance in their cognitive abilities. As blind people reach abstract propositional thinking, their spatial representation improves markedly.

Ochaita (1993; Ochaita & Huertas, 1993) suggests that, taken together, the results of the latter studies point to the greater difficulties that blind children seem to have in the access and processing of figurative types of representations. According to Ochaita, these difficulties are due to the fact that blind children use sensorial systems, such as touch, own body movement perception, and hearing, which are less efficient than the visual system to gather and process information. Thus, blind children form inadequate images of a given space, or inadequate images of objects that cannot be entirely perceived because of their size, such as vehicles or buildings. Only later does the abstract use of language and verbal reasoning allow blind adolescents to surmount these difficulties in figurative representation.

None the less, in spite of these difficulties, adult blind people seem to have space representations and orientation similar to sighted people. Passini and Proulx (1988) found that 15 adult blind subjects could learn, remember, and complete a complex route in a similar way to a comparison group of 15 sighted subjects. In addition, the blind subjects' ability to represent the route they followed, and their capacity to suggest short cuts, were similar to those of the sighted subjects. Easton and Bentzen (1987) observed that blind subjects, much like sighted subjects, were able to represent (through space images) the information about a route provided to them verbally. The results of the latter two studies do not give support to the opinion of those authors (Hartlage, 1976; Warren, 1984) who state that blind people are not able to have space representations, or, at least, that their space representations are deficient. Further evidence of adult proficiency comes from the study by Carreiras and Codina (1992). These authors observed that blind adults could estimate path and straight-line distances between different locations of a small-scale model similarly to sighted adults. The authors suggested that spatial representation of blind people is not qualitatively different from that of sighted people, and, thus, spatial representation seems to be amodal.

Generally speaking, it seems that blind children's cognitive development is delayed during the first years. Probably, this is so because during the first months of life the exploration of the environment is based on the information coming from the use of senses and their coordination, as well as from children's actions. For this very reason, blind children are at a disadvantage as compared to sighted children who can perceive external reality and the results of their actions on it in a more complete way. For example, for the concept of object to develop a great deal of touch exploration is needed. Nevertheless, touch exploration requires a slow process of development to become useful and offer reliable information on objects. Therefore, the promotion of touch exploration experiences with objects has special relevance for blind children, as we will see in Chapter 7. However, as blind children achieve a certain level of language development, they can use language as an extremely important tool to gather information about the external world, and, thus, language and communication with others compensate blind children's lack of visual information, which results in adult proficiency in a number of cognitive domains.

CHAPTER THREE

Social interaction, the beginnings of communication, and the development of a theory of mind

This chapter is comprised of two sections. In the first section we review research on sighted and blind infants' early social and communicative development. By way of an introduction we discuss the development of social interaction, the development of the self, and the beginnings of communication in young children without visual deficits. We contrast this information with what we know about congenitally blind children. Particular attention is paid to two different points of view. The first suggests that blind children have severe deficits in social interaction and early communication, which are similar to those presented by children with autism. The second argues that blind children and their parents develop alternative forms of social interaction and early communication, which are able to provide different routes for the development of the child as a social, communicative being. We emphasize the crucial compensatory role that language plays in blind children's development and we argue that through learning and use of linguistic symbols blind infants begin to understand persons as intentional agents.

SOCIAL INTERACTION AND THE BEGINNINGS OF COMMUNICATION IN SIGHTED AND BLIND INFANTS

Early social interaction, the development of the self, and the emergence of communication

It is evident that young infants without visual deficits use vision as the primary sense modality to learn about themselves and the environment. It appears that the visual system is organized in such a way that it assures that infants attend to those elements of the environment that are most important to development and survival.

Thus, Haith (1980) found that infants visually search for things to look at and explore. Infants also coordinate visual information with experiences from other sensory modalities. For example, upon hearing a sound, infants search and look for the source of that sound; while tactually manipulating an object they also visually inspect it (Spelke & Cortelyou, 1981; Streri, 1991/1993). Thus, it appears that vision affords easy intermodal transfer of information given that many attributes of the physical environment perceived in other modalities such as shape, movement, location, and rhythm are shared in vision. In addition, infants can more actively control the level of visual stimulation they receive compared to that from other modalities. Infants can exercise more control over visual stimulation—they can look away or close their eyes if visual stimulation is too overwhelming (Stern, 1985). Such regulation is more difficult for other sensory modalities such as hearing, touch, smell, and taste. Imagine a non-locomotor infant exposed to loud noise or wanting to grasp for a dropped object.

It is also evident that, in the beginning, young infants come to our interactive world with an interest in the behaviours of other humans. Young infants prefer the acoustic signals that are similar to the human voice and they synchronize their bodily movements with adults' speech (Jusczyk, 1997). They are also interested in visual configurations that are or resemble the human face and they are able to imitate mouth movements (Meltzoff, 1988; Meltzoff & Moore, 1993). The young infant is also able to use eye-gaze, smiling, and crying behaviours that are interpreted by the adult as intentional social signals. Although the transition into intentional communication remains a qualitative jump, the fact that adults interpret such behaviours as intentional helps them eventually become so. Thus, young infants manifest simple behaviours that are mere contingent reactions to maternal signals such as facial expressions or vocalizations, which are interpreted as intentional by the adult. Young infants thus learn to discriminate special people in their world and they turn to them with a smile, a "greeting" in the form of a vocalization, or a bodily "reaching out" to them in anticipation of a pleasurable, familiar interaction. There are two important lessons that are being learned here. Young infants are learning about their own selves and how their actions have predictable consequences in the world. They are also learning about other people as intentional agents capable of initiating and carrying out actions.

Knowledge of the self develops most easily in early social interaction. The action–reaction interchanges between an adult and an infant begin to form interactive sequences or cycles of interaction that become more complex with time. Caregivers respond contingently and consistently to the infants' behaviours (Watson, 1985). The regularity with which these cycles occur and their repetitive nature will help the young infant to learn most readily the association between their own action and what goes on in the social environment. Young infants develop expectations and anticipate specific consequences of their actions. In Neisser's terminology (1991, 1993) they develop their "interpersonal" self, which connects and separates the self from other people. For example, between 3 and 4 months of age, infants become distressed if mothers become still-faced during face-to-face interaction (Tronick, Als, Adamson, Wise, & Brazelton, 1978) or if they are exposed to delayed (and thus non-contingent) video playback of their mothers (Murray & Trevarthen, 1985).

There is also another aspect of the self, Neisser's "ecological" self, which is also developing in the young infant at this time (Neisser, 1991, 1993). This aspect of the self is also specified through perception. This time the emphasis is placed on the particular perceptions of the self in activity with the physical environment. The ecological self connects and separates the self from the physical environment through experience with objects and events. In this way, young infants develop knowledge of the environmental effects of their own actions. For example, young infants learn in the first 4–6 months of life what objects are reachable in space and what objects are not. Visual information and feedback are extremely important for the development of the ecological self, especially with respect to spatial understanding. Many of the experiences of the young infant with the physical environment can be facilitated and fostered by caregivers and interactions with them. For example, caregivers may provide interesting hanging toys that are reachable for the infant to explore. Within caregiver–infant social interactions there are also opportunities for the infant to gain knowledge of the environmental effects of their own actions. Consequently, there are important social aspects to the experiences of young infants with their physical environment and thus the development of the ecological self.

Returning to early social interaction, we have argued that young infants develop the capacity to anticipate and predict the behaviour of significant others. This capacity is first observed in very familiar, specific contexts that the young infant has been engaged in, for example, face-to-face interactions with mother. With time, infants begin to generalize from these specific contexts to other situations. At the beginning, the ability to anticipate behaviour is anchored on the adult's action. It is the adult who initiates interaction with action and it is the adult who acts as a guide within the interactive sequence. Later, the young infant will be able to take the role of initiator in social games or action routines (peep-po, give and take) and it will be the young infant who determines the pace of the interaction (Bruner, 1978, 1982, 1983).

It has been argued that the capacity to predict and anticipate the behaviour of other is a necessary prerequisite for the infant's understanding of another person as an intentional agent capable of initiating and carrying out actions. Furthermore, in this interactive process the child becomes aware that attention on some external thing is shared with another; it is inter-subjective (Baldwin, 1995). What happens is that this capacity is initially limited to a few familiar contexts. When the infant is about 9–12 months of age this capacity to predict and anticipate has become established and the infant's understanding of inter-subjectivity and of others as intentional agents emerges (Carpenter, Nagell, & Tomasello, 1998). This is evident in behaviours where there is coordination of attention to persons and to objects

(Sugarman, 1984; Trevarthen & Hubley, 1978). The previously established dyadic, adult–infant, interactive dyad becomes a triadic, adult–object–infant, social interactive, inter-subjective system (Dunham & Moore, 1995). Now, the young infant is able to share the same perspective with the adult. The child will, for example, look at the same objects the adult is looking at, observe the adult's emotional reaction to the new object or person, attribute meaning to that reaction and behave accordingly. Such phenomenon whereby emotional information about an object/person/event is conveyed from adult to an infant has been referred to as social referencing (Campos & Stenberg, 1981; Hornik, Risenhoover, & Gunnar, 1987; Sorce, Emde, Campos, & Klinnert, 1985). Infants also engage in gaze monitoring at this stage. The infant turns in the same direction that another person is looking at and then shows gaze alternation, checking back and forth a few times as if to make sure that the other person and himself/herself are both looking at the same thing thus establishing joint attentional focus on the same object (Butterworth, 1991; Scaife & Bruner, 1975). Gestures such as pointing and reaching accompanied by gaze alternation also take an important role at this time. The prelinguistic child between 12–14 months of age will begin to use what have been called protoimperatives to solicit adult help in obtaining a desired object or activity and protodeclaratives to direct adult attention to an object or activity of interest (Baldwin, 1995; Bates, Camaioni, & Volterra, 1975). The pointing of this period followed by gaze alternation is an excellent example of prelinguistic children's understanding of others as intentional beings. In other words, when a prelinguistic child points, be it declaratively to direct attention or imperatively to direct behaviour, he or she is not only attempting to obtain a desired object or activity, but is attempting to change the adult's intentions so that they become aligned with his or her own (Tomasello, 1995). Furthermore, at this stage infants engage in imitative learning of new behaviours involving actions on objects. Perhaps the most illustrative example of this is provided by Meltzoff (1988). In this study 14-month-old infants watched a researcher bend at the waist to touch his forehead to a panel which activated a light. The infants reproduced the action, even though they might more plausibly have used their hands to produce the same result. This study and other evidence suggests that young infants are involved in following adult behaviour and attention and are tuned to the adult's strategy in producing a change of state in an object. Young infants therefore seem to be able to understand others as intentional beings with their own point of view. This understanding is thought to be an essential component for the development of language and for our capacity to "read" other minds (Gómez, 1991; Tomasello, 1999).

It is evident that young children without visual deficits undergo significant development in the way they socially relate to the world and to their primary caregivers (usually mother) during the first year of life. We have argued that, during this time, changes in mother–child interaction can be observed that suggest that the dyad progressively engages in more complex interactive behaviours. Thus, new forms of early interaction are based on previous advances and as such are best described as a constructive process where qualitative "jumps" are evident (Lamb & Easterbrooks, 1981; Rivière & Coll, 1987). In addition, the advances made by young infants in the first year of life appear robust, but they are highly dependent on the primary caregivers' sensitivity in interpreting the infant's behaviours as communicative and adequate for the situation. To reiterate, primary caregivers provide the infant with routines, that is, scaffolded experiences in familiar situations with restricted, predictable, repetitive formats that help the child anticipate, predict, and understand the world around him or her (Bruner, 1983). In turn, these advances are also dependent on the infant's ability to use information, and, undeniably, visual information plays an important role in this process.

Given the previous information, a number of questions arise: What if any is the effect of lack of vision on the development of prelinguistic communication? Are blind infants able to develop joint attention? Do they develop an adequate sense of self? Do they understand others as intentional agents? Can they use gestures to communicate? In the following sections we will attempt to provide some answers to these important questions.

Effects of lack of vision on prelinguistic development

Blindness denies some infants of the many opportunities for eye contact and reciprocal gazing that normally draw sighted infants and their primary caregivers together in the early stages of their developing relationship (Ainsworth, Bell, & Stayton, 1974). Towards the third month of life most sighted infants are able to show signs of emotional expression such as smiling at the sight of the mother's face (Kaye, 1982). Thus, frequently one encounters the situation where mother approaches the baby, comes close to his or her face, talks to him or her, the baby responds with a smile, which in turn provokes a further reaction from the mother who touches or tickles her baby and continues to talk, the baby may vocalize and kick, and so on. These chains of turn-taking in interaction were referred to as protoconversations by Bateson (1979).

The situations just described where the infant's behaviours are contingent on those of his or her mother, depend on the infant being able to see the mother's face and her facial expression as well as hear her speech. In the case of the blind infant there is a great barrier between mother and infant as the child has no visual clues to help him or her engage in interactive behaviours. Thus, cycles of interaction involving alternate emotional expressions between the blind infant and his or her caregiver may be compromised or may not occur often enough (Als, Tronick, & Brazelton, 1980b). The blind child will not be able to produce a contingent smile as he or she is unable to see the mother's face or if he or she uses it it may not be contingent or adequately related to maternal reactions. Furthermore, as shown by Rowland (1983, 1984) the blind child's vocalizations will not be produced as responses to previous parental behaviours as is the case with sighted children (Messer, 1994). Interestingly, blind children often react with silence and stillness when listenening to their primary caregivers' speech and other communicative behaviours (Als et al., 1980b; Burlingham, 1964). This reaction can give caregivers the impression that the infant is unable to understand or express emotions, which usually creates anxiety in caregivers who may feel at a loss of what to do. As a result, blindness from birth can make it difficult for there to be conventional cycles of interaction between blind infants and their caregivers. There may be opportunities for non-visual anticipatory games, but the problem is that there is often too much surprise and lack of control on the child's part. This may make the blind child reluctant to participate or fearful in social encounters. The blind infant and his or her caregiver are not tuned together in interaction as the infant is unable to see the appropriate, contingent reactions of his or her interactive partner. But the problem here may be partly the adult's and not the infant's. There are various cues the blind infant can use to engage in reciprocal interaction based on sound, touch and vestibular stimulation, provided the adult is attuned. The immediacy of vision makes it difficult to understand and use the information provided by other senses.

Thus, blind infants and their caregivers are not able to easily establish face-to-face interactive routines. This makes it difficult for the blind infant to experience the regularity and turn-taking nature of parental contingent behaviours. This in turn, makes it hard for the blind infant to anticipate and predict what is about to happen. We have argued that this capacity to anticipate and predict one's own behaviours and the behaviours of others is related to the infants' development of the self and their understanding of another person as an intentional agent capable of initiating and carrying out actions. Consequently, both the development of self and the social understanding of others is more of a challenge to the blind infant than it is for the sighted infant. As discussed earlier, blind infants are typically passive and learn to be helpless. They do not demand much of caregivers and are content to lie in their cots seemingly uninterested in social and environmental stimuli. But it is important to underline that this learned helplessness is not necessarily due to the lack of vision on the part of the child. An alternative explanation for passivity can be found in the lack of affordances in the environment that would otherwise draw the child's interest and action and perhaps even in the relatively clumsy (and to a degree, insensitive) way people sometimes play with infants who are blind. Fraiberg (1977) suggests that for blind infants, persons and objects manifest themselves in a random, unpredictable way, "emerging from the void only to fade back into the void". Interestingly, the passive behaviour of blind infants is precisely the type of behaviour that would be expected of humans who have no known way of predicting or controlling their environment (Hiroto & Seligman, 1975). Blind infants have difficulty discovering themselves, their bodies, and the effect their behaviour has on the social and physical environment around them. For example, Fraiberg (1977) in her observation of 10 congenitally blind infants does not observe instances of blind infants watching their hands or discovering their feet. As discussed in Chapter 2 on motor and cognitive development and on Chapter 7 on intervention, blind children can suffer major delays in reaching motor developmental milestones such as reaching for an object, crawling, and walking without sensitive help or intervention. Consequently, blindness presents a challenge to the development of the interpersonal and ecological self.

It has been suggested that the ecological self is the most at risk in blind infants. Blind infants have particular difficulties in understanding themselves in relation to the physical environment and this represents a major hurdle to their development of the ecological self (Bigelow, 1995). Despite their difficulties in early social interactive experiences, blind children seem to be able to develop an interpersonal self more readily. Observation of older blind children who use spoken language suggest that they are able to engage successfully in social interaction and understand themselves as being the object of others' thoughts, feelings, and desires (Bigelow, 1988; Landau & Gleitman, 1985; Pérez-Pereira & Castro, 1994). In contrast, many studies of older blind children and adults have shown that congenitally blind infants have continued problems with spatial understanding and the relationship between themselves and the physical, spatial environment (Bigelow, 1991a; Dodds, Howarth, & Carter, 1982; Fletcher, 1981; Rieser, Hill, Talor, Bradfield, & Rosen, 1992).

None the less, some difficulties with the development of the interpersonal self are evident in blind infants. At around 6–9 months there is another major change in the development of sighted infants. The infant is able to sit and/or crawl. The infant's universe opens as the infant is able to take in a wider view from the upright position and use his or her limbs more effectively to reach, take objects, offer objects, and, when self-produced locomotion is possible, to go and get them. This is the time when simple games such as peep-po, "give and take" with favourite toys, building towers and smashing them, emerge. Researchers working with blind infants have found an absence of such conventional social games (Als et al., 1980b; Preisler, 1991; Rowland, 1984; Urwin, 1984). This is not surprising given that the format of such games are heavily dependent on visual information. It is difficult for the blind infant to take an object that is being offered when the blind infant can not see the offering gesture, nor is it possible for the blind infant to maintain an expectant attitude when his or her mother hides behind a cloth in a peep-po game or to greet her with a smile and laughter when she shows her face again.

During this period of 6 to 9 months caregivers are introducing objects and toys to blind infants none the less, the blind infant has difficulties using gestures such as pointing with gaze alternation to direct attention or direct behaviour, reaching to demand an object, offering or showing objects. This makes it very difficult for caregivers to know the preferences and interests of the blind infant (Rowland, 1983; Urwin, 1978, 1983). The blind infant's lack of vision make it difficult for him or her to refer to external events (for example, via pointing or reaching) or to engage in social referencing or gaze monitoring. Thus, the blind infant appears uninterested in the outside world and this may discourage the caregivers from initiating activities involving external referents such as objects and events. Indeed, as mentioned earlier young blind infants do not appear to use protoimperative or protodeclarative gestures (Preisler, 1991; Rowland, 1984), suggesting that they are not able to easily share joint attention with their caregivers nor understand them as intentional agents until much later in life when they begin to use language (Bigelow, 1997; Preisler, 1991). It needs to be noted that Iverson's recent work (Iverson & Goldin-Meadow, 1997, 1998; Iverson, Tencer & Goldin-Meadow, 1998) indicates that children who are blind exhibit a variety of gestures. These researchers studied congenitally blind children longitudinally between 14 and 28 months of age. They found that these children used gesture during the prelinguistic period despite the lack of visuo-gestural input. Thus, the emergence of communicative gesture does not appear to be determined by exposure to visual information. Interestingly, the frequency with which gestures were used to communicate in blind children was reduced relative to sighted control children. The nature of early gesture use in blind infants was also different than that observed in sighted infants. Blind children's gestures tended to be more body-centred, consisting primarily of indications of objects that were close at hand or conventional gestures. Sighted children's gestures tended to be deictic (points or shows) and were used to refer to both proximal and distal objects with roughly equal frequency. However, the question of whether gestures play a role in early routines or joint attention episodes with blind children remains to be answered as Iverson's studies examined older subjects for whom early routines and joint attention were no longer a main concern.

This review of the literature suggests that blind children may have some difficulties in the use of gestures and behaviours related to the development of joint attention. Does this mean that blind infants are not able to establish social interaction routines with their caregivers and communicate prelinguistically?

The ability to compensate and to develop alternative routes

The sombre picture presented earlier for blind infants is not in any way generalizable to all blind infants. To the contrary, such developmental patterns are not commonly found in blind infants today given that alternative forms of social interaction and prelinguistic communication are developed by young blind infants and their caregivers. Fraiberg (1977) was perhaps right when she said "it is the exceptional mother who can help her blind children circumvent major handicaps without counseling". There is little doubt that early intervention and counselling have had a major impact on the patterns of development now observed in blind infants and their caregivers (for further discussion on intervention see Chapter 7). Caregivers learn to look in different places and use different modalities to reach the blind infant and enable interaction to ensue.

Based on the work of Als et al. (1980b) it is apparent that caregivers learn to interpret the reaction of quietness and stillness of their blind infants not as a sign of lack of interest or attention but as a way of indicating more concentration and attention. The reaction of stillness is indicating to the caregiver that the infant is ready to focus his or her attention exclusively on what stimulation is offered by the caregiver. This starting point is an essential first element to the establishment of social interaction between blind infants and their caregivers. But this is not sufficient. In addition, caregivers establish alternative modes of developing routines and cycles of interaction that do not require visual support. The use of touching, tickling and other forms of physical contact as well as vocalizations and the use of language have been thought to provide good alternative routes to early interactions (Urwin, 1984a). In this way, caregivers can hold the blind infant's hand and perform regular rhythmical movements accompanied with vocalizations/ language which can be turned into games, and this can be done from very early on.

From the start, caregivers provide alternate support for their blind infants so that they can begin to understand and predict forthcoming events. Thus, everyday routines such as feeding, bathing, changing are routinized to signal to the child that a series of events are coming. For example, taking the blind infant's hand and putting it into the water before starting a bath will eventually become part of a routinized sequence of actions, which the infant will begin to anticipate. Similarly with changing clothes, following the same pattern will eventually result in the blind infant participating actively in the routine, for example, by lifting up the arms to have their top taken off. Like most caregiver–child interactions, at the beginning it is the caregiver who does most if not all the work. But, as the events become routinized the child has an opportunity to engage fully in the routine and divert some attentional focus from the task at hand to others present and involved in the activity. Attention can also be diverted to the language being used and the gestures that accompany the event. In this sense, anticipation derived from routines is important for communicative development. In these examples the goal is not simply to acquire a particular living skill (e.g. take a bath, change clothes) but to engage in interactions that afford joint attention and communication.

It appears that vision is not an essential requirement for successful social interaction exchanges in infancy. However, vision does contribute towards the spontaneity, ease, and frequency with which these exchanges take place. Thus, adults engaging with blind infants have to be more aware of the need for establishing routines and cycles of interaction and also they need to be more patient and careful in detecting responses and signs of engagement on the part of the blind infant. Blind infants have more difficulties in detecting patterns in social interaction and their responses to such interactions are often less obvious than those expected of sighted infants and may often be idiosyncratic (Preisler, 1991, 1997; Urwin, 1984a). For example, instead of turning to face the direction of the sound source, blind infants may drop their heads or slowly swing their heads from side to side. Similarly, when spoken to, blind infants do not always raise their heads but instead may turn to one side facing away from the caregiver's vocalizations. When approached by caregivers, blind infants may move their arms and legs but they also may use the same movement to show their intentions and desires (e.g. to be picked up). The blind infant who remains turned away from the caregiver may move the arms and hands excitedly upon hearing the caregiver's voice and become still and quiet upon hearing a stranger's voice. Caregivers are thus presented with a major challenge in recognizing and mutually negotiating responses and engagement in social interaction with their blind infants. In addition, as Preisler (1997) emphasized, caregivers interacting with blind children need to always be audible, readable, and predictable. It is here where caregiver language can play an enormously important compensatory role (Peters, 1994). Oral language makes it possible for caregivers to sustain contact with their infants and to express and share emotion with them.

Another important goal is to have the blind infants explore their environment actively. This should happen from the start. Thus, caregivers place the blind infant's hand on their lips when talking to them, allow blind infants to tactually explore their faces, and the environment around them. In addition, caregivers enrich the child's experience by introducing a variety of sensory stimulation: sounds, smells, textures, and shapes. Towards 6–7 months the development of reaching and searching for objects is fostered by the use of sound-making objects (Bigelow, 1986; Urwin, 1984a). Caregivers encourage the blind infant in this via games and verbally and/or tactually coaching them as to where to reach or touch. A bit later, around 9 months, blind infants and their parents develop social games that circumvent vision. For example, they will play pat-a-cake, clap hands, or this piggy went to market, they will engage in vocal imitation, and they will have tickling or kissing games that have strong physical contact and a predictable sequence. During these games what stands out is the ability of caregivers to adequately interpret the reactions of blind infants and their bodily and facial expressions, and caregivers' continual use of language to reflect changes of mood, shifts in attention and to explain current and forthcoming events (Lewis & Collis, 1997a; Webster & Roe, 1998).

Moving towards the end of the first year of life, we have already discussed the low frequency of conventional gestures such as pointing, offering, and showing in blind infants and their difficulties in perceiving what others are attending to and their emotional reactions to novel objects and events. This does not mean that blind infants are unable to engage in joint attentional episodes with their caregivers. For example, social referencing can occur between the blind infant and the caregiver when the infant is allowed to explore the caregiver's facial expression when confronted with novel objects or learn to interpret the caregiver's different tones of voice. Furthermore, it needs to be noted that a great deal of social referencing comes as a consequence of parent and child doing things together in both joint and turn-taking patterns. For example, picking up something together, shaking together, passing back and forth, moving together, touching together. These joint and/or turn-taking activities also provide opportunities for meaningful language to be exchanged. Similarly, joint attention can be shared via touch, by taking the caregiver over to an object and putting his or her hand on it. Furthermore, conventional gestures such as pointing with the finger can sometimes be substituted by more idiosyncratic movements/gestures such as pointing with the head or the upper part of the body (Preisler, 1991, 1995). The function of conventional gestures such as pointing may also be substituted by language use, thus, a blind child may say: Look what I have! or See camera! (Landau & Gleitman, 1985). The key to advancement at this stage of development is to provide opportunities for the blind infant to engage in non-visual joint attentional episodes with the caregiver. Once again, the use of other sensory modalities and language is essential. It appears that for blind children, language becomes the most important compensatory mechanism in this respect. That is, it is through learning and use of linguistic symbols that blind infants begin to understand other persons as intentional agents (see Tomasello, 1995 for a discussion of this same point with respect to sighted infants). In addition, language can also help in such mundane activities such as finding one's way. In the absence of other cues that are not readily available, blind children code directions linguistically and use language as their mental map (Iverson, 1998, in press).

In this section, we have argued that prelinguistic communication develops through alternative routes in blind children. Blind children have opportunities to develop socially and communicatively within the context of interactions where other sensory modalities other than vision are used and explored. We have also emphasized the crucial compensatory role that language plays in blind children's development and the positive effects of early interactive, joint attention routines can have in the development of the child as a social, communicative being. In the next section we turn to a specific aspect of social cognition—theory of mind. We begin with a brief historical review. Then, we move to discuss the development of theory of mind in normal children and children with autism. These discussions provide the context for an evolution of (1) blind children's theory of mind abilities, and (2) the superficial similarities that are sometimes observed between blind children and children with autism. The chapter then ends with some brief concluding remarks.

THE DEVELOPMENT OF A THEORY OF MIND

The evolutionary interest of prelinguistic communication: Prelinguistic communication and theory of mind

Interest in the development of a theory of mind began with the study of non-human primates. Do non-human primates have a theory of mind? Premack and Woodruff (1978) asked precisely this question of a chimpanzee and a great deal of research has followed since (see Povinelli & Eddy, 1996 for a detailed discussion of what chimpanzees know about seeing; see Tomasello & Call, 1997 for an excellent review of primate cognition). The issues raised by the work with non-human primates formed the basis for the experimental work, which followed involving normal children (Wimmer & Perner, 1983). This in turn led researchers interested in atypical populations to ask the theory of mind question of a variety of populations (children with mental retardation and Down's syndrome, Baron-Cohen, 1989; deaf children, Peterson & Siegal, 1995; congenitally blind children, Minter et al., 1998); and, most notably, of children with autism (Baron-Cohen, 1995; Baron-Cohen, Leslie, & Frith, 1985). Thus, since the early 1980s there has been a growing interest on the study of theory of mind abilities and this interest has spread to include questions such as: What are the precursors of a theory of mind? Is there a relationship between prelinguistic communication skills and theory of mind abilities? We will address these questions from a three-way comparative perspective in which information from three populations relevant for theory of mind research will be considered, that is normal infants, children with autism, and congenitally blind children.

Normal infants

In order to understand the thrust of theory of mind research we need to begin with the original Wimmer and Perner (1983) study. These authors developed the now well-known Sally–Anne task. In this task there are two doll protagonists, Sally and Anne. Sally comes into a scenario and places a marble into her basket. Then, she leaves the scene and the marble is transferred by Anne to a hidden box. When Sally returns, the experimenter asks the "Belief Question": Where will Sally look for the marble? If the children point to the previous location of the marble (in Sally's basket) then they pass the belief question as they appreciate that Sally could not possibly know that Anne has moved the marble. Children understand Sally's false belief. If, however, children point to the marble's current location in the hidden box, then children fail the belief question as they fail to take into account Sally's own beliefs. Two further questions are usually included in the task in order to further understand the child's representations of the events: Where is the marble really? ("Reality question") and Where was the marble at the beginning ("Memory question"). The importance of false belief is essentially methodological. False belief tasks allow the subject and another individual to have different beliefs/knowledge and for these to be tapped experimentally. It has been argued (Leslie, 1987) that failure on this task demonstrates an inability to form representations of representations (metarepresentations), that is, I know that Sally believes that the marble is where she left it last. It is only at around 4 years of age that normal children pass this task which has been considered the "acid test" of theory of mind. It is thought that 4-year-old children are able to pass the Sally–Anne task as they understand that the false belief of other persons will determine their subsequent behaviour. They fully understand about people's desires (Sally wants to find the marble), beliefs (Sally thinks the marble is where she left it last), and emotions (she is surprised not to find the marble where she left it last). Thus, by approximately 4 years of age children have an "adult-like" belief-desire psychology within which they can coordinate belief and desire to explain and predict behaviour (Cassidy, 1998).

Interestingly 3-year-olds are not as successful as 4-year-olds in the Sally–Anne task. Bartsch and Wellman (1989) provide some insight as to why this may be the case. Their proposal involves a desire-based account of theory of mind development. They suggest that 3-year-olds' failure on standard false belief tasks is the result of their reliance on desire to predict behaviour rather than the result of an inability to understand false belief. Children have a desire-belief psychology at 3 but they use desire as their primary tool to understand and explain behaviour. Consequently, many 3-year-old children when confronted with the Sally–Anne task respond by having Sally look at where the marble actually was hidden, disregarding the fact that Sally could not possibly have known this (Wellman & Estes, 1986).

Looking further back in developmental time we find that 2-year-olds have a naive psychology based purely on desire (Bartsch & Wellman, 1989). At this age, children do not yet understand beliefs. Two-year-olds use desires as their main source of information on how to predict and explain behaviours. Desires are conceived as drives towards objects (Wellman & Woolley, 1990) and perceptions are at first understood as awareness of objects (Flavell, 1988). It is thought that knowledge of representation is limited in 2-year-olds but enough is available for the child to separate objects, events, and desires in the world and their representations. Thus, 2-year-old children are able to engage in pretend and symbolic play behaviours at this stage. As symbolic play behaviours also appear to be based on the ability to build representations, researchers such as Leslie (1987) have argued that pretend-play is an early manifestation or precursor of the development of a theory of mind.

Once this type of reasoning got started, the search for earlier and earlier precursors of theory of mind development began. Thus, prior to pretend play, it was found that infants around 9–12 months of age engage in prelinguistic intentional communication. As described earlier in this chapter, infants develop communicative gestures to regulate interactions with caregivers in relation to external objects. They will engage in triadic adult–object–infant social interactions including social referencing, joint attentional behaviours, imitative learning, protoimperative requests and protodeclarative calls for attention. These behaviours seem to entail some level of understanding by the infant of the mental processes of other people, that is, of considering people as intentional beings and understanding other people's understanding (Grice, 1957). Thus, prelinguistic intentional communication, especially the ability to use protodeclaratives and imitative learning, have also been thought to be a precursor of the development of a theory of mind.

In summary, evidence from the development of normal infants suggests that theory of mind development involves a number of stages: the development of infant intentional communication at the end of the first year of life; the ability to pretend and engage in symbolic play at around the age of 2 years; the presence of desire/belief understanding at around the age of 3 years; and the development of a full metarepresentational system capable of understanding false beliefs at around the age of 4 years. Let's now turn to children with autism. It has been argued that insights from atypical populations can often illuminate much about typical or normal development (Tager-Flusberg, 1994a). With this in mind we now turn to two atypical populations and ask the same theory of mind questions of children who do not appear to be developing in the normal way.

Children with autism

In 1985, Baron-Cohen and colleagues asked the question: Does the child with autism have a "theory of mind"? They went about answering this question by giving children with autism the acid test of theory of mind—the false belief, Sally–Anne task. Interestingly, children with autism were unable to pass this false belief task. This lead Baron-Cohen and co-workers (Baron-Cohen, 1991a, 1991b; Baron-Cohen et al., 1985; Frith, 1989) to propose that the characteristics of autism derive from a problem with the development of a "theory of mind" and has to do with an inability to read other people's minds or intentions. Hence, the condition of autism being referred to as "mindblindness" (Baron-Cohen, 1995).

Interest in the precursors of a theory of mind was also evident in the work with children with autism. Thus, in 1987, Baron-Cohen found further evidence for the absence of a theory of mind in autism when he found that children with autism have severe impairments in their symbolic play abilities. Authors interpreted these findings as evidence of a connection between pretence and theory of mind via metarepresentation (Leslie, 1987). Impairment in metarepresentational abilities would affect both symbolic play and one's ability to understand other people's minds and children with autism showed major deficits in both areas.

Children with autism also present major difficulties with language use. Approximately 50% of children with autism do not learn to use language at all. The other half, although able to use language, do not do so appropriately. Their speech tends to involve a great deal of echolalia (mimicking repetitions) and pronoun reversals (*you* for *I*) and is seldom socially relevant (Loveland, 1991, 1993; Loveland, McEvoy, Tunali, & Kelley, 1990).

But how about earlier precursors? Children with autism also appear to have deficits in prelinguistic intentional communication. Children with autism have difficulty with imitation and furthermore appear to be unable to reproduce any behaviour that is novel (Dawson, Hill, Spencer, Galpert, & Watson, 1990; Jones & Prior, 1985; Mundy, Sigman, Ungerer, & Sherman, 1986; Stone, Lemaneck, Fishel, Fernandez, & Attemeier, 1990). In line with their difficulties with imitative learning, children with autism also have problems with joint attention and perspective taking. Traditionally, children with autism were considered to have problems with eye contact in terms of lack of eye contact and avoidance in eye contact (Frith, 1989). Recent research, however, has suggested that the deficit is not in eye contact *per se* but in the coordination of eye contact and gesture in action. Children with autism do not appear to be able to coordinate gaze behaviour in order to share attention with another person on a third thing or object. In other words, it appears that the deficit in children with autism is in joint attention itself (Gómez, Sarriá & Tamarit, 1993; Hermelin & O'Connor, 1970; Sarriá, & Rivière, 1991). Consequently, children with autism develop what Gómez and colleagues (1993) refer to as contact gestures, that is, gestures that involve establishing contact with a person such as leading a person by the hand to a desired place or object but they do not develop joint attentional gestures such as the emblematic protodeclarative pointing (Baron-Cohen, 1989). When children with autism use pointing they seem to do so protoimperatively, to request objects or actions.

The difficulties in children with autism discussed earlier appear to be related mainly to their social cognition (Tomasello, Kruger, & Ratner, 1993). Other aspects of the cognition of children with autism appear to be adequate such as tool use or object permanence (Curcio, 1978; Rivière, Belinchón, Pfeiffer, & Sarriá, 1988). Thus, children with autism appear to have a specific deficit in the area of social cognition and consequently the development of a theory of mind.

Now we turn to the population of interest in this book, blind children. Is it possible that blind children due to lack of vision also suffer from mindblindness as children with autism do?

Congenitally blind children

Lack of vision and mindblindness.   Some classic authors have suggested that a proportion of blind children also suffer from mindblindness (Keeler, 1957). Others have adopted a more psychoanalytic perspective and have pointed out the difficulties blind children have in developing a sense of self (Burlingham, 1965; Wills, 1979). Based on this underdeveloped-self perspective, authors have provided explanations for other behaviours of blind children such as echolalia and difficulties with the use of personal pronouns (Dunlea, 1989; Fay, 1973) and delay in the use of symbolic play (Fraiberg & Adelson, 1973). Blind children have also been noted to have stereotypes, mannerisms, and ritualistic behaviours (Chess, 1971; Wills, 1979). Interestingly, these same characteristics are seen in children with autism (Frith, 1989; Hobson, 1993a) and Hobson, Brown, Minter, and Lee (1997) have gone as far as to suggest that the characteristics of congenitally blind children include substantial numbers of autistic-like clinical features. Thus, it appears that the line that separates mindblindness and congenital blindness is getting more and more blurred. Blind children can have difficulties in their social and early communicative development and in the nature of their difficulties they resemble children with autism. Is this really the case?

There are two lines of research that need to be separated here. First, it is theoretically interesting to find out if congenitally blind children are able to develop a full-blown theory of mind and its precursors. Are blind children like normal children in this respect or are they more like children with autism? Second, there is the question of whether blind children are autistic-like in their language use and behavioural characteristics. In other words, does lack of vision predispose children to autism or autistic-like behaviours? We will address these two issues separately.

We will begin with the theory of mind question. Do blind children develop a full blown theory of mind? There is a dearth of research in this area but what is available has been highly suggestive. We will start with the precursors of theory of mind and work our way to the acid test of theory of mind, the false belief tasks. As our previous reviews point out, congenitally blind children can experience difficulties in the development of joint attention and shared reference because they have problems following a line of gaze and using gaze alternation. As a consequence protodeclarative pointing may be absent or severely delayed in congenitally blind children. None the less, it is important to underline that caregivers and blind children can establish joint attention and shared reference using alternative modes of interaction. In blind children, shared reference with significant others is most often achieved via verbal interactions (including prelinguistic vocalizations in the part of the infant) as well as touch and audition (Als et al., 1980b; Mulford, 1983; Urwin, 1979). Thus, the absence or delay in protodeclarative pointing does not necessarily reflect difficulties with one of the precursors of theory of mind. In the blind, we need to look at alternative modes of interaction which perform the same function as protodeclarative pointing. Blind children do not spontaneously point protodeclaratively because the pointing gesture is visually guided and derives from our ability to visually share information with others. Once caregiver–infant routines are underway, blind children should be able to use sound/hearing and touch protodeclaratively, for example, by taking the hand of the caregiver and putting it on a particular object, and protoimperatively, by crying/whining to request that an object be given or returned (Pérez-Pereira & Castro, 1995; Rowland, 1983; Urwin, 1983). This is an important clarification to make. The information we have from blind children helps us understand that in theory of mind development it is not the pointing *per se* that is important, but *its function*, the fact that protodeclarative pointing represents an interest in sharing attention without regard to the consequences that the behaviour itself may bring. Which gestures are used to perform this function is of relatively minor importance, perhaps exaggerated because of the fact that it happens to be the pointing gesture that initially performs this function in most prelinguistic sighted infants across the world. It needs to be made clear that reference is not modality dependent. Visually based joint attention is not essential for reaping the possible benefits of joint attention in language acquisition, nor is protodeclarative pointing essential for triggering adult linguistic input about the names of things.

In this sense, research on prelinguistic abilities of blind children has used sighted infants's development as the yardstick with which to measure blind children's progress. Although this perspective is necessary and informative, it is also relevant to try to understand development from the perspective of blind children themselves. Without vision nor language, how would one secure an adult's attention to an object? Pointing will not be at the top of the list, but sounds/hearing and touch will be. Like Urwin (1983) said many years ago, we need to uncover the process of adaptive development. What we should be studying in detail is blind infants' alternative ways of engaging in interaction with significant others to try to understand how some blind children are able to achieve excellent progress in early prelinguistic and later linguistic development.

Later on, symbolic play and perspective taking can be delayed in blind children (Andersen et al., 1984; Bigelow, 1988, 1992a; Fraiberg & Adelson, 1973). None the less around 3 years of age most congenitally blind children have developed symbolic play, and shortly after 3 years role play is also evident (Pérez-Pereira & Castro, 1994; Urwin, 1984a). Urwin's (1983) work also suggests that delays are not always evident. In the case of Suzanne, a congenitally blind child with optic atrophy, Urwin observed fantasy play at 2;3 years and use of language that was similar to that expected of a sighted infant of a similar age. Suzanne named and requested objects frequently, she referred to places beyond her range of touch, she commented on other people's possession of objects and on their actions. It is thought that Suzanne's experience and use of language played an important role in developing her understanding of her "self" and "others" and in extending her surrounding context beyond her immediate range of touch. In this sense, language played an important compensatory role in the development of this blind infant, especially with respect to symbolic play and perspective taking. In turn, this blind infant had access to language experience through a sensitive and conducive communicative environment which provided her with opportunities to engage in cycles of interaction. It is important, therefore, for us to question the necessity of developmental delay in blind infants as the environment can play an important compensatory role in their development.

But how about the acid test of "theory of mind"? McAlpine and Moore (1995) carried out an experiment using an adaptation of the false belief task. They used containers with tactile familiarity, a MacDonald's styrofoam container and a cardboard milk container. The child was presented with the container and asked to guess what was inside it. After answering that it contained a hamburger or the like, the child was asked to open the container where a sock of the approximate weight of a hamburger was found. Next, a friend or parent or teacher was called to the area; as the person approached the child was asked what he or she thought the other person would answer when asked what was inside the container. The second task repeated the same procedure with the milk container, which was in reality filled with water. McAlpine and Moore (1995) tested 15 blind subjects aged 4–9 years of average to above-average intelligence. These authors found that the majority of blind children passed both tasks (10 out of 15 children), one child passed one task but not the other, and four children failed both tasks. The four children who failed both tasks had worse visual acuity and they were also in the younger age range in the sample (5–6 years). Unfortunately, these authors did not test any control sighted children; none the less, it has been found that sighted children are able to succeed in this type of task around the age of 4;6 years or over.

More recently Hobson and his colleagues (Hobson et al., 1997; Minter et al., 1998) have completed a study of false belief with congenitally blind children. They studied 21 blind children and 21 sighted control children of similar chronological (5–9 years) and mental ages (mean verbal mental age for each group 6;10 years). The children were asked to feel a warm teapot and to guess its contents. They were then shown that it contained sand, not a drink. The children were then asked two questions: What they first thought was in the teapot? And what would a peer (who had not seen the demonstration) would think was in the teapot. Interestingly, not all the sighted children passed the false belief question; 10% did not in this task, despite the fact that the youngest sighted child was 4;7 years. The blind children performed worse, with only about half the blind children passing the false belief question. If Hobson and colleagues would have done no more than this experiment, we would have concluded that blind children have significant problems developing a theory of mind. Interestingly, Hobson and colleagues did another task, this time more dependent on touch as boxes had been covered with material that differentiated a rough box from a soft-covered box. Children were asked to predict in which box a person would look for a pencil when the pencil was moved from one kind of box to another kind of box, without the person having witnessed the change. Interestingly, the blind children did much better in this task with 80% of the children passing the false belief question. The sighted children were all able to pass this task.

These results on theory of mind tasks with blind children underline the complexities involved in comparing the performance of blind and sighted infants. Hobson et al. (1997) acknowledged that when undertaking the tasks, the experimenters had to be extremely careful in communicating with the blind children through language and touch. They also found it difficult to interpret some of the blind children's responses. Basically, the authors are acknowledging the possible detrimental effect that a stranger experimenter may have on having successful communication with a blind child. This difficulty, of course, is problematic when we are trying to have successful communication in order to get at theory of mind abilities in blind children. In addition, the discrepant results from the two tasks used by Hobson point out the enormous methodological difficulties that exist in interpreting performance in particular tasks as evidence of theory of mind abilities in blind children. There is little doubt that the second task, the box task, was more accessible to blind children and they therefore performed better. Methodologically, we need to learn from the work of Hobson, to include at least two tasks before conclusions are reached. But we can go further. Recall that blind children only have language and touch information to work with to make their decision, whereas the sighted peers have vision to provide them with cues as well. Thus, we would suggest, that a third control group is necessary: sighted children who perform the task under blindfolded conditions. It is only then that we can make some sense of the role that vision plays in understanding instructions and in creating joint reference necessary for evaluating theory of mind abilities. In this respect we have much to learn from methodologies used by Povinelli and colleagues with non-human primates (Povinelli & Eddy, 1996).

This discussion underlines a number of important points. Blind children are not like children with autism in that they do not appear to have major deficits in theory of mind development nor in its precursors. It is clear that as scientists we need to look for alternative ways in which blind children can show us what they know, otherwise we may reach the wrong conclusions. Some blind children are delayed in the development of theory of mind and its precursors, but a longitudinal view suggests that these delays are surmountable with time and relevant experience, which is not the case for children with autism. Finally, in the case of children with autism, it is the theory of mind capacity that is severely damaged. Consequently, exposure to conducive learning environments for the development of a theory of mind should have much smaller effects for children with autism than for blind children.

Lack of vision and autistic-like behaviours. We now turn to our second question. Does lack of vision predispose blind children to autism or autistic-like behaviours? Interestingly, Hobson and colleagues (Brown et al., 1997; Hobson et al., 1997) have been addressing this precise question in their recent research. Hobson (1990, 1993b) has argued that there may be functional overlap in the developmental psychopathology of children with autism and blind children. This claim is based on Hobson's theory of interpersonal relatedness. According to this theory, blind children, like children with autism, have difficulties in comprehending and identifying with other people's attitudes. In the case of blind children, it is a peripheral problem—lack of vision that leads to lack of social-emotional experiences such as visually experiencing caregivers' emotional reactions to particular objects and events. In the case of autism, there are more central mechanisms that are impaired. Thus, Hobson and colleagues have a theoretical motivation to look for similarities between children with autism and congenitally blind children.

Is there a higher prevalence of autism in the population of congenitally blind children? The answer to this question is not simple nor easy to investigate. Researchers have varied in their definitions and uses of terms like "autism" and "autistic-like" and reports vary in terms of methodologies used and amount of information they provide. There are a number of clinical-anecdotal accounts of blind children presenting the syndrome of autism (Blank, 1975; Curson, 1979; Elonen & Cain, 1964; Green & Schecter, 1957; McGuire, 1969). In general, these descriptive accounts tend to be particular case studies where methodological details make it difficult to make generalizations. On the other hand, Fraiberg (1977) found that 7 out of 27 blind children exhibited a clinical picture closely resembling autism (26%) but other researchers have not found such a high incidence in their studies (Gillman & Goddard, 1974; Jan, Freeman & Scott, 1977; Norris et al., 1957). For example, Jan et al. (1977) found only 3 out of 92 blind children exhibited psychotic-autistic type syndrome (3%). More recently, Hobson and colleagues (Brown et al.,

1997) found that 2 out of 24 congenitally blind children would warrant a confident diagnosis of Kanner-type autism (8%) whereas 10 out of the 24 congenitally blind children in their study could be described as exhibiting autistic-like behaviours (42%).

Where does this information leave us? The incidence of autism in the general population is approximately 0.1% or 1 per 1000. Thus, even if we take the smallest percentage found in congenitally blind children, i.e. 3%, this is substantially higher than what would be expected from the general population. Can we then conclude that the prevalence of autism is higher in congenitally blind children due to their lack of vision? We think this would be rather premature. We need to go further and be confident that it is blindness, and not something else, that accounts for the findings. With this in mind, we looked at other populations with sensory and other deficits. We looked at deaf children, deaf-blind children, and severely mentally retarded children. Interestingly, there is an increased incidence of autism in all these populations, suggesting that one can arrive at autistic-like behaviours through so many different routes. Jure, Rapin, and Tuchman (1991) found that 46 out of 1150 deaf children (4%) met the DSM-III-R criteria for autism. A figure not unlike that found by Jan et al. (1977) with blind children (3%). None the less there was one important variable that needed to be taken into consideration before the findings could be understood fully. The authors found that the severity of the autistic behaviours found in the deaf children were related to the severity of the mental handicap of the deaf children in their sample. They found that less than one-fifth of the deaf children with autism had near normal non-verbal cognition. Thus, it appears that cognitive abilities may well play a role in the presence or absence of autism in deafness, and this may also be the case in other populations as well. Let's now turn to deaf-blind children. In a recent American study (Baldwin, 1993) it was found that 10% of deaf-blind children were also considered to exhibit the syndrome of autism (as defined by DSM-III-R criteria). No information on the relationship between cognitive abilities, autism and deaf-blindness was provided in this study. Continuing our comparisons, we found that the prevalence of autism (as defined by DSM-III-R) in children with mental handicap has been found to be 8.9–11.7% (Nordin & Gillberg, 1996). These findings suggest once again that cognitive abilities may well play an important role in the presence of autism in populations with sensory impairments.

If we look back at some of the studies we reviewed before, we find that Hobson's 2 out of 24 blind children who were also considered to exhibit autism also had significant cognitive deficits (Brown et al., 1997). Both blind children with autism in his study had verbal IQs lower than 70 as measured by the Weschler Pre-school and Primary Scale of Intelligence (WPPSI). Putting aside the methodological difficulties of using the WPPSI with blind children (Tillman, 1963, 1973) as opposed to using more appropriate scales such as the Reynell–Zinkin scales (Reynell, 1978), Slossen scales (Slossen, 1984), Binet–Simon scales, or others (Hayes, 1942, 1950; Tobin, 1994), it is important to note that Hobson and colleagues did provide information on the cognitive abilities of the children in their sample. Furthermore, when trying to ascertain whether blind children also exhibited autism, these authors used as a control group children with autism with similar poor cognitive abilities, thus comparing like with like, so to speak. We, in turn, think that one further comparison group in the Hobson study was necessary, namely, children with poor cognitive abilities without autism. With this third control group of children with mental handicap, it would have been possible to begin to ascertain whether the presence of autism in blind children was related to the lack of vision or their cognitive impairment or both. At this stage, we can not simply talk about the presence or absence of autism in blind children. Future research needs to consider further the role of cognitive abilities and other variables in this relationship. We venture to speculate that such data will show that there is no necessary relationship between congenital blindness and autism. It is our opinion that there needs to be an additional handicap in blind children, be it in the form of mental handicap as suggested previously, severely impoverished environmental provision with no alternative routes for communication explored, or coincidental psychopathology of autism for the presence of autism in blind children to occur. In the latter case, that is, coincidental psychopathology of autism, one would expect the incidence of autism to be skewed towards blind boys rather than blind girls as is the case in the general population. One would also expect prognosis to be poor and intervention to have limited success. Autism or autistic-like behaviours as a result of a combination of handicaps such as blindness and mental handicap or blindness and environmental impoverishment, should not present such a skew towards boys and, furthermore, should show greater likelihood of improvement with intervention.

This review has shown clearly that superficial similarities between blind children and children with autism are deceptive and misleading. First, the "autistic-like" behaviours reported in blind children may not reflect the same underlying mechanisms as those observed in children with autism (a point emphasized in Chapter 1 about much of blind children's behaviours). Second, "autistic-like" behaviours in blind children may have different functions for blind children and may in fact be adaptive. For example, we suggest that repeated head turning and rocking back and forth may provide blind children with proprioceptive feedback that can give information about the position of their bodies in space. In the same vein, Blass, Freedman, and Steingart (1974) have noted that repeated hand stroking may facilitate lexical retrieval and verbal fluency in blind adults. Third, the population of blind children is extremely heterogeneous and the vast majority of blind children have other deficits such as deafness, cerebral palsy, or mental handicap. Thus, when reporting data from studies of blind children researchers need to be sure to describe carefully the composition and characteristics of the sample used. As discussed previously, cognitive impairment is certainly one route to arrive at autistic behaviours. Thus, studies including blind children with poor cognitive abilities are much more likely to find "autistic-like" behaviours in their sample than studies who include blind children with better cognitive abilities.

CONCLUDING REMARKS

We would like now to return to the issues of variability in the social and early communicative outcomes of blind children. Due to the fact that even minimal degrees of vision, or short periods of vision in early life, may make a significant difference to the development of visually-impaired children (Preisler, 1991), we have tried as best we could to limit our discussion to congenitally blind children. Despite these efforts, it is likely that new students to the field of blindness as well as parents and professionals find the literature on early social and communicative development in blind infants highly confusing. There appears to be a spectrum of outcomes for congenitally blind children, from excellent development with no apparent delays in social and communicative interaction as was the case of Suzanne (Urwin, 1983) to major delays in social and early communicative interaction with autistic-like behaviours as described in a number of case studies (Blank, 1975; McGuire, 1969). We argue that there are at least two key factors which affect the outcomes of congenitally blind children. One is the child's own cognitive resources, and the other is the extent to which the environment provides the child with alternative means of engagement in social interaction and communication. Furthermore, we highlight the need for research with blind children to focus on the process of development, rather than in particular behaviours such as pointing or passing a particular theory of mind task. In the same vein, we suggest that although sighted children's development is an important yardstick with which to measure progress in blind children's development, there is a need for research to focus in more detail on blind children's own alternative developmental routes to understanding themselves, others, and the world around them.

CHAPTER FOUR

Language development in blind children (1)

There is a great deal of information available on blind children's language development. With this in mind, the discussion is presented in two separate chapters. The first chapter introduces this topic by presenting methodological and theoretical considerations of previous research on blind children's language. In addition, this chapter has three sections devoted to phonological, lexical, and morphosyntactic development. The second chapter (Chapter 5) covers the following topics: personal reference terms, pragmatic development, verbal routines, and imitative speech, and a final section on blind children's language and language acquisition theories.

PREVIOUS RESEARCH ON BLIND CHILDREN'S LANGUAGE

Introduction

For a long time, very little was known about the development of language in blind children. Practically until the 1970s no systematic research was done on the topic, with the exception of Maxfield's study (Maxfield, 1936), and the controversy surrounding Cutsford's work (Cutsford, 1951) on verbalism or the lack of meaning of blind children's words. Before this time, there were partial reports on language acquisition, but the majority were not the result of organized research but came from unsystematic observations carried out by clinicians (Burlingham, 1964, 1965; Keeler, 1957; Nagera & Colonna, 1965; Wills, 1979). In the case of Norris et al.'s study (Norris et al., 1957), the data came from a large-scale assessment of a number of developmental schedules. The impetus of this type of large-scale research on the development of blind children has its origins in the substantial increase of blind children born between 1940 and 1954 as a consequence of retrolental fibroplasia (RFP), caused by an overexposure to oxygen of premature infants (Norgate, 1996). The first in-depth studies, such as Urwin's (1978, 1979, 1984a), arose in the 1970s probably as a consequence of the vitality of the research on language development with non-handicapped children at that time. However, the study of blind children presents additional methodological difficulties, which probably have had consequences on the present state of the art of what we know about language development in blind children.

This late interest in the language acquisition of blind children is striking because of the possible theoretical relevance of data on blind children for any theory of language acquisition and for increasing our understanding of psychological development. Theoretical interest in this matter goes back to the time of empiricism, when it was considered that experience was the base of knowledge. Thus, if blind children lack an essential experience, namely vision, then their concepts may be different from those formed by sighted children. Consequently, if we assume that conceptual development is the basis of language, then language development is likely to be deficient in blind children. But, is this the case? Do blind children exhibit delayed or deficient language development? Is there a relationship between blind children's cognitive development and language development? The study of blind children's language development is an excellent realm to test whether these hypotheses are true or not (see Landau & Gleitman, 1985).

Methodological considerations

As already indicated, the study of the acquisition of language by blind children has been informed by former studies with sighted children, not only because a great deal of information and theoretical interpretation were provided by the studies of non-handicapped children, but also because they provided methods to study blind children's language. However, the task of studying blind children's language is not a simple one, nor is it straightforward to directly apply the methods, procedures, and interpretations used with sighted children to the study of blind children. In addition, the characteristics of the population of blind children present additional difficulties to researchers. First, the majority of studies with blind children have been carried out with very small numbers of subjects. Most longitudinal studies have focused on a few cases, usually not more than five blind children. For instance, Dunlea (1989) studied two blind children, two visually impaired children, and two sighted children, Urwin (1978, 1984a) studied two blind children and one visually impaired child, and Pérez-Pereira and Castro (1994) studied three blind children, one visually impaired child, and one sighted child. The small samples used are due in part to the fact that congenitally blind children without other deficits are rare. Other studies that used a larger number of blind children were not devoted to the study of language acquisition (Fraiberg, 1977), or, in most cases, were cross-sectional studies (Norris et al., 1957).

The point about using such small numbers of children is that it is problematic to generalize the results found in one study to the larger population of blind children. This is particularly the case given the heterogeneity of the population of blind children. Blindness may have different causes and aetiologies, and this may result in children presenting not only blindness, but, in many cases, other additional problems, which are not always easy to detect or assess. In other cases (particularly in retinopathy of prematurity, ROP, formerly referred to as retrolental fibroplasia, RLF), prematurity is highly associated with blindness, which makes comparisons based on chronological age problematic, even if correction for prematurity is introduced. In addition, blindness is defined by the degree of visual acuity. The threshold of blindness is not the same in all countries, since its legal definition has consequences regarding social services, benefits, access to education, etc. Furthermore, there are great differences among the children who are defined as blind. Many children who are defined as legally blind have residual vision, and the extent to which they can use it may vary a great deal. Moreover, blindness can occur at different times during life. Regarding children, visual loss can happen after birth, or before birth (congenital). In the first case, the amount and length of visual experience available to the child before blindness is extremely important. Thus, it is difficult to speak of blindness as a homogeneous category. Heterogeneity is probably higher in the population of blind people than in non-visually impaired people, because of the higher proportion of blind people with other additional handicaps (Rosa & Ochaita, 1993; Webster & Roe, 1998). This makes it even more necessary to have an approach that pays due attention to individual differences (Warren, 1994). Although the majority of the existing longitudinal researchers tried to study congenitally blind children without any additional handicaps, this obviously does not ensure the similarity of their samples, and this constitutes a difficulty in making comparisons between them.

Second, there are differences in the categories used to analyse blind children's productions, even though scholars have tried to focus on the same phenomena. For example, not all researchers interested in blind children's first words have used the same category system: Some of them (i.e. Bigelow, 1987; Landau & Gleitman, 1985; Mulford, 1988) have applied the categories originally devised by Nelson (1973), whereas others have introduced a few changes in them (Dunlea, 1989). Similarly, the studies analysing the pragmatic functions of blind children's language (Dunlea, 1989; Pérez-Pereira & Castro, 1992) have used different category systems. This makes comparisons between studies difficult, and in addition creates discrepancies and contradictory findings that can be attributed to the different ways in which the data were categorized in the first place.

Third, a number of scholars have been insensitive towards blind children's behaviours and as a result have underestimated their abilities. A number of scholars have used tasks and techniques to assess blind children abilities that are inappropriate for such a population. For example, Brown et al. (1997) used the WISC to analyse the intelligence level of a sample of blind children in order to classify the children into two groups with different IQs. It is clear that the use of a test which requires the processing of visual information and the handling of material with visual clues is not appropriate for assessing blind children. Furthermore, other instruments exist which are better adapted to blind children's abilities (see Tobin, 1994). In the same vein, Norgate (1996) calls our attention to and criticizes Dunlea's (1989) use of a task to test the ability of blind children to sort a set of same and different objects. On the basis of her results, Dunlea concluded that blind children have difficulties treating the members of a category as the same sort of thing. In Norgate's opinion, this technique is inappropriate for use with blind children because, as Landau (1997) has indicated, blind children might have extra difficulties keeping track of which objects they had or had not explored. This sequential touching and grouping task is useful for sighted children, but it does not have the same value for blind children. Norgate (1996) suggests that blind children are able to demonstrate that they treat category members as the same type of things provided that haptic scans are taken into account. Therefore, suitable measures of blind children's abilities must be developed by researchers. It is not appropriate to rely on techniques and tasks designed for sighted children.

In a similar vein, researchers have underestimated blind children's abilities and have not been sensitive enough to the meaning of blind children's behaviours. This can occur, for instance, whenever a behaviour that apparently is similar to that of sighted children has a different function for blind children, or when blind children use alternative or different means than sighted children to fulfil the same function. Some authors have considered the use of imitations by blind children as parroting, echolalia, or using words without any sense (Burlingham, 1964, 1965; Nagera & Colonna, 1965; Wills, 1979). Nevertheless, other authors have shown that blind children use imitations as a tool to analyse language, and to convey conversational and pragmatic functions (Kitzinger, 1984; Pérez-Pereira, 1994; Peters, 1987, 1994). Whereas Andersen et al. (1984, 1993) and Dunlea (1989) have claimed that blind children rely heavily on stereotypic speech and that stereotypic speech has no apparent developmental role, Peters (1994) and others (Pérez-Pereira, 1994; Pérez-Pereira & Castro, 1997) have shown how blind children use verbal routines and stereotypic speech to keep in touch with other people, and to interact socially and participate in shared activities. As for the use of alternative means to fulfil a given function, Als et al. (1980b), Preisler (1991), Rattray (1997), Rowland (1984), and Urwin, (1978, 1984a), found that blind children first used tactual and vocal means to participate in social interactions, and later on they use social play and communicative acts to achieve the same end. However, these children did not use conventional gestures to communicate their intentions or participate in social exchanges. The interpretation of the functional value of such behaviours requires a certain degree of sensitivity on the part of researchers, who have to adopt the child's perspective and try to understand their intentions. Otherwise, blind children's abilities are likely to be underestimated.

Fourth, in a number of studies the interpretations and conclusions put forward by researchers are not well grounded in data, and, sometimes, generalizations are offered without enough data to support them. An important limitation of a number of studies of blind children's language acquisition is the relatively small size of the speech samples on which data analysis and conclusions are based. It is not uncommon to find studies of blind children's language development relying on very short corpora. For instance, Moore and McConachie (1994) studied verbal interaction between blind and visually impaired children and their parents based on 15 minutes speech samples of 16 children. The same authors (McConachie & Moore, 1994) studied the development of expressive language and the relationships between cognitive and language development based on the application of a few scales of the Reynell–Zinkin test to 18 severely visually impaired children. Although, as a first step, it may be acceptable to draw conclusions from transcriptions of speech that are a few minutes long, there is no doubt that it is rather risky to make general statements on any subject, based on such a small database.

On other occasions, scholars have proposed interpretations which are not based on rigorous analysis of their data. For instance, the belief that blind children produce an abnormally high number of pronoun reversal errors, proposed by several authors (Andersen et al., 1984; Dunlea, 1989; Fraiberg & Adelson, 1973), has not been based on quantitative analysis of children's pronoun productions (see Pérez-Pereira, 1999, for a criticism). On the contrary, conclusions are based on a few examples or anecdotal observations. Although it is certainly true that in some cases examples are extracted from many hours of observation, we cannot forget that the scientific method requires systematicity and should be open to the possibility of the data being checked and verified by other researchers. Moreover, although some studies do provide quantitative results, statistical analyses are rarely undertaken in order to show statistical significance (e.g. Dunlea, 1989). Thus, there is a pressing need to present quantitative as well as qualitative data when reporting studies with blind children (see McCune, 1991 for similar arguments).

Finally, as is well known (Miller, 1987), cross-sectional research cannot tell us much about individual changes across time, nor about differences in the patterns of development between individuals. Thus, whether our goal is to see if blind children follow a different route from that of sighted children in their linguistic development, or if we are exploring possible differences between blind children, longitudinal research is needed. Otherwise we can only appreciate differences between individuals at a given point in time, but can not understand developmental trends. Thus, the use of cross-sectional designs may hide existing differences in developmental patterns. The use of longitudinal methods is very time consuming and expensive in relation to cross-sectional studies. However, if we want to know how blind children change across time, longitudinal (or longitudinal sequential) methods are the designs most suited for this purpose. Furthermore, since individual differences seem to be even greater between blind children than between sighted children, the use of cross-sectional methods can lead researchers to recruit non-equivalent age samples. As differences among blind children are great, it is easy for a bias on different aspects of development (e.g. motor, cognitive) to be introduced among the age groups studied. This may result in the findings being contaminated by these differences. As should now be clear, all these factors make research on language acquisition in blind children a complex and difficult task.

Theoretical considerations

The study of language development in blind children has interesting theoretical implications for our understanding of the role of vision in language acquisition. The vast majority of previous studies on the topic have adopted the view that language development is based on cognitive abilities. According to this view, clearly inspired by the Piagetian tradition, the beginning of language depends on previous cognitive developments, such as the acquisition of notions such as object permanence, means–ends relationships, or the capacity of representation. This dependence between cognition and language affects not only the emergence of the first words, but also the meanings expressed by children in their first language productions, as classical researchers of language acquisition have proposed (Brown, 1973; MacNamara, 1972; Slobin, 1973). As for later development, even certain aspects of grammatical development (such as the use of comparative terms in coordinated structures to describe differences in two dimensions) are considered to be dependent on specific cognitive achievements (such as reversibility and operational thinking) (Cromer, 1991). According to this view, given that blind children have difficulties in their conceptual development and knowledge of reality, then, their language development is also expected to be subject to deviations from the normal path. Usually, this standpoint has adopted a monolithic view of development (akin to the Piagetian view), with minimal consideration of individual differences. Consistent with this view, any differences found between blind children and sighted children are interpreted as deviant, pathological, or not normal language development. Nevertheless, even when scholars use the latter less pejorative expression of not normal, the differences remain unexplained. Thus, the possibility that certain features of the language of blind children may have different functions is not contemplated; neither is the possibility that there may exist different routes to acquiring language.

This view that there is a cognitive basis for language acquisition has been predominant in the field until very recently and can be observed in many accounts of blind children's language development. Many characterizations of blind children's language are anchored in the assumption that blind children's conceptualization of reality cannot be the same as that of the sighted children. Consequently, their difficulties in conceptualizing reality result in specific features of their language.

One of these difficulties is that young blind children do not describe characteristics of objects, or their locations. In other words, they show a great difficulty in describing external reality. In tune with this, it was also considered that, in general, blind children do not make reference to actions performed by other people, but only to their own actions (Andersen et al., 1984, 1993; Dunlea, 1984, 1989; Urwin, 1978, 1984a). Precisely because of this, a number of authors concluded that blind children's speech was egocentric or self-centred, and not externally oriented.

Apart from being egocentric, some scholars claim that blind children's speech is less creative compared to that of sighted children. This lack of (or severely reduced) creativity is shown in the absence of idiosyncratic terms invented by the children themselves, the absence of overextensions in their speech, and their enormous use of stereotypic and formulaic speech (Andersen et al., 1984, 1993; Dunlea, 1989; Miecznikowski & Andersen, 1986). Finally, it is argued that due to blind children's difficulties in perform deictic shifts, blind children produce many reversal errors when using pronouns (Andersen et al., 1984; Dunlea, 1989).

The account of blind children's language offered by authors who were impressed by the so-called cognitive basis for language coincides with the descriptions and interpretations of blind children's language given by psychoanalytically oriented scholars. In a way, it can be said that the cognitively based authors offer a newer version of proposals made by earlier authors, who had clinical experience with blind children. Thus, there is a clear link between a number of early studies of blind children, clearly influenced by psychoanalytic theory, and those of more recent scholars who are more cognitively oriented. For example the characterizations of blind children's language as parroting, speaking without meaning, or echolalic speech by earlier authors (Burlingham, 1961, 1965; Nagera & Colonna, 1965; Wills, 1979), show a clear resemblance to the descriptions of formulaic speech by more recent researchers (Dunlea, 1989). Similarly, there is a resemblance between recent accounts of pronoun use by blind children Andersen et al. (1984), Dunlea (1989) and earlier accounts by (Fraiberg, 1977; Fraiberg & Adelson, 1973), although Fraiberg explained the later and mistaken use of personal pronouns as being based on blind children's difficulties with the development of self, whereas Andersen, Dunlea, and colleagues gave a somewhat different explanation rooted in difficulties with deixis. As for self-centred, egocentric speech, there are obvious parallels between psychoanalytically oriented scholars (Burlingham, 1961, 1964, 1965; Nagera & Colonna, 1965; Wills, 1979) and those who are cognitively based.

In a certain sense, the cognitively based view of language development has also a precedent in Cutsford (1951), who considered that blind children's words are meaningless, and that they show a sort of verbalism. Cutsford's view, as well as Dunlea's, has a strong empiricist basis: Since blind children do not share the same type of experience with sighted children, their concepts, and as a consequence their language, cannot be the same.

Recently, and in direct connection with earlier psychoanalytically oriented authors, Hobson and colleagues (Brown et al., 1997; Hobson et al., 1997) have conceptualized blind children's language as having autistic-like features. Among these features are errors with pronouns, imitative and formulaic speech, and children's inability to initiate conversation. These authors, however, related these autistic-like features to the problems blind children have in the development of self, in achieving a normal pattern of interpersonal relatedness, and in their knowledge of others' mental processes (theory of mind). According to Hobson (1993a, 1993b), the development of a theory of mind is based on previous perception of the facial expression of emotions by others, which is an indication of their attitude towards external objects and events, and on interpersonal relationships, all of which are restricted in blind children.

Recently, against this predominant view of blind children's language acquisition, a few researchers have begun to offer a different interpretation of the data observed, and to perform new analysis of apparently well-known phenomena. In addition, more rigorous methods have also been employed by some researchers in their analyses, leading to different interpretations. This new point of view does not deny that there are important links between cognition and language. What is put into question is that there exists a direct mapping of cognitive achievements onto specific achievements in language acquisition.

One of the topics which has attracted recent attention has been semantic development. Landau and Gleitman's seminal work (1985) demonstrated that blind children are able to learn the meaning of certain words (look, see) without direct sensory experience. According to them, this achievement is possible thanks to the syntactic information that children are able to process. By observing the position occupied by certain words, and the words that accompany them, blind children can draw inferences about their meaning. This theory is currently known as the syntactic bootstrapping theory of word meaning (Gleitman, 1990; Landau, 1997). In a similar vein, other authors (Pérez-Pereira, 1994) have indicated that blind children are able to analyse the position of the words in the utterances, extract regularities, and learn grammatical rules (Lieven, Pine, & Baldwin, 1997). Language experience is viewed as especially relevant to blind children, who are deprived of visual input, and it is suggested that blind children pay special attention to language as a formal problem space (Pérez-Pereira, 1994; Pérez-Pereira & Castro, 1997). Blind children's initial use of imitated whole phrases, and subsequent analysis of their components, suggests that blind children are using a strategy of language learning closer to the Gestalt style of language acquisition than to the analytic style.

In addition, language is also viewed as a means to obtain knowledge about external reality. Blind children can also learn utterances that are appropriate for certain circumstances, making frequent use of imitation, which promotes their social interactions and their knowledge of external reality (Peters, 1994). Thus, well-known phenomena, formerly considered as aberrant or not useful to promote language development, such as the frequent use of stereotypic speech, imitations, and repetitions, are now considered as useful to further language development in blind children, to convey many pragmatic functions, and to keep conversational interaction going (Pérez-Pereira, 1991, 1994; Peters, 1987, 1994).

Similarly, many statements put forward by psychoanalytically oriented and cognition-based scholars on a number of features of blind children's language have been put into question. Among them, the topic of pronoun use stands out (Andersen et al., 1984; Dunlea, 1989; Fraiberg, 1977). New quantitative analysis suggests that pronoun reversal is not a general feature of all blind children. Only a relatively small percentage of blind children produce reversals to a large extent, whereas the majority of blind children rarely produce pronoun reversals. On the other hand, and contrary to previous considerations, reversals are scarcely produced in imitation of other's speech (Pérez-Pereira, 1999).

This new perspective on blind children's language acquisition adopts a compensatory view (Pérez-Pereira & Castro, 1997), and considers that blind children's language acquisition is not delayed, nor aberrant, but follows a different route, by exploiting other resources to a greater extent than sighted children. For example, blind children seem to show evidence of better verbal memory, which allows them to retrieve verbal expressions used in past circumstances and apply them to similar but new circumstances; they seem to use verbal play (which manifests itself in an abundancy of modified repetitions) to a greater extent than many sighted children, probably as a way of analysing language.

In spite of the data and arguments offered by these authors who propose an alternative route, there are many criticisms and resistance against their position. For instance, Davison (1990) believes in the "unshakable tradition", in Landau and Gleitman's words (1985, p. viii), that blind people must be defective in their learning. Davison criticizes those academics and clinicians who are against this view. There is also a clear bias in recent books on blind children's development to ignore those standpoints criticizing the "unshakable tradition" view of the language acquisition of blind children. In some cases there is a complete disregard of authors who disagree with this predominant point of view, to the point, not admissible from a scientific point of view, that their works are ignored and not quoted (Warren, 1994; Webster & Roe, 1998). What seems paradoxical is that many blind adults show a more than acceptable adaptation to social requirements, excellent knowledge and cognitive abilities, and surprisingly good language. How can all this come true if they have had such defective learning? How is it possible to accept a theory of acquisition that is in disagreement with the longitudinal, later results of the process of acquisition? It is clear that any theory of acquisition must be compatible with later stages of development, that is to say, adult usage.

In this chapter we will try to disentangle what is supported by data and what is not in this debate. In the following, we will attempt to review the many topics embraced under the heading of language acquisition on which there is some existing research.

THE ACQUISITION OF PHONOLOGY

Perception

The acquisition of phonology in blind children is a topic that has received little attention in spite of its potential contribution to our understanding of how blind children process language. Because blind children lack visual information accompanying the speech they hear, it is reasonable to suppose that they may pay more attention to the purely auditory stimuli coming from the speech they hear. Thus, blind children's abilities to perceive speech may well be more developed than those of sighted children. However, some gestures and mouth movements accompanying speech cannot be perceived by these children. Thus, it may be fair to assume that blind children may have more difficulties in discriminating and producing those sounds which have visually perceptible articulation (e.g. labials). In addition, they may have difficulties in the use of conventional gestures and body movements that sighted children use when they are engaging in conversational interaction.

There have been no speech perception experiments carried out with blind infants similar to those that have been carried out with sighted infants (see Vihman, 1996 and Menn & Stoel-Gammon, 1995 for recent reviews). The only information we have on speech perception by blind infants comes from records made by researchers using observational methodology in longitudinal studies or from anecdotal observations and clinical experience.

Als et al. (1980b) and Fraiberg (1977) reported that from the first month of life blind children react to their mothers' voice by head turning or extending their arms, smiling, or quieting. Reactions to other noises, such as plastic keys, were observed at 4 months of age. These reactions have been taken to mean that blind children can hear these stimuli. However, no discriminative reaction has been clearly established until the children are over 2 or 3 months old. At this time they begin to react in a different way to the mothers' or other familiar people's voices in contrast to a stranger's voice. But again no reliable behaviour has been established until they are 4 months old. Blind children tend to react to their mothers' voice with a smile and movements of arms, whereas they do not react at all to strangers' voices (Fraiberg, 1977, Freedman et al., 1969; Rogers & Puchalski, 1988; Rowland, 1984). When they are 8 months of age, coinciding with the fear of strangers in sighted children, blind children have a freezing reaction to a stranger's voice (Fraiberg, 1968). Finally, at around 10 months of age, blind children show reaching behaviours to sounding toys (Fraiberg, 1968), which suggests a clear differential pattern of reactions and relationship towards objects and people.

In summary, the scarce evidence so far gathered suggests that sound discrimination development in blind children is not different from that of sighted children (Warren, 1994). However, as we have pointed out before, we know of no single experimental study on the discrimination of phonemes by blind children.

We can only assume that blind children discriminate phonemes as sighted children do (Vihman, 1996).

Production

Concerning sound production, there is more valuable information, although it is also scarce. Mills' research (1983, 1987b) is the most reliable source of evidence on blind children's development of phonology. Previous studies (Dodd, 1979; McGurk & MacDonald, 1976) had shown that sighted children are able to lip-read from an early age (well under 4 months), and Kuhl and Meltzoff (1982) observed that 5-month-old infants show some ability to match vowel sounds to the sight of appropriate mouth movements. Therefore, vision may play an important role in the acquisition of speech perception and production abilities. Speech perception seems to involve not only the processing of auditory cues, but also lip-reading information, which is visually available.

Mills (1983) studied a blind German-speaking girl between 1;9 to 2;1, and two sighted English-speaking children. The phonological development of one of the sighted children had been observed and transcribed by Smith (1973). In her study, Mills compared the production of the initial consonants of the words produced by the children, differentiating those consonants that manifest a visually perceptible articulation (b, p, m, f, and v) from those consonants that do not (dentals, palatals, velars, and glottals). She analysed the substitution errors produced by the children, and found that the blind child produced a higher percentage of substitution errors. In addition, the blind child tended to replace a consonant with another consonant from a different visual group, that is to say, by a consonant with a perceptually different articulation. Therefore, although the two sighted children produced articulation errors within the same group (i.e. b instead of p), the blind child made more errors across the visual groups (i.e. t instead of p). Mills concluded that sighted children learn articulatory movements that they can see with less error than those they cannot see. In contrast, although the blind child seemed to present slight problems with the acquisition of those sounds which have an observable articulation, she did not present a delay in the acquisition of those consonants that do not have clearly visible articulation. Similar findings were also obtained by Dodd (1983), who compared the same 100 words produced by one blind child between the ages of 21 and 23 months and one sighted child between 17 and 27 months of age. Her results indicate that, whereas the sighted child was more likely to substitute a sound from the same visual category (with a similar observable articulation), the blind child was more likely to substitute a sound from a different visual category (with a different observable articulation). Taken together these data seem to point to the fact that blind children cannot use lip-reading, and that they may show a higher incidence of phonological delays, although only in so far as sounds with visible articulation are concerned.

Subsequently, Mills (1987b, 1993) widened her sample, presenting data from three blind children and three sighted children with MLUs between 1.0 and 1.6. Again, she analysed the initial consonants of the words produced by the children. The author found that 41% of the blind children's productions of sounds with visible articulation were errors, against 21% of the sighted children's productions. In contrast to these findings, there was no difference between blind and sighted children regarding their production of sounds without visible articulation. Both groups of children produced a similar percentage of errors (51% and 52% for sighted and blind children, respectively). In addition, Mills (1987b, 1993) analysed the type of substitution errors produced by the children. She found that 90% of the substitutions produced by sighted children belonged to a sound from the same category and only 10% of them consisted of a sound from a different category. The results found in the blind children were rather different: 66% of the substitutions were sounds from the same visual group and 34% of the substitutions belonged to a sound from a different category. These results give support to previous findings reported by Dodd (1983) and Mills (1983).

In a similar vein, Mulford (1988) analysed the number of words that have labial, dental/palatal, and velar consonants as their initial consonant. Of those categories, labial is the one with the highest visual distinctiveness, and Mulford found that visually deficient children produced a significantly lower proportion of labials (31%) than sighted children (40%). (See Table 4.1 for an overall summary of these findings.)

In summary, the results so far reported suggest that blind children may be slightly delayed in learning those sounds that have clear visual articulation. However, older blind children show normal use of speech sounds, suggesting that blind children in due course can make use of acoustic information to correct their substitutions and to achieve standard adult pronunciation. Research carried out by Brieland (1950) supports this proposal. Brieland (1950) analysed the oral performance of 84 congenitally blind children ranging in age from 12 to 18 years and of a matched group of 84 sighted children. The children heard a story and 10 days later had to re-tell it. The children were judged by 10 university teachers specialized in speech, who rated the children using a five-point scale. Among the variables studied were general effectiveness, vocal variety, pitch modulation, use of loudness, bodily action, lip movement, and memory. It was found that the blind children were significantly better than the sighted children at pitch modulation, whereas the

TABLE 4.1

First consonants of the words produced by blind and sighted children.
(Adapted from Mulford 1988)

	No. of subjects	Labial	Dental/palatal	Velar	Other
Blind	11	31%	45%	15%	9%
Sighted	9	40%	36%	12%	12%

sighted children were better at lip movement and, as expected, in the bodily action ratings. There were no significant differences in any of the other variables, although the blind children obtained higher mean ratings in their use of loudness. The results indicate that, contrary to expectations based on very early development, blind children are as able as sighted children to use their voice. It is also interesting to note that blind children's diminished use of lip movements in articulation do not appear to have a negative effect on their use of voice.

Interestingly, Brieland (1950, p. 103) suggested that the superior ability of blind children to modulate pitch and to use loudness "may result from their reliance upon more verbal means of expression in order to present their ideas". This suggestion is in agreement with the general idea that blind children pay more attention to speech as an outstanding source of stimulation to them.

In conclusion, the development of the sounds of speech in blind children do not appear to differ greatly in terms of the pattern nor the rate of development found in sighted children, with the possible exception of early production of sounds that have clear visual articulation. This has interesting implications for our understanding of the way blind children learn to talk. In addition, research with deaf children has shown that vision alone may not be much help in developing articulation skills (Mogford, 1993).

Other paralinguistic features

Hand and arm movements are closely related to speech, this coordination producing a more expressive way of speaking, partly because these movements may offer some kind of information that is complementary to that provided by language itself (for example, when indicating directions in a route, or explaining the qualities of objects, such as shape or size).

Although early studies indicated that congenitally blind children hardly use hand and arm movements to accompany their speech, thus rendering their speech less expressive (Harper, 1978), recent research seems to provide a different picture. In this respect, Iverson and Goldin-Meadow (1997) compared the hand and arm gestures produced by a group of 4 blind children to those produced by a group of 20 sighted children who were distributed under two different conditions, blindfolded or sighted. All the children were between 10 and 12 years of age. The authors observed the gestures that these three groups of children produced in three different discourse situations: (1) a Piagetian conservation task, (2) a direction task, in which the children had to give directions to a series of known locations, and (3) a narrative task, in which the children had to retell a story. The results indicated that the blind children produced a higher frequency of gestures than the sighted children in the conservation (although the blind children also produced more speech than the sighted children). There were no differences between the children in the narrative task, where both sighted and blind children tended to produce low rates of gestures. In addition, the sighted and the blindfolded children produced significantly more gestures in the direction task. Iverson and Goldin-Meadow conclude that, although blind children use gestures, they do not use them in all of the contexts that sighted children do. However, a remarkable fact is that the blind children do use gestures as an accompaniment to speech, in the absence of visual experience with gestures. Moreover, these children use gestures to express the same kinds of information as sighted children, and their gestures take the same form as those of the sighted children. Iverson and Goldin-Meadow (1998) have found that blind children used gestures at a comparable rate when talking to sighted or blind dyads. These results seem to indicate that visual experience is not essential for gesture development. Gestures appear to be an important element in communication, but their use does not necessarily depend on the experience that children may have with them as listeners. As observed in previous studies with younger blind children (Preisler, 1991; Rowland, 1984; Urwin, 1984a), Iverson and Goldin-Meadow (1997) also found that blind children rarely used the pointing gesture. However, they suggest that blind children are able to use other gestures, for example a palm handshape with four fingers spread.

Iverson and Goldin-Meadow (1997) also found something extremely interesting. They observed that the blind children in their study produced significantly more words on each of the three tasks than did the sighted children (whether blindfolded or not). In their opinion, this reveals that the blind children produce a greater amount of speech than their sighted mates because they make more efficient use of verbal memory and rely on verbal information to a greater extent. This indicates that blind children appear to use and process language and linguistic information to a greater extent than sighted children. Similarly, Pring (1988), who found that blind children recalled pairs of related words better than sighted children, suggests that blind children pay more attention to linguistic input than sighted children because language is more salient to them. In Chapter 5 we will have the opportunity to comment again on this characteristic feature of blind children's behaviour.

LEXICAL DEVELOPMENT

Introduction

The acquisition of words and their meanings by blind children has traditionally been a controversial topic in the field. From very early on it has been argued that blind children give different, often unreal, meanings to words than sighted children (Cutsford, 1951). More recently, other scholars (Andersen et al., 1984, 1993; Dunlea, 1984, 1989; Webster & Roe, 1998) have claimed that in acquiring the meanings of words blind children follow a different and defective path compared to sighted children. In contrast to this defective viewpoint, Landau and Gleitman (1985; Landau, 1983, 1997) have suggested that blind children are able to give words' meanings which, substantially, are the same as those of sighted children.

This debate between defenders and critics of a similarity between blind and sighted children in lexical development has its roots in different conceptions of how meanings are acquired. Those who deny that blind children give the same meaning to words as sighted children, particularly at the beginning of their lexical development, consider that word meanings are cognitively based (MacNamara, 1972; Piaget, 1971) and that first word meanings are based on concepts and notions built by children during their sensorimotor stage of development. Therefore, assuming that the lack of visual information will cause problems for blind children in constructing cognitive notions and obtaining an understanding of the world, blind children would have to build their first meanings on a different and more limited knowledge of objects and their relationships. As has been shown in Chapter 2, blind children do show greater difficulties than their sighted counterparts in acquiring such sensorimotor notions as object permanence, means–end relationships, causality, space, and time (Bigelow, 1986; Fraiberg, 1977; Rogers & Puchalsky, 1988). Thus, it might be reasonable to suppose that the delay in cognitive development blind children experience may have an effect on these children's acquisition of the meanings of words.

In contrast, Landau and Gleitman (1985, Gleitman, 1990; Landau, 1997) attribute an important role to the structural sources of word meanings in blind as well as sighted children. From this point of view, a relevant component of the meaning of a word comes from the position it occupies in a sentence and the other words that accompany it. In this respect, blind children should not be at a disadvantage in relation to sighted children since they do not receive a smaller amount of verbal information. Similarly, from a strongly nativist point of view, Bloom (1994) argued that even young children possess mappings from grammatical categories, such as "noun phrase", "count noun", or "mass noun", to abstract semantic categories. Thus, semantic meaning does not have its only origin in the experience children may have with objects, actions, and relationships, but also on syntactic knowledge. Although Bloom's view and Landau and Gleitman's view are not the same, they coincide in the importance given to syntax as a source of information about word meanings. Landau and Gleitman's view does not call for the child to have innate semantic mappings.

There have been three main topics within the debate on lexical development in blind children: (1) the characteristics of the first words produced by young blind children in comparison to those of sighted children, (2) the usage of the first words by blind children with special reference to their generalization, and (3) the meanings underlying words, including the verbalism issue. We will review each of these topics in turn.

First words of blind children

Following the seminal work of Nelson (1973), several researchers studied the content of the first 50 (or 100) words that blind children used with the aim of comparing the types of words used by them with those used by sighted subjects or the sighted children studied by Nelson. The rationale for this interest was that, because blind children lack visual information, other aspects of reality perceived through other senses may be more salient to them than to their sighted age mates, and this may be reflected in the content of the first words they use. Related to this, some scholars (Andersen et al., 1984, 1993; Dunlea, 1989) have suggested that the meanings underlying blind children's first words may be different from those of sighted children because the concepts they form may be different.

The results of the studies carried out using maternal reports of first appearance of words are, however, not homogeneous. Some investigations (Bigelow, 1987; Landau, 1983; Landau & Gleitman, 1985) have used exactly the same semantic categories as used by Nelson (1973), that is to say, specific nominals, general nominals, action words, modifiers, personal-social, and function words. Others have used somewhat different systems of categories. For example, Dunlea (1989) used the following categories: objects, people and family pets, sounds, actions and states, relational terms, qualities, routines, social expressions, deictics, and miscellaneous; whereas Pérez-Pereira and Castro (1994) used specific nominals, general nominals, action words, modifiers, personal-social, expressing words, function words, deictics, pronouns, routines, and miscellaneous. However, the use of particular category systems does not explain the differences found. Those researchers using the same category system found different results for the blind children they studied (e.g. Bigelow, 1987; Landau & Gleitman, 1985), and different results were even found in the same study for different blind children (e.g. Landau, 1983; Landau and Gleitman, 1985). On the other hand, not all the studies used the same number of words. Whereas some of the studies analysed the first 50 words produced by children, others analysed the first 100 words. In addition, some studies did not use a maternal report instrument (Nelson, 1973) to obtain the vocabulary produced by the children, but the first words recorded by the researcher through direct observation of the children (Pérez-Pereira, 1994). All these variations in methods contributed to the differences in the results obtained.

Regarding the age of acquisition of the first 50 words there seems to be no delay in blind children compared to sighted children. For instance Bigelow (1990) found that her three blind subjects acquired their early vocabularies between the ages of 1;4 and 1;9 years, while Nelson's subjects did the same between 1;3 and 1;8 years. Similar results were also reported by Mulford (1988). Mulford (1988) also tried to summarize the findings of different researchers, and proposed several features common to blind children's vocabularies. The mean percentages she obtained for all nine children are shown in Table 4.2. In this table the results obtained with blind children by Bigelow (1986), Landau (1983; Landau & Gleitman, 1985), Dunlea (1989; Andersen et al., 1984), and Pérez-Pereira and Castro (1994) are shown. In the case of the results from the studies by Dunlea (1989) and Pérez-Pereira and Castro (1994) some adjustments to the category system of Nelson (1973) were made. In these cases, the categories of personal-social expressions and routines were combined as personal social, and the categories of deictics, pronouns (in the case of Pérez-Pereira and Castro's study), and qualities or modifiers were put

TABLE 4.2

Type of words used by blind and sighted children (percentages)

Study	Child	Type	Specific Nominal	General Nominal	Action Words	Modifiers	Personal-Social	Function Words
Mulford	9 (mean)	blind	21	38	25	5	11	1
Bigelow	3 (mean)	blind	25	44	21	5	4	0
Landau	Kelli	blind	15	60	5	11	7	0
Landau	Carlo	blind	34	11	25	0	29	1
Dunlea	Teddy	blind	13	43	19	2	17	0
Dunlea	Lisa	blind	10	35	21	0	12	2
Dunlea	Julie	part sighted	10	35	31	3	15	0
Nelson	18	sighted	14	51	13	9	8	4
Nelson	10	sighted referential	13	62	12	7	5	1
Nelson	8	sighted expressive	15	38	15	12	11	8
Pérez-Pereira	Ernesto	part sighted	13	30	15	20	11	10
Pérez-Pereira	Alicia	blind	10	27	15	19	18	9
Forján et al.	Mar	sighted	20	38	16	10	14	2
Forján et al.	Andrea	sighted	20	46	14	8	12	0
Forján et al.	Nuria	sighted	40	29	14	7	10	0
Forján et al.	Anxo	sighted	8	64	14	10	4	0

together as modifiers. In Table 4.2, the results of the group of sighted children studied by Nelson (1973) are shown as well, differentiating between the two groups of expressive and referential children. For purposes of comparison with the blind children studied by Pérez-Pereira and Castro (1994), the results obtained for the first 50 words used by four sighted children, who were speakers of the same languages (Spanish and Galician), and who lived in the same region as the blind children, are also shown (Forján, García, & Pérez-Pereira, 1995). These four children completed the 50 first words when they were between 1;4 and 1;9.

Having compared the mean results obtained from different studies with those obtained by Nelson (1973) in a group of 18 sighted children, Mulford (1988) concluded that blind children use a relatively higher proportion of specific nominals and action words, and a lower proportion of general nominals. Moreover, there is an almost total absence of function words in blind children. Initially, these results show the difficulties that blind children may have in generalizing the use of a word to the referents of a category. Looking at their low percentage of general nominals and the relatively high number of personal-social words, the blind children are similar to the expressive group of sighted children. However other features, such as the practical nonexistence of function words, or the higher percentage of action words in the blind children than in the sighted group, do not fit precisely with the expressive style as defined by Nelson. Therefore, it is difficult to classify blind children into the expressive-referential dichotomy.

Regarding the semantic content of general nominals, Mulford (1988) found that the most important differences between blind and sighted children concerned the lower percentage of words for animals in the blind children than in the sighted children (8% v. 20%, respectively), and the higher proportion of furniture and household items in the blind children (22% in the blind v. 9% in the sighted group). As Mulford suggests, furniture and other household items are more salient or interesting for blind children than for the sighted children. Probably this is so because they can explore them or hear them (in the case of telephone, radio, clock ...) and need to take them into account in relation to their movements. On the other hand, many words for animals are learnt by sighted children with reference to pictures and books, and not directly related to their own experience with real animals. It is clear that this type of experience is not common with blind children. Analysing the semantic categories used by blind and sighted children, Bigelow (1987) found that many items blind children chose to label were characterized as having sensorimotor properties (change of sensation related to tactual or hearing experiences).

The point to be made here is that the mean results of blind children offered by Mulford (1988) hide a great deal of variability among individuals, which is clearly shown in Table 4.2. For example, Bigelow (1987) obtained results so different from Mulford's in the three children she studied regarding the low use of personal social terms (4%), that she refused to characterize blind children as expressive. Similarly, McConachie and Moore (1994), studied 10 children and found that specific nominals was a weaker category for the blind group than the visually impaired group, contrary to what would be expected from Mulford's study. These scholars also found a lower proportion of action words in their blind subjects compared to Mulford's. Landau (1983; Landau & Gleitman, 1985) also found important differences between the two blind children she studied (Kelli and Carlo) and concluded that it is impossible to find a common pattern for their first words. Even the most general feature observed, that is to say, the relatively low percentage of general nominals, is not uniform, since Kelli, the child studied by Landau (1983; Landau & Gleitman, 1985), produced a great deal of general nominals—as many as 60% of her 50 words fell into this category. Something similar can be said for the use of personal-social and function words. In addition, the comparison of the results obtained by Pérez-Pereira and Castro (1994) with blind children and by Forján et al. (1995) with sighted children from the same area and language community points to a surprising similarity between them.

Probably the most cautious conclusion we can draw from the studies of the first words used by blind children is that there is no common pattern of development, and that it is difficult to find clear and consistent differences with sighted children. Individual variation, rather than a specific effect of vision, appears to account for the differences between subjects.

First word usage

Regarding the second issue, Dunlea and colleagues (Andersen et al., 1984, 1993; Dunlea, 1984, 1989) have claimed that although blind children apparently use the same type of words as sighted children (referring to the first 100 words), in reality there are qualitative differences regarding the use of the words and their underlying meanings.

First, the blind children these authors studied (Andersen, et al., 1984, 1993; Dunlea, 1984, 1989) did not seem to invent idiosyncratic words as observed in some sighted children. Dunlea could not find any examples of child-created terms in the two blind children she studied. She considered this to be enough evidence to suggest a general lack of creativity in blind children's language development. According to Dunlea, this feature is complemented by the absence of mortality of unconventional words that must be progressively replaced by conventional words. However, we want to make some comments regarding a possible bias in the method Dunlea used to collect the words and the opportunities the blind children had to show their capabilities at lexical creativity. The method used by these authors to gather the 100 first words may have led to an underestimation of idiosyncratic words, because the mothers may have tended not to report such words. Moreover, the blind children probably had fewer opportunities to invent words referring to aspects of the external world because they had more restricted experiences of objects, actions, and events than sighted children. As a counterexample to Dunlea's claims on the lack of self-invented words in blind children, Pérez-Pereira (1991; Pérez-Pereira & Castro, 1994) found at least two examples of idiosyncratic words in two Spanish blind children. It is noteworthy that, in contrast with Dunlea (1989), these examples were obtained using the method of direct observation and recording with video. In the first example, one girl used the term *piquito* with the meaning of collar (necklace) (Pérez-Pereira, 1991, 1994). It is certainly true that she was somewhat older (3;1,27) than the children studied by Dunlea; however, the second example was observed in another blind girl whose first words were recorded between 1;10,19 and 2;0,13. She produced an idiosyncratic form, *yeya*, for abuela (grandmother) (Pérez-Pereira & Castro, 1994). In this regard, Peters (personal communication) has reported that one blind child, Seth, invented quite a number of idiosyncratic words (20 between 15 and 19 months of age). She attributes this finding to the fact that Seth was observed by his father, who, moreover, was a very accommodating conversational partner, and tried very hard to assign meanings to Seths's idiosyncratic words. Seth's father's effort contributed to these idiosyncratic forms eventually achieving fairly stable meanings that lasted for 2 or 3 months, until they were replaced by more conventional words (Peters, personal communication).

In addition to these counterexamples, the point made by Andersen et al. (1984, 1993) and Dunlea (1984, 1989) does not make much sense given that not all sighted children use idiosyncratic words. Therefore, the absence of idiosyncratic words in blind children cannot be used as evidence of something "missing" in their linguistic system. Furthermore, the issue of the lack of mortality of blind children's words appears to have been over emphasized.

Second, Dunlea (Andersen et al., 1984, 1993; Dunlea, 1984, 1989) found that blind children's words are tied to their original context of use. That is to say, they do not use the words to refer to other instances of the concept. The word is used only with the original instance with which it was learnt for a protracted period of time. Dunlea claims that this is due to a lack of conceptual meaning underlying blind children's words. In support of her claim, Dunlea (1989) offered as evidence the fact that blind children have fewer lexical extensions and overextensions than sighted children. She found that only 8% and 13% of blind children's first 100 words were overextended, whereas the sighted child she studied showed 41% overextensions, which is in itself an unusually high percentage for sighted children (Dromi, 1987; Rescorla, 1980). Dunlea (1989) reported that blind children's overextensions were mainly based on perceptual features such as texture and shape. For instance, Lisa said the word *cookie* not only as applied to cookies and crackers, but also when she was feeling small rough surfaces on a piece of paper, sniffing a sweet fragance from a pine tree, or feeding herself small bits of food. In addition she affirmed that approximately half of the first 100 words of the two blind children were generalized, whereas the sighted child used 95% of their first words beyond the original context. In her opinion, blind children's lack of generalization of their first words beyond the original context of use to other instances of the same class indicates that, in reality, their first words act as if they were "names" for specific people or food.

It is reasonable to suppose that blind children's opportunities to generalize in the absence of sight might be restricted. However, this does not mean that they are incapable of decontextualizing words. They have this capability, although it is restricted because they have reduced access to external information. In this connection, Norgate (1996) suggested that overextensions by blind children may be underestimated because (1) scope for extensions depends upon the emergence of particularly suitable referents, which are restricted for blind children, and (2) the greater difficulties in establishing joint attention in the absence of vision make it more difficult to be sure of the referents of blind children's words. Moreover, the context-bound usage of words is also usual in young sighted children (Barrett, 1986, 1995; Dromi, 1987; Nelson, 1985), especially during the first weeks of use of a given word. At first, the words children use are tied to specific contexts, and are not generalized. The context-bound use of first words seems to be, thus, a general feature of language development, independent of children's visual acuity. An event representation basis for words' usage is not the only explanation of the restricted use of words in young children. It is also well known that prototypical representation leads to a restricted use of words to specific exemplars of the concept, and that many children go through a phase of prototypical use of words[10] (Barrett, 1986, 1995; Barrett, Harris, & Chasin, 1991; Bowerman, 1978). Considering both event representation and prototypical representation processes together, lexical development seems to follow a developmental course from specific to general. This implies that, at the beginning of lexical development, restricted uses of words to certain contexts or instances can be very usual. In addition, we have to remind ourselves that children's early words can exhibit an enormous variety of different developmental profiles (Barrett, 1995). Therefore, a smaller percentage of overextensions and extensions to wider concepts is not necessarily an index of language acquisition problems. Probably, blind children's problems do not seem to reside in their capacity to form concepts, but in the opportunities they have to encounter more than one instance of the concept (Bigelow, 1987; Urwin, 1984a, 1984b). As Landau and Gleitman (1985) suggest, the important question is whether the blind child is able to generalize when the appropriate circumstances (haptic rather than visual resemblance) arise. This is exactly what blind children seem to do: to generalize on the basis of tactual information, as Dunlea has reported (Dunlea, 1989).

Norgate, Lewis, and Collis (1997) have suggested that if we closely examine the contexts of routines in which blind children produce words, we may detect subtle ways in which words are used in a generalized way over time. For example, Lottie, a 15-month-old blind child, produced the utterance "oh she's posh" when her mother was brushing her hair. Subsequently she used the same utterance in a range of circumstances that involved a change to her appearance, such as putting shoes on, wearing her mother's watch, and having her face wiped. Interestingly, these authors hypothesize that infants who adopt a strong holistic style of lexical functioning may be less likely to generalize, since their utterances describe an object/action/event specifically, that is to say, they use utterances for specific routines and situations.

To conclude, the supposed restricted capacity of blind children to generalize appears to be an extreme interpretation, which is decontextualized from the background of the processes of lexical development, and does not take into consideration the actual conditions under which a blind child can put into action his or her ability to generalize.

Third, a specific restriction on the use of words by blind children is the use of action words to describe a child's own actions, but not to describe the actions of others. Dunlea (Andersen et al., 1984, 1993; Dunlea, 1984, 1989) deems this egocentric use of action words to be a qualitative difference between blind and sighted children. According to her (Dunlea, 1989, p. 59), "there is no evidence of decentration in word use" by the two blind children she studied. She also mentions Urwin's findings in support of her view (Urwin, 1978, 1979, 1984a, 1984b). Nevertheless, non-handicapped young children at first use action words as an accompaniment to their own outgoing actions or the actions they are to perform. Later, they will use these words in relation to the actions performed by others (Barrett, 1983). On her part, Urwin (1984a, 1984b) pointed out that a totally blind child could also talk about other people's actions and possessions of objects when these actions and objects were familiar to them by 2;3 years. This fact suggests that as blind children grow older they surmount the initial restrictions in their use of action words. In any case, it is logical that blind children might have more difficulties than sighted children in perceiving others' activities, and, consequently, that they will talk about them less often than sighted children. As Warren (1994, p. 137) rightly stated, "without vision, the blind child is less likely to perceive the actions of other people, unless those actions are directed to him- or herself". Thus, the fact that the two blind children studied by Dunlea showed an egocentric use of action words does not mean that all blind children behave in the same way. Warren (1994) has convincingly argued in favour of individual differences between blind children, and other researchers (Castro & Pérez-Pereira, 1996; Pérez-Pereira & Castro, 1992) have reported that blind children can talk in a decentred way about the actions performed by others. In this regard, Maxfield (1936), who established a coefficient of egocentricity for the language samples of eight blind children between 38 and 73 months of age, found that the older blind children (average 68 months old) showed a notably lower coefficient of egocentricity[11] than a group of sighted children of similar age. As for the three younger blind children studied (average 40 months old) they showed such great variability that it was impossible to find a clear trend.

Taking all these qualitative differences together, Dunlea (1989, p. 62) affirms that "the mechanisms that allow sighted children to take an active creative role in vocabulary development (...) are not functioning at the same level for blind children at the onset of language". The idea that blind children's language is not (or is less) creative is a recurrent theme in the work of Dunlea and her colleagues Andersen and Kekelis. Talking about the morphological and syntactic development of blind children Dunlea and colleagues also suggest that blind children show a lack of creativity (Andersen et al., 1984, 1993; Dunlea, 1989; Dunlea & Andersen, 1992).

In conclusion, the strong hypothesis defended by Dunlea (Andersen et al., 1984, 1993; Dunlea, 1984, 1989) appears to be an excessively radical interpretation of the data. What seems to be certain, however, is that blind children need a longer period of time experiencing the world to be able to extend words to other referents of the same sort, and to be able to talk more frequently about the actions performed by other people. Nevertheless, this does not represent a lack of capacity, or a qualitative difference in ability, but a restriction derived from blind children's lack of visual information regarding surrounding objects and events. This conclusion can also be extended to the two other qualitative differences Dunlea and colleagues (Andersen et al., 1984, 1993; Dunlea, 1984, 1989) have proposed with respect to blind children, namely lack of creativity and egocentricity. To summarize, there is no clear evidence that blind children use their first words in an underextended and less creative way than sighted children.

The meanings of words

Generally, words represent concepts agreed upon by adults. However, there is no guarantee that two persons using the same word give it the same meaning. The end point of having shared meaning for words is the result of a long process involving conceptual as well as linguistic development. In the previous subsection we have reviewed some topics related to the process of lexical acquisition and use, which are clearly related to the construction of adult, conceptual meanings. Now we will review other topics more directly related to the issue of the meanings underlying the words blind children use. First, we will see what is probably the first controversy that arose in the field—that of the meaningless use of certain words by the blind, also called verbalism. Second, we will review other studies on the meanings of certain sorts of words, such as visual terms, colour terms, locative prepositions, and so on.

The verbalism issue

Probably one of the first characterizations of blind children's meanings of words was that of Cutsford (1951). According to him, blind children's words must be meaningless, because blind children tended to give definitions for words couched in visual terms but such experience is inaccessible to blind people. He concluded that their underlying concepts must be empty, and in no way based on real experience. Cutsford called this characteristic "verbal unreality of words" or "verbalism". The author drew this conclusion from an experiment with 26 congenitally blind children, between 8 and 21 years of age, who had to respond with the first quality they thought of when they heard the names of objects on a list. The list consisted of words varying in their degree of sensory availability, ranging from words for objects practically inaccessible to blind people, such as a star, to words for objects that are experienced daily by blind children through touch, taste, hearing, and smell, such as milk or oranges.

Although there were wide individual differences, Cutsford (1951) observed that nearly 50% of the blind children's responses were the names of visual qualities (for instance, *red* for blood), about 33% were qualities having to do with touch, 7% referred to taste or smell, and about 3% to hearing. The remaining 7% were abstract qualities such as "expensive", or "nice". The use of visual qualities showed that blind children use visually based concepts instead of concepts based on other sensory experiences more meaningful and familiar to them, thus not reflecting their own experience. In addition, there was a large number of inappropriate visual responses (for instance, *blue* for cotton). Cutsford (1951, p. 69) concluded that "a predisposition toward the unwarranted use of meaningless visual terminology demonstrates a strong tendency toward unreality in which valid relationships are utterly disregarded. The inevitable result is that nothing but incoherent and loose thinking is possible".

Coinciding with Cutsford's findings, other psychoanalytically oriented scholars, such as Burlingham (1961, 1964, 1965) or Nagera and Colonna (1965), in their clinical experience with blind children, observed that they tend to use words in an imitative fashion without an appropriate understanding of their meaning. These authors used the term *"parroting"* to label this phenomenon of parrot-like repetition of words without understanding their meaning. However, their reports are characterized by subjective impressions, lack of methodological systemacity, and lack of information on the characteristics of their subjects, all of which makes it difficult to interpret their observations.

In a penetrating review of the concept of verbalism, Dokecki (1966) criticizes Cutsford's conception of meaning, according to which the meaning of words derives solely from sensory experience. Dokecki (1966, p. 526) argues that the meaning of words is not solely dependent on sensory experience and its symbolization, but that "language itself is important in the creation of meaning". He argues that most people obtain knowledge of the world, not through direct experience, but through linguistically conveyed information. Nevertheless, this fact does not mean that non-sensory-based concepts are meaningless. The relationships between words and other words is an important factor in learning the meaning of words, together with the relationships between words and things. In addition, Dokecki (1966) also suggests something that was later developed by Nelson (1985), that is to say, that certain words take on meaning for the children (blind and sighted children) because they are repeatedly used by others in social interaction. Therefore, there are other avenues for meaning, apart from sensory experience. Consequently, Dokecki (1966), agreeing with Harley (1963), disagrees with Cutsford's position that the use of words with visual referents must be avoided in the education of blind children.

It is clear that Cutsford's study is open to many criticisms. First, in his analysis there is a confusion between the real meaning of a word in use and the conscious lexical access and analysis (definition) of a word. The latter implies a certain degree of metalexical or metalinguistic knowledge, but this is not the case with the spontaneous use and comprehension of a word (Gombert, 1992). Up to a point, we cannot infer the actual meaning of a word from its metalinguistic definition. They are different things. Second, Cutsford's conceptualization of meaning is rather limited, that is, he does not take into account other sources of meaning besides direct experience, such as sense relationships, as in the case of antonyms (Lyons, 1977), or grammatical relationships (Bloom, 1994; Landau & Gleitman, 1985; Gleitman, 1990; Landau, 1997). Third, Cutsford did not use a control group of sighted children to compare the results obtained with blind children. Fourth, the selection of the sample used by Cutsford was not done particularly carefully, since there were subjects with some residual vision, who could have made use of visual information (Caputo, 1973), alongside congenitally blind children. Fifth, the word stimuli used, as well as the warm-up examples and the details of the instructions, appear to bias the children to provide responses containing visual information (Dokecki, 1966). Furthermore, the results of Cutsford's experiment on verbalism are in disagreement with the results obtained by other researchers. We will turn to these studies next.

Harley (1963) studied a sample of 40 blind children between 6;11 and 14;3 (mean 11;4). The children were scored on several measures: chronological age, IQ (using the WISC or the Hayes–Binet scales for blind children), experience with objects (measured through a verbal self-report by the subjects), social adjustment (measured through the Tuddenham Reputation Test), verbalism, and visually oriented verbalism. Verbalism (VE) was defined as the inability to identify accurately an object labelled by the word by some sensory means (the children had to identify the correct referent of a word among several objects); whereas visually oriented verbalism (VV) existed when a child employed a word referring to colour or brightness to define the name of a given object from a list of 39. Harley obtained only negative correlations between verbalism scores, on the one hand, and age, IQ, and experience, on the other. All other correlations were insignificant. These results suggest that verbalism tends to decrease with age, which is related to increased opportunities for blind children to interact with their environment. In addition, verbalism decreases as IQ and experience with objects increases. The significant negative correlation between chronological age and verbalism "suggests that verbalism may not be an enduring problem among blind children", according to Harley's (1963, p. 23) opinion. Harley observed that visually oriented verbalisms were very low in the group he studied, since only an average of 2.19 words of the list of 39 (SD 1.70, and range 0–7) were defined using visually oriented descriptions. This result markedly contrasts with Cutsford's findings that 50% of descriptions by blind children used visual expressions. Although Harley's results are markedly different from Cutsford's, Dokecki (1966) suggests the possibility that Harley's VE was not really a measure of verbalism but of tactual discrimination ability. If this were the case, Harley's results could not be considered as valid, either.

In another study, Demott (1972) tested three different groups of subjects, 41 blind subjects, 41 visually impaired subjects, and 61 normally sighted subjects. Normally sighted individuals were matched on age, grade, sex, and IQ, with blind or severely visually impaired subjects. The subjects ranged in age from 6 to 19 years. An advantage of Demott's study over other studies on verbalism in blind children is that he also used a group of sighted children to make comparisons. He obtained two measures: a verbalism score and a measure of meaning. In order to obtain the verbalism score, Demott used a collection of 39 objects and a vocabulary list with the names of those objects. A verbalism measure was obtained by subtracting the number of objects correctly identified from the number of words correctly defined. To measure meaning, Demott used a five-point semantic differential scale and 15 pairs of adjectives (such as slow–fast; happy–sad; heavy–light; pretty–ugly, etc.). Fifteen words representing concepts were judged for each pair of polar adjectives.

The results did not show significant differences between groups in the factor analysis for the adjective scales. Therefore, the results showed that normally sighted individuals did not assign significantly different meanings to concepts as compared with blind and visually impaired subjects. Indeed, this result was the same for concepts having a visual component (such as clouds, or fire). As for the measure of verbalism, there were no differences between groups. Thus, verbalism does not seem to be a typical feature of blind children's lexical development, contrary to Cutsford's (1951) claim. From these results Demott (1972) concluded that blind youngsters, just as sighted children, learn the meanings of many words through their verbal context and their use within language discourse. Demott supports the view that meaning is a function of language, and that a difference does not exist between blind and sighted individuals regarding the meaning of their words.

More recently, Civelli (1983) studied verbalisms in a sample of 10 blind and 10 sighted Italian adolescents. The blind subjects, who ranged in age from 13;0 to 16;6 years, were blind from birth or shortly after, with no associated handicaps, and had normal IQs. The sighted adolescents were of similar ages. The subjects were given a list of 28 words referring to objects, animals, movements (verbs), and facial expressions, and were asked to describe them. No significant differences were found between blind and sighted children, regarding correct definitions, although a trend was observed in verbs of movement, in which the blind group showed a better performance than the sighted group. Civelli concludes that no general differences exist in the language of intellectually normal sighted and blind adolescents, and that verbalism affects only certain areas of language, or, to be precise, certain semantic fields.

Von Tetzchner and Martinsen (1981) studied verbalisms in a sample of eight legally blind subjects and eight sighted children. The authors used the same definition of verbalism as Harley (1963), that is to say, the inability to recognize an object by sensory means. These authors used two tasks, a word explanation task and an object recognition task, with 200 words (and their corresponding objects) from eight different semantic domains (25 words per domain). The sighted children took the recognition task blindfolded. In order to score the responses, Von Tetzchner and Martinsen differentiated three types of definition: concrete, general, and incorrect definitions, as well as three types of recognition of objects: precise naming of the object, general naming, and wrong naming. They found that the blind group tended to define objects less precisely that the sighted group (50.3% v. 63.6% of precise definitions, respectively), and the blind group tended to give general definitions more frequently than the sighted group (36.6% v. 26.6%, respectively). Regarding the recognition task, the sighted blindfolded children obtained higher scores than the blind children (75.9% v. 69.1%). According to the authors, the lower capacity for recognizing objects by touch in the blind children indicates that the proposal that blind children can use compensatory strategies is a myth, and that blind children's low recognition scores may be due to lack of visual cues. Comparing the results obtained in the verbal definition task and the recognition of objects task, Von Tetzchner and Martinsen found that the blind group showed more verbalisms than the sighted group (22.3% v. 17.8%, respectively). Besides, the difference between groups in verbalisms used was higher for precisely defined objects (20% in the blind v. 14.2% in the sighted group) than for the words defined in a general manner (25.5% of the blind v. 26.5% of the sighted children). The authors concluded that the percentage of verbalisms found was in accordance with Harley's findings, which "paints a rather depressing picture of the possibilities of a blind child's familiarising itself with its surroundings" (1981, p. 60).

However, different interpretations may be derived from the aforementioned results. It seems reasonable to think that blind children have less experience than sighted children with some of the items (e.g. tools) used by Von Tetzchner and Martinsen (1981). Therefore, it is not surprising that they achieved lower results in the recognition tasks than the sighted children. This in turn affected their verbalism scores. In any case, the differences found in verbalism scores by Von Tetzchner and Martinsen (22.3% v. 17.8%) were not large and are unlikely to represent statistically significant differences. Unfortunately, the authors did not offer any statistical comparisons of the data. Another weakness of this research relates to the selection of the sample. As they indicate, the group of blind children was formed by eight "legally blind children", but, as discussed previously, this could well mean that some of the children had residual vision. If this were the case, there would be no guarantee that the children in the blind group were not making use of their visual experience.

In our view, the research on verbalism does not support the view that blind children's words are meaningless. This is not only because the results of most studies (Civelli, 1983; Demott, 1972; Harley, 1963) disagree with Cutsford's (1951) findings, but suggest that verbalism does not have such a high incidence in blind children, but also because of the limited conception of meaning underlying the verbalism proposal. It has been argued that other sources of meaning exist, apart from the sensorial or experiential one (reference), such as the word to word or intralinguistic relationships in the semantic structure of the language (sense), or the structural sources of meaning. Therefore, the position that blind children have different meanings for words than their sighted counterparts, and live in a meaningless world, seems to be untenable.

The issue of verbalism, however, does not cover other interesting aspects of the meaning of blind children's words. Words that have attracted the attention of researchers include visual terms such as the verbs *look* and *see*, or colour adjectives.

The acquisition of conventional meanings

One of the most striking studies on the acquisition of meaning by blind children is Landau and Gleitman's research on the acquisition of visual and colour terms by Kelli, a congenitally blind girl (Landau & Gleitman, 1985). The authors observed the first uses of the words *look* and *see* by Kelli at about age 28 months. By 36 months she used these words consistently and frequently in conversation. At this age, Landau and Gleitman began an intensive study of the comprehension of these verbs, administering a series of tasks or experiments (in the Piagetian sense) to Kelly and four sighted children of the same age, who were blindfolded, in order to study their comprehension of *look* and *see*. The first experiment on *look*, showed that the blind girl understood this word with the meaning of "contact with the hands", instead of the meaning that sighted children showed of "turn one's nose toward". For instance, Kelli's response to "look up", "look down", "look behind you", "look in front of you", and so forth, was to move her hands, not her eyes and head, in the direction indicated by the command. In the second experiment, when she was told to look at an object, the child manually explored the object extensively, running her hands over all its surfaces. She was able to differentiate between *touch* and *look*. When she was told to touch an object she simply touched, stroked or banged it with her fist. Kelli clearly showed in this experiment that whereas touch was understood as "contact", *look* was interpreted as exploring or apprehending (manipulating, feeling all over, pretending to eat, or smell). The exploratory behaviour was only elicited by *look*, not *touch*. The blindfolded sighted children simply oriented their eyes towards the object. In addition, other experiments showed that Kelli differentiated between *look* and other perceptual verbs such as *listen*. Only the former was understood as haptic exploration, whereas the other verbs implied apprehension by other means.

The experiments with *see* showed that Kelli understood that seeing can take place at a distance, but that in order to see the correct face of an object it must be positioned in the viewer's line of sight and with no barriers. For instance Kelli showed an object when she was asked to "let Mommy see the car", or hid it in her pocket when she was asked to "make it so Mommy cannot see the car". Similarly, the child turned around as a response to the command "let me see the back of your pants". Kelli showed a differentiation between *see* and other verbs such as *give* or *let touch*. In the latter cases, she always physically extended the object towards the target person.

In spite of Landau and Gleitman's experimental results, Bigelow (1991b) found that older (6- to 8-year-old) totally blind children still showed difficulties in making inferences about whether a person could or could not see an object, provided that the distance between the person and the object was longer than one metre, and that there were objects in between the target object and the person. These results indicate some difficulties that blind children may have in representing Euclidean space, and, thus, in correctly understanding the meaning of *see* under certain conditions. Contrary to Landau's (Landau, 1991; Landau et al., 1984) suggestions, the majority of the studies on spatial representation development in blind children indicate that an Euclidean representation is not acquired until adolescence (Bigelow, 1991a, 1996; Millar, 1988; Ochaita, 1984; Ochaita et al., 1991).

Landau and Gleitman (1985) in addition offered examples of spontaneous productions and elicited descriptions and definitions of *see* and *look* that seem to support the idea that Kelli was able to learn the right meaning of these verbs without direct experience. Thus, if extralinguistic information was not available to her, but the child understood and used correctly these visual verbs, how did she learn them? Landau and Gleitman, for the first time, proposed that the child was able to learn these visual words because she could process information that existed in the linguistic environment itself, that is to say, the linguistic context in which the words appeared, their position and the other words that accompany them, provide useful information from which meaning could be derived.

Furthermore, Landau and Gleitman (1985) analysed the contexts of occurrence of perceptual verbs such as *look, see,* and others, and other non-perceptual verbs, such as *get, hold, give, come, go, play, put,* and others, in the speech of Kelli's mother. Specifically, they analysed the spatial context of use of these verbs, attending to three different circumstances: (1) their production when the child had an object in hand or near her hand, (2) their production when there was an object far from reach, and (3) their production when there were no objects. In this way, Landau and Gleitman tried to test whether the spatial context in which a word was produced by the mother may give some clue to the child to understand the meaning of the word. Landau and Gleitman found that these spatial contexts alone could not explain how Kelli learned the meaning of verbs, particularly the similarity between *look* and *see,* and the difference between *look* and other verbs that encode manual activity, such as *put* or *hold.* Therefore, in order to look for other explanations, Landau and Gleitman analysed the kinds of sentences in which the verbs occurred, under the assumption that children can extract useful information for word meaning from the linguistic context in which words are heard. They observed that there were differences regarding the subcategorization frames of the verbs, namely attending to the phrasal material that followed them. Their main finding was that the most frequent verbs used by Kelli's mother occurred in highly distinctive syntactic frames. A subset of these syntactic environments were restricted to *see*:

(1) Only *see* appeared in deictic interjective queries ("See?" or "See?, That's a circle").
(2) Practically, only *see* appeared with sentential complements ("Let's see if Granny's home").

A different subset of syntactic frames was restricted to *look*:

(3) Only *look* appeared in deictic interjective commands ("Look!", or "Look, that's a book").
(4) Only *look* appeared deictically with a free how relative ("Look how I do it").
(5) Only *look* appeared in constructions with *like* ("You look like a kangaroo in those overalls").

As Landau and Gleitman (1985, p. 113) remarked "*look* and *see* are in some ways distinct from all other verbs and distinct from each other". In addition, other frequent verbs, not to be commented on here, appeared in syntactic frames, which were disallowed for *look* and *see*.

Combining the results of spatial and syntactic analysis for look and see, the proportion of use of *look* in its distinctive subcategorization frames and when an object was near rose to 1.00 (from 0.73 in the spatial analysis) and that for *see* rose to 0.72 (from 0.39 in the spatial analysis only).

Thus, Landau and Gleitman (1985, p. 119), conclude that, together with their contexts of occurrence, the syntactic subcategorization frames of occurrence of verbs offer valuable information about their meanings. Their explanation, which they named "syntactic bootstrapping" was later reaffirmed again by Gleitman (1990) and Landau (1997), separately.

In a similar vein, Landau and Gleitman (1985) proposed that syntactic frames provide important information for a blind child's understanding of the meanings of colour terms. In particular, they affirmed (p. 170) that Kelli learned that 10 colour terms (yellow, red, black, green, orange, and so forth):

- belong to a single domain whose superordinate is colour;
- are used in adjectival positions in sentences;
- can be applied only to concrete objects;
- do not map onto certain perceptual property domains available to her, such as size or form;
- map onto a domain property that Kelli could not figure out.

The evidence Landau and Gleitman provide is based on Kelli's spontaneous use of colour terms, as well as in two comprehension experiments between 3;7 and 6;0 years. The latter are better described as metalinguistic experiments, because she had to answer questions such as "what terms are colour terms?", or "what can be coloured?".

Other researchers have also reported examples of blind children's use of colour terms which are in agreement with Landau and Gleitman's earlier affirmations. For instance, Pérez-Pereira (1991) related that one blind girl (with minimal perception of light) at around 5 years of age was playing with her sighted sister with blocks of wood of different forms, sizes, and colours. In a fairly routine way, both of them were naming the colours of the blocks: "this one is blue", "this other is red", and so on. Unexpectedly, at a given moment, the blind child asked her sighted sister "Andrea, what colour is this?" From this utterance, it can be inferred that the blind child knew: (1) that colours make reference to some quality of objects, (2) that objects may have different varieties of this quality, and (3) that the child knew that her sighted sister could perceive such features of objects that she could not. It is likely that the properties of colour terms could only be inferred by the blind child through the position these words occupy in sentences, which is an adjectival position ("This circle is yellow", "Give me the yellow circle"). Obviously, as Landau and Gleitman (1985, p. 173) rightly point out, the semantic knowledge that totally blind children can get of colour terms is restricted in many ways.

Landau and Gleitman's (1985) book none the less has received a number of criticisms. The book was thought to be a manifestation of nativist arguments which were not well grounded in the data (Davison, 1990; Mills, 1987a). However, it has not been sufficiently acknowledged that these authors have tried to provide a balanced explanation of the learning of visual and colour terms by blind children based as much on the information they extract from the environment (the contexts in which words are produced) as on the information provided by syntactic structures in which these words are embedded. Furthermore, they adopt a comprehensive view of the "variety of contrivances and principles" that are needed to arrive to a satisfactory theory of language learning, despite their nativist preference (Landau & Gleitman, 1985, pp. 155–156).

In connection with the conceptual basis of words, Peraita, Elosúa, and Linares (1992) carried out one experiment to test the characteristics of underlying concepts of words in blind children. In this experiment, the children had to tell all the characteristics they knew with reference to 27 words. On the list there were superordinate, basic-level, and subordinate words. The words belonged to two wide semantic fields: biological/natural (for instance, animal, bird, parakeet), on the one hand, and non-biological/appliances (vehicle, car, sports car, for instance), on the other. The children were 33 children blind from birth or shortly after birth, from 7 to 15 years of age. The authors did an inventory of features to analyse the responses given by the children. It was found that blind children, especially the youngest ones, used many tactual features to describe words. There were hardly any references to colour terms in the children's descriptions, until they were 10 years old. Until this age, the children scarcely knew supraordinate categories (animal, plant, vehicle) and the taxonomic organization of the words. As the children approached 14 years of age, they produced a greater number of features for each word. The oldest children used many sorting strategies, which were not idiosyncratic but "scientific". One finding common to all the children was that they all seemed to know better the features for biological than for non-biological items, and, for all categories, they had more information about basic-level items than for superordinate or subordinate ones, in that order. According to Peraita et al. (1992) the blind children used the same types of conceptual features underlying words as the sighted children in a previous study, particularly after 10 years of age. This is so because, thanks to language, there are shared concepts. In the authors' own words, "it can be said that children 'see' the world through language" (1992, p. 103). Language organizes the process of categorization and shaping of knowledge about the world. In spite of this, Peraita and collaborators found a chronological age gap between the abilities of blind and sighted children.

What Peraita and colleagues' research suggests is that the concepts underlying words are fundamentally the same for blind and sighted children, and that language plays an extremely important role in the process of acquisition of knowledge for blind children. In a certain way, reality is seen in the way we see it because of language.

Although this standpoint is somewhat different to the perspective that considers language as a very important source of information for the construction of language itself, and a formal problem space for children, Peraita's perspective also highlights the importance of language for blind children's development.

Finally, another study was carried out on the comprehension of spatial prepositions by blind children. It was considered that blind children, due to their restricted experience of spatial relationships, may construct different meanings for spatial prepositions. Bigelow and Bryan (1982) related the results of one comparative study of blind and sighted children on the comprehension of the prepositions "in", "on", and "under". Three children who were born totally blind but without other handicaps, were asked: (1) to put themselves "in", "on", or "under" various objects, such as a table, a box, etc., that allowed two or more spatial positions; and (2) to put toys "in", "on", and "under" the same objects. The aim of the study was to test the comprehension of self in relation to an object and of two objects in relation to each other, respectively. The blind children were presented with the tasks monthly between the time they were 2 and 4 years old. Bigelow and Bryan found that the blind children were able to correctly place themselves "in", at 33 months, "on" at 33 months, and "under" at 38 months. Nevertheless, the correct location of an object in relation to another object was reached a little later: at 34, 34, and 45 months for "in", "on", and "under", respectively. "Under" was more difficult to understand than any of the other prepositions. The conclusion of the authors was that blind children initially understand spatial terms egocentrically.

In order to test whether the initial egocentric construction of space was deviant from normal development, Bigelow and Bryan (1982) asked 36 sighted children between ages 1;6 and 3;0 years to demonstrate their understanding of these prepositions in tasks similar to those administered to the three blind children. Although the sighted children were a little younger than the blind children, their results showed that, similarly to the blind children, self-placement was easier than object placement for each of the three spatial prepositions. In addition, "under" was also found to be more difficult to understand than the other two spatial prepositions. These results, taken together, suggest that blind children do not seem to be atypical in their understanding of the spatial relations expressed by "in", "on", and "under". Obviously, in the case of these prepositions, the spatial relations conveyed by them are within the reach of blind children's representational capacities.

To summarize, old conceptions about the meaninglessness of blind children's words do not seem to be well grounded. Blind children seem to have meanings similar to those of sighted children, especially if we look at later points in development. None the less, although the developmental process they follow does not seem to be atypical, it is likely that blind infants take a longer time to construct conceptual meanings of some words, as Dunlea and colleagues (Andersen et al., 1984, 1993; Dunlea, 1984, 1989) and Urwin (1979, 1984a) have proposed. One of the reasons why some researchers have considered blind children's use of words to be atypical was their lack of consideration of individual differences in lexical development. In considering the sources of word meanings, Landau and Gleitman's

(1985) research suggests that, in addition to direct experience of the external world (extralinguistic experience), children, and especially blind children, may rely on the use of the information presented by language itself (intralinguistic information).

DEVELOPMENT OF MORPHOLOGY AND SYNTAX

Developmental processes in morphological acquisition

Few studies have been devoted to morphological development in blind children, if we disregard the studies on the acquisition of pronouns, which will be reviewed separately due to their empirical and theoretical relevance.

Dunlea and Andersen (1992) compared the acquisition of several morphemes in a blind boy, a partially sighted girl, and a sighted boy. The children were systematically recorded at home every month. They began the analysis of morpheme production when the children productively used one of Brown's 14 morphemes (Brown, 1973): This was at 1;8 years for Teddy, the blind child, at 1;9 years for Brett, the sighted child, and at 1;6 years for Lydia, the partially sighted girl. The analysis spanned the next eight sessions. Although Dunlea and Andersen used Brown's criteria to analyse the time of acquisition of the first morphemes in the blind child, they discarded the results they obtained, arguing that Brown's criteria present methodological problems. Among them they highlight: (1) that these categories are too broad, and, thus, scarcely sensitive to the different types of morphemes when various forms are possible (for example collapsing all the possessive pronouns together); (2) that Brown's procedure does not allow one to analyse the functions a form may serve (such as the use of *on* or *in* as verb particles or as locative prepositions); and (3) that this traditional method conflates clearly productive uses with imative and formulaic uses. Using Brown's criteria, Dunlea and Andersen found that, apparently, the blind child had acquired all but 2 of the 14 morphemes by 3;6 years. Nevertheless, using what they called an "emergence analysis", the results were rather different. A particular morpheme was credited as emerging if it was used by the child at least four times in spontaneous productive utterances during a single session. In contrast, Brown suggested that a morpheme was acquired if the child used it in 90% of its obligatory contexts during three consecutive sessions. Therefore, it must be emphasized that the results of the two analyses are likely to be very different, given the differing criteria used. Dunlea and Andersen were more interested in analysing the emergence process or first regular uses of a particular morpheme than examining the end product of this process. In analysing the data, they scored separately spontaneous and appropriate use, misapplication, omission, and imitative or formulaic uses of each morpheme. However, they did not specify in advance the possible functions of a particular morpheme in their category system. Therefore, there are several features of Dunlea and Andersen's research that make us cautious about their findings. In addition to the aforementioned comments, the exclusion of imitations and formulas from

Dunlea and Andersen's analysis is problematic, since there is no guarantee that they teased apart those imitations that introduce modifications on the modelled utterance from those which represented non-creative imitations. The former should not have been excluded from the analysis, due to their creativity. In addition, methodologically it is very difficult to identify formulaic utterances and separate them from creative productions, as we will discuss later.

The main findings Dunlea and Andersen (1992) obtained were the following. The sighted child began to regularly use the plural morphemes, the locative prepositions *on* and *in*, and the third person of present indicative well before the blind child. Nevertheless, the blind child did use these morphemes earlier in formulaic structures and imitations, that is to say in "non-productive" utterances. In their opinion, the later appearance of these morphemes in the blind child was based on cognitive difficulties in conceptualizing the number of entities in the external world, their spatial relationships, and the agency of others. Moreover, there were differences in the use of some of these forms between the two children. Thus, the first uses of *on* by the blind child were as verb particles (put on, get on), and only later did the child use *on* as a locative preposition. In contrast, the sighted child first used *in* and *on* as locative prepositions, and later as verb particles. In addition, the blind child not only started to use possessive pronouns later than the sighted child, but also incorrectly, without introducing the deictic shift, which the sighted child always introduced.

In contrast, other morphemes, such as the regular past, the present progressive and contractible auxiliary *be* were used by the blind child earlier than the sighted child. Regarding the use of regular past tense forms, Dunlea and Andersen (1992) indicated that they were correctly used from the beginning by the blind child, who even produced over-regularizations of irregular forms, such as *goed, throwed,* and *singed,* between 1;11 and 3;0 years. These over-regularizations show the productivity of this morpheme. The early mastery of regular past morphemes by the blind child is probably due to an adaptive strategy of the child, who used to talk about past events that established a shared knowledge with the caregiver and could well be a common focus of attention, in a similar way as non-handicapped children talk about the here and now (Andersen et al., 1993; Dunlea, 1989; Dunlea & Andersen, 1992; Wilson & Peters, 1988). As for present progressive and contractible auxiliary *be,* it was found that they were mainly used when the blind child talked about his ongoing or intended actions, to express his wishes, or in unanalysed forms. Other morphemes emerged in both the sighted and the blind child at a similar time. These forms were the contractible copula and articles, and the irregular past, which appeared a little later.

As for the partially sighted child, Dunlea and Andersen (1992) found she was midway between the blind child and the sighted child. As one of her most characteristic features, she first used *in* and *on* as verb particles, as the totally blind child did, but, at the same time, she had an earlier use of *in* and *on* to encode locations than did the blind child. Nevertheless, her first uses of *in* and *on* as locative prepositions were not finely grained, and she seemed to use them in a "generic" or undifferentiated way. Based on visually impaired children's difficulties in talking about locative relationships, but, at the same time, on their facility in talking about past events, the authors suggest that as visual impairment increases (thus reducing information about locative relationships), time tends to be expressed before space, just the opposite of what happens with sighted children (Weist, 1991).

Taking all these results together, Dunlea and Andersen (1992, p. 112) conclude that: "morphological development in the two visually impaired subjects is neither delayed nor impaired in comparison to sighted children. It is different."

Nevertheless, the same conclusion does not seem to be shared by Miecznikowski and Andersen (1986), in spite of the fact that they studied the same visually impaired child. Miecznikowski and Andersen aimed to study the transition from formulaic speech to analysed speech in the morphological development of Lydia, the visually impaired girl. They studied the use of four morphemes, contractible copula, progressive, articles and the preposition *on*, by Lydia from 1;6 to 3;6. These scholars observed that the child simultaneously passed through the same three different stages in the acquisition of each of these four morphemes. In the first stage, between 16 and 20 months of age, she used these morphemes correctly in grammatically correct unanalysed, formulaic utterances. The morphemes were not produced in other combinations except the formulae. A fixed formulae is an utterance which is repeated often in a fixed form with no internal changes. For instance, Lydia produced *what's that* in a fixed order, and never changed the form to *what is that* or *what's this*; or Lydia also produced the formulaic utterance *I'm gonna beat your butt* very frequently and from very early, but no other utterance with present progressive. In addition, these formulae were closely tied to specific contexts. In the second stage Lydia started to use these morphemes in new combinations, but now she omitted the morphemes in most of her analysed utterances. During this stage correct formulaic uses of the morphemes coexisted with incorrect creative uses. However, Lydia's productions changed to include more varied formulae, although less frequently used than in the first stage. The second stage spanned from 20 to 25 months of age. Finally, in the third stage, after 25 months, the girl began to use the morphemes in her analysed, creative sentences, in a systematic and correct way. Now she did not omit the forms in obligatory contexts, although earlier formulae still survived. According to Miecznikowski and Andersen (1986, p. 199), at this stage, Lydia's general use of the morphemes in creative sentences indicated full acquisition of the morphemes. Interestingly, the authors point out that the acquisition of morphemes in this visually impaired child did not involve overgeneralizations. According to these authors, this might be indicative of a lesser capacity of morphological analysis in visually impaired children than in the sighted children, who usually show over-regularizations of irregular forms.

In spite of Miecznikowski and Andersen's interesting observations, in our opinion their conception of formulae is subject to criticisms, as they use a very broad definition of formulaic utterances, which includes utterances that could well be considered as truly creative by other authors (especially in the case of "variable" formulae: *it's a cat*, in which *it's* is a fixed form, with the word *cat* replaceable by other NPs like *the dog*). They themselves say (Miecznikowski and Andersen, 1986, p. 201): "at some point, the breakdown of formulae and the analytic buildup of language would meet, and at that point, it would become difficult, if not impossible to distinguish formulaic from analytic utterances". Additionally, these authors affirm that, in part, formulaic expressions are not creative because their production is tied to particular contexts. Whereas this affirmation seems to be correct, we must remind ourselves that this context-bound characteristic is not only typical of formulae, but of early language in general. Therefore, at first it is difficult to separate formulae from other productions at early stages of development. On the other hand, it seems to us that there appears to be an essentially negative view of formulae in Miecznikowski and Andersen's work. As Pine and Lieven (1993) have convincingly shown, there is a tendency to view the acquisition of unanalysed chunks as essentially negative, because of their lack of creativity. The use of unanalysed units or formulae is characteristic of the pronominal style of language acquisition (called by Miecznikowski and Andersen, Gestalt style), in contrast to the nominal style. Nevertheless, the pronominal style is not devoid of analytical capacity. Similarly to Pine and Lieven, Pérez-Pereira (1994) has shown how children with Gestalt or pronominal style, and blind children in particular, also demonstrate active processing of language, although in a different way from nominal or analytic children.

In order to further investigate whether blind children do not produce over-regularizations of irregular morphemes, as Miecznikowski and Andersen (1986) claimed, Pérez-Pereira and Castro (1997) compared the over-regularization errors produced by a blind child and her sighted fraternal twin sister between 2;5,28 and 5;3,23. The authors carried out monthly, hour-long recordings of the speech of these children. They found that, during this period, the blind child produced 33 over-regularization errors and her sighted sister produced 21. Moreover, the types of irregular verbs over-regularized by the girls were very similar. In addition, the blind girl started to produce her first errors earlier than her sighted twin sister (3;1,2 against 3;3,13). Over-regularization errors are considered to be the application of a general rule to forms which are exceptions. These errors imply the abstraction of a rule from linguistic experience, and, this in turn is indicative of a capacity for morphological analysis (Bowerman, 1982; Pérez-Pereira, 1989; Slobin, 1973). Therefore, the blind child studied by Pérez-Pereira and Castro (1997) does not appear to be deficient in relation to her capacity for morphological analysis, and as a result puts in question the view that blind children are less creative than their sighted peers in constructing language (Andersen et al., 1993).

In summary, the results of several investigations show that blind children are not deficient in their morphological development. What existing differences remain seem to be the result of processes adaptive to the absence of visual information.

The acquisition of syntax by blind children

Two broad hypotheses have been put forward as explanations for the role of visual experience in the acquisition of language in general and of syntax in particular. According to the first, lack of vision hinders the acquisition of language, and therefore the syntactic development of blind children is delayed with respect to that of sighted children. Fraiberg (1977), for example, reported that the blind children she studied began using two-word combinations later than sighted children, and she attributed their syntactic deficiencies (which she judged to have disappeared by the age of 3 years) to limitations in experience due to lack of vision. In the same vein, Wills (1979) reported delays in the development of blind children's language. Authors studying other aspects of language acquisition by blind children have also maintained that the absence of visual information affects their cognitive development and their comprehension of reality, and that a consequence of this is that their linguistic development is slow and in some respects deficient (Andersen et al., 1984, 1993; Dunlea, 1989). Similarly, Dunlea (1989) argued that lack of vision will lead to an impoverishment in conceptual development, which, in turn, will cause deficiencies in the language learning of blind children (cf. McCune, 1991 for a criticism of this position). This view can be considered an extension of the theory that conceptual development sets the pace for linguistic development (MacNamara, 1972). Andersen et al. (1993) point out that, besides being visually deprived, blind children generally receive less appropriate linguistic input than sighted children, and that it is the combination of these two factors that gives rise to their poorer linguistic development. Some researchers have pointed out the importance of the amount of maternal talk children experience for their linguistic development (Hoff-Ginsberg, 1992; Huttenlocher, Haight, Bryk, Seltzer, & Lyons, 1991; Snow, 1994), and Snow (1994) suggested that handicapped children, such as blind children, may be considerably more dependent than non-handicapped children on the availability of optimal input if they are to show normal language acquisition. Nevertheless, as far as we know, there is no comparative study of the linguistic input received by blind and sighted children,[12] with the exception of those studies (only indirectly related) on mother-infant conversational interchanges, which themselves have provided controversial results (Conti-Ramsden & Pérez-Pereira, 1997, in press; Kekelis & Andersen, 1984; Moore & McConachie, 1994; Pérez-Pereira & Conti-Ramsden, submitted), as is reviewed in Chapter 6.

   In contrast to the previous view, other researchers have concluded that the syntactic development of blind children is not delayed relative to that of sighted children (Landau, 1997; Landau & Gleitman 1985; Pérez-Pereira, 1994; Pérez-Pereira & Castro 1992, 1997). This conclusion is based on the idea that linguistic development is relatively independent of cognitive development, and that in acquiring language children not only combine linguistic and non-linguistic input but also employ specifically linguistic analytic strategies to solve the problems posed by the linguistic system to be acquired. The idea that there exist specific linguistic mechanisms for learning language is compatible with different theoretical views, such as a nativist (Bloom, 1993), a neo-constructivist (Karmiloff-Smith, 1992), or a neo-connectionist (Elman, Bates, Johnson, Karmiloff-Smith, Parisi, & Plunkett, 1996) view. All these views defend a domain-specific view of development. In some cases, researchers have identified mechanisms and strategies for linguistic analysis that are abundantly used by blind children. These mechanisms and strategies show blind children's capacity to extract the meaning and function of the elements of language from the linguistic context in which they occur, by paying attention to the regularities the children observe (Gleitman, 1990; Landau & Gleitman, 1985; Landau, 1997; Pérez-Pereira, 1994; Peters, 1987).

Therefore, from the latter point of view, but not from the former, it sounds reasonable to suppose that blind children may show a profile of syntactic development similar to that of sighted children, provided they have enough linguistic experience. Next we will review those studies that specifically focus on blind children's syntactic development.

Several longitudinal studies calculated the MLU measures for blind and sighted children. It is thought that the mean length of child's utterances (MLU) is a consequence of the growth of underlying linguistic competence, in such a way that MLU grows as morphosyntactic complexity of language increases. Landau and Gleitman (1985) compared their blind subjects' rate of growth in MLU to those of Bloom, Lightbown, and Hood's (1975) and Brown's (1973) sighted subjects. The children were between 18 and 42 months of age. Even though two of the three blind children showed a delay in their MLU measures in relation to the sighted children for the first few measures, thereafter in the rate of progress increased and they rapidly caught up with the sighted children. By 36 months blind children's measures were equal to those of the sighted children group, and by the fourth birthday blind and sighted children's MLUs were above 4.0. In spite of the fact that the authors did not perform any statistical analysis, Landau and Gleitman (1985) conclude that MLU development of blind children was normal.

Similar conclusions may be drawn from the results obtained by Dunlea (1989). Although the data she reported were not so detailed, it appears that the MLU indexes of her two blind subjects were higher than those of their visually impaired and sighted peers.

Furthermore, Pérez-Pereira and Castro presented data on the MLU of different blind subjects in several investigations (Pérez-Pereira & Castro, 1992, 1994, in press). These authors studied MLU measures of three blind children, one partially sighted, and one sighted child, at different ages. Table 4.3 shows the results obtained. In addition, the authors applied a two-tailed Mann–Whitney U test, to compare the results across subjects at specific periods where sufficient data were available. The results of this analysis indicated that the only significant differences were between Subject 4 (blind), on the one hand, and Subjects 3 (blind) and 5 (sighted), on the other, from 29 to 41 months of age. This result suggests that there was more rapid morphosyntactic development in Subject 4 than in Subjects 3 or

TABLE 4.3

MLU's development
(adapted from Pérez-Pereira & Castro, in press)

Age (months)	1 Partially sighted	2 Blind	3 Blind	4 Blind	5 Sighted
19	1.31				
20					
21	1.34				
22	1.69	1.21			
23	1.33	1.42			
24		1.43			
25	1.83	1.58			
26		2.05			
27		2.07			
28		2.04	2.04		
29			2.60	2.24	2.80
30		2.26	2.55		
31		2.10	2.51		
32		2.08	2.39	2.52	2.11
33		2.39	2.31		
34		2.53	2.08	2.74	2.37
35			2.81	2.73	2.42
36			2.46	3.37	2.77
37			2.53	3.85	2.98
38				3.50	2.82
39			3.11	3.67	3.04
40			3.02	3.61	3.18
41			3.99	3.57	3.02
42				3.54	1.63*
43				3.41	3.78
44				4.76	4.00
45				4.37	5.31

*This session is not useful for comparison due to Subject 5's tantrum.

5, during this period of time. However, if we consider the whole period of time on which there was overlapping data (29 to 45 months) there were no significant differences between Subjects 4 and 5 (the blind and sighted twin sisters). In addition, no differences were observed between the youngest children (Subject 1, partially blind, and Subject 2, blind). Therefore Pérez-Pereira and Castro's data suggest that blind children are not at a disadvantage in relation to sighted children with regard to morphosyntactic development as measured by MLU (and, what is more striking, that some blind children are even more advanced than their non-impaired peers). The agreement of these results with those of other studies indicates the robustness of this claim.

Landau and Gleitman (1985) studied early word combinations in their three blind subjects (Angie, Kelli, and Carlo), specifically the thematic relations expressed in predicate-argument structures. In order to analyse the semantic relationships conveyed in the children's word combinations, Landau and Gleitman used the categories proposed by Bloom et al. (1975), and compared the results of their blind subjects to those children studied by Bloom and colleagues. The results of the study indicate that the blind and sighted children were very much alike. Both groups of children predominantly talked about actions and states at the early stages of language learning, and, to a much lesser extent, talked about possessions, attributions, and existence.

Landau and Gleitman (1985) also analysed the internal complexity of children's utterances, such as the number and complexity of noun phrases (the doll) and verb phrases (hit the ball), and they found that the blind children were comparable to the sighted children of equivalent MLU from Newport's study (Newport, 1977) in this regard. Nevertheless, the blind children were delayed (though not deviant) compared to the sighted children regarding verb-auxiliary structure, that is to say, the mean number of morphemes that appear in verb + auxiliary frames. For instance, the blind children tend to say *I eating the pizza*, instead of the correct *I am eating the pizza*. In that case the verb + auxiliary structure would have two morphemes (eat/ing), instead of three (am eat/ing). This was the only systematic exception to the pattern of normal growth of syntactic structures in blind children. According to these authors, this delay is due to the speech that the blind children received from their mothers, where there was a high proportion of imperatives (see also Kekelis & Andersen, 1984; Moore & McConachie, 1994) and a very low proportion of yes/no questions (e.g. Will you go to the kitchen?), compared to sighted children. This kind of speech to blind children does not provide these children with the optimal syntactic information, because the use of imperatives precludes the use of auxiliary verbs. In this respect, Mills (1993) has also found that the prolonged use of imperatives by the mothers of German-speaking sighted children lead to a non-adult positioning of the verb at the end of the utterance. Mills suggests that cases like these point to the role of input on syntax acquisition, although she considers that there is no indication that the children suffer any permanent damage from this temporary delay. In any case, this delay in verb + auxiliary structure may have an effect for English-speaking children, but not necesarily for speakers of other languages where the use of auxiliaries is less important, as is the case in Spanish. Furthermore, many auxiliaries in English have low phonetic substance and are thus more prone to being left out by young normally developing children as well as children with specific language impairment (Leonard, 1998). In the case of blind children learning English, some effect of phonetic substance may also be at work.

In spite of the verb + auxiliary delay and the later onset of the first combinations of words, Landau and Gleitman (1985, p. 49) conclude: "Over and above these differences we are struck by the normalcy of the blind child's language development on all the other measures we have taken. The two populations are essentially indistinguishable from each other by the third birthday, including internal organization of syntax, thematic relations, and vocabulary."

Similarly to Landau and Gleitman (1985), Dunlea (1989) analysed the thematic roles or semantic relations of words using a classification system based on case grammar. Dunlea, following a Piagetian cognitively based theory of language acquisition (Cromer, 1991), formulates the hypothesis that "if the claim is valid that semantic relations reflect the child's prior schematization of events perceived in the world, it should follow that children whose conception of the world is necessarily different as the result of visual impairment will express qualitative different relationships in their early utterances" (Dunlea, 1989, p. 90). She found that the eight core case relationships[13] plus four frequently occurring three-term constructions (Agent + Action + Object; Agent + Action + Location; Agent + Object + Location; Action + Object + Location) accounted for 68% of the utterances produced by the verbal sighted child (Brett), and 64% and 72% of the two visually impaired children. In contrast, these core relationships accounted for 31% and 34% of the two blind children. This percentage rose to 50% in both blind children if stereotypic utterances were excluded.

In addition, the sighted child was the only one who produced all eight of the core relations. Some of them were absent or very rare in the blind children. This was the case with Entity + Attribute, not observed at all in one visually impaired child (Lydia) as well as the other visually impaired child, Julie, although she, with a lower development of language, produced instances of only four semantic relationships. Cases where Entity + Attribute were observed in two blind children tended to be "common associations" such as "nice bath" and "little horse". Dunlea's impression was that these children had not abstracted attributional features from the items with which they were initially associated and that the phrases containing them were unanalysed units (Dunlea, 1989, p. 94). However, it is necessary to say that Brett (sighted) produced very few instances of Entity + Attribute as well. Dunlea reported that Action/State + Location was not observed in the two blind children and one visually impaired child (Julie). However, these children produced instances of Entity + Location, although almost all of them were produced in questions asking about the location of something. The conclusion she drew from these data was that blind children did not talk about novel information concerning the location of objects or actions, or about the qualities of objects.

Similarly, Dunlea reported that both blind children used Agent + Action/State in a self-centred or egocentric way, where they themselves were the agent. This was not the case for the sighted child, who always referred to actions performed by someone else. Something similar happened with the semantic relationships Action/State + Object, and Possessor + Possession, which were always used in an egocentric way by the blind children, but not so egocentrically by the sighted child. In spite of Dunlea's interpretation that blind children speak in a self-centred way, there are some facts which cast some doubt on Dunlea's interpretation. For instance, the single exception of self-centred Agent + Action relations was Teddy's expression "Linda burp(ed)" (Dunlea, 1989, p. 100). Interestingly, the action performed by Linda was an audible one, and, thus, could be reported by Teddy (blind). In this connection, Dunlea reported as well that Demonstrative + Entity relations were used by blind children when they were holding an object, but also, and this is the interesting observation, for audible objects, for example, "that (a) motorcycle". In our opinion, Dunlea should have noted the fact that blind children are able to use their language to make reference to other's agency or to external entities when the action is performed by another person or when entities have some audible quality. It is obvious that blind and severely visually impaired children have many limitations in talking about visually perceived actions performed by others at a distance, visual qualities of objects, locations of actions, or identifications of entities, unless these actions and entities are accompanied by information that can be perceived through senses other than vision. Furthermore, it is well known that the identification of qualities of objects, actions, and events through senses other than vision takes a longer time, because visual processing is qualitatively different from the discontinuous perception via audition or touch (Rosa & Ochaita, 1993). In this connection, Maxfield (1936) reported that activity terms relating to self were more abundantly used by her youngest group of blind children (average 40 months) than by the oldest group (average 68 months), and that reference to the activity of other persons showed a regular increase with age.

Dunlea (1989) claimed that the data she reported show that blind children have different conceptions of events from sighted children. Conceding that this may be relatively true at first, the important point is to understand how blind children can arrive into a world of shared meanings, as they in fact do, with only minor delays. In addition, Dunlea's semantically based frame of reference (case grammar), which is centred on the thematic relations expressed by the children, has little to say about syntax and syntactic relationships, such as order, agreement, government, etc. In this connection, McCune (1991), reinterpreting Dunlea's data, found that Teddy, the most visually impaired child, leads Brett, the sighted child, in MLU and number of combinations at each month of age. Thus, McCune (1991, p. 101) states that, contrary to Dunlea's conclusion, early grammatical development can proceed quite well in blind children.

In another study, Pérez-Pereira and Castro (in press; see also Pérez-Pereira & Castro, 1994 for a shorter and partial account) analysed the coordinate and subordinate clauses produced by the same children used for the MLU analysis, with the exception of the partially sighted boy, who still was too young to produce complex sentences. Therefore, three totally blind children and one sighted child were compared, from 1;10 to 3;5. All the different types of coordinate and subordinate sentences produced by these children were categorized, according to the categories available in Spanish grammar. The results showed that the syntactic development of the blind children was not delayed as compared to that of the sighted child, whose language development was within the normal range. An unexpected result was that subordinate clauses were found to be used more abundantly than coordinate ones by all the children, although the percentage of complex sentences (coordinate plus subordinate) was low, on a par with other studies with blind and sighted children of the same age (Maxfield, 1936). The main significant difference found indicated that the blind twin girl (Child 4) produced significantly more subordinate clauses than the other children. The analysis of the type of subordinate clauses produced by the children showed that this difference was essentially due to the higher proportion of infinitival noun clauses she used in comparison with the other children. These clauses were predominantly used to express wishes and intentions ("quiero coger uno grande," "I wanna take a big one"). Some individual differences regarding the most frequently used types of subordinate clauses were found, but these appeared to have little to do with differences in vision. Although the percentage of coordinate and subordinate clauses in the speech of all these children was low, the blind children began to use them very early. Longitudinal studies on the acquisition of complex sentences by Spanish children have shown that they begin to use them shortly before 30 months of age, and that Spanish children seem to have produced nearly all the variety of subordinate sentences at 36 months of age or a few months later (Aguirre, 1995; Aparici, Capdevila, Serra, & Serrat, 1996; Hernández-Pina, 1984). Two blind children (Child 2 and Child 3) in Pérez-Pereira and Castro's study (in press) began to use subordinate sentences before 30 months of age, and before they were 36 months of age they could produce a high variety of subordinate sentences, such as subordinate noun clauses (*Dile a Mercedes que no haga ruido*—"Tell Mercedes not to make any noise"), relative clauses (*Mira lo que cogí*—"Look what I got"), and adverbial clauses of cause, manner, and conditional, and comparative clauses (*Espera que tengo que jugar un poco*—"Wait, I've got to play a bit"; *Estoy tieso como una piedra*—"I'm as stiff as a stone"; *Vete a la calle si quieres*—"Go out if you want"). The other blind child (Child 4) started to use subordinate clauses shortly after 30 months of age, and by 39 months of age she produced an important variety of subordinate sentences. The pattern of acquisition of her sighted twin sister (Child 5) was quite similar. Based on these findings Pérez-Pereira and Castro (in press) conclude that the ability to analyse linguistic structures does not appear to be impaired in blind children.

In summary, the results of the studies on the acquisition of syntax are conflicting, especially those focusing on the semantic relationships expressed by blind children. Whereas Dunlea (1989) claims that there are differences between blind and sighted children in this respect, Landau and Gleitman (1985) claim that there are none. One possible source of the differences found may be the different stages of linguistic development of the children analysed in the two studies. Dunlea's subjects had a lower MLU than Landau and Gleitman's, and it may be the case that blind children take a longer time to express the same type and percentage of semantic relationships as their sighted peers. The data gathered by Landau and Gleitman (1985) show that, as blind children grow, differences with sighted children vanish.

It also appears that the analysis of the semantic relationships expressed by blind children can not tell us much about the development of syntax. The analysis of more specifically syntactic aspects of language indicates that lack of vision in itself does not cause delay. There is general agreement that morphosyntactic development, as measured by MLU, is not delayed in blind children. In addition, the analysis of the emergence and percentage of use of coordinate and subordinate clauses shows that blind children follow a normal pattern of development as compared with sighted children (Pérez-Pereira & Castro, in press). The only difference found concerns the verb-auxiliary structure, which may be temporarily delayed in blind children (Landau & Gleitman, 1985), this apparently seems to be caused by characteristics of maternal input that blind children receive, not by the visual impairment itself (Mills, 1993). Moreover, this delay is probably specific to blind children acquiring English, and may not be the case for children learning other languages, such as Spanish.

CHAPTER FIVE

Language development in blind children (2)

In this second chapter on language development in blind children we discuss in some detail the acquisition of personal reference terms, pragmatic development, verbal routines, and imitative speech, as well as a more general discussion of blind children's language and language development theories. We now turn to examine the controversial area of blind children's use of personal reference terms.

PERSONAL REFERENCE TERMS

The acquisition of personal reference terms, and pronouns in particular, has been considered as one of the most distinctive features of blind children's language. According to several researchers who have had an important impact on the field, these children produce many reversal errors, such as *you* instead of *I*. However, as we will see, this conclusion is far from universal.

In the present section, we will be concerned with the semantic and pragmatic properties of personal reference terms, as well as with the emergence of person marking, but not with other morphological aspects of personal reference terms, such as the emergence of case and gender distinctions, or the anaphoric uses of pronouns in connected discourse. Under the label of personal reference terms we will consider not only personal pronouns (*I, you, he/she* ...), but also possessive pronouns (*mine, yours, his/hers* ...) and adjectives (*my, your, his/her* ...).

Like other deictic terms, personal reference terms do not have a fixed referent as other words have. Common and proper names are good examples of words with fixed referents (for instance, *table* or *bicycle*, refer to specific objects, or *Mary* to a particular person). On the other hand, other personal reference terms designate different speech roles, such as speaker, addressee, and non-participant (anybody who is neither the addressee nor the speaker). These conversational functions are accomplished by the first person, the second person, and the third person, respectively. Thus, the shifting of reference (Benveniste, 1974; Chiat, 1986; Clark, 1978; Jakobson, 1968;   Levinson, 1983) is the most distinguishing feature of personal reference forms—the particular individuals they identify in a given conversational context shift depending on who is speaking. A particular person may be *I* when he or she is speaking, but *you* when the speaker is talking to him or her, or *he* or *she* when two other persons are talking about him or her.

Therefore, it has been generally assumed that personal reference terms in particular, and deictic terms in general, show greater complexity than non-deictic reference terms and, thus, are more difficult for children to learn (Clark, 1978).

Theories of the acquisition of personal reference terms by sighted children

Before reviewing the acquisition of personal reference terms by blind children, it is important to review how non-handicapped children acquire these terms, in order to have a point of reference for comparison.

According to several naturalistic studies (Hernández-Pina, 1984 and Shum, Conde, & Díaz, 1992 for Spanish-speaking children; and Clark, 1978 and Chiat, 1986, for English speakers), children between 18 and 25 months usually start to use a few first- and second-person singular forms. Third-person singular forms appear shortly after, and the emergence of plural forms does not follow a clear-cut order. In any case, an across-the-board acquisition of personal reference terms does not occur. Therefore, although there is not complete agreement within naturalistic studies concerning the order of emergence, the order of acquisition previously described seems to be the most common one. However, the first forms that children use as personal reference are proper names, which coexist with the earliest pronoun forms for a few months, before being abandoned (Chiat, 1986; Pérez-Pereira, Forján, & García, 1996).

Another area where there is wide agreement deals with the fact that first personal reference forms are used in unanalysed phrases or stereotyped contexts, such as *I wanna x*, *Give it to me!*, *Give me x*, etc., that the children produce as unanalysed wholes. Only later are these forms used in other linguistic contexts (Chiat, 1986; Loveland, 1984).

Three different theories have been proposed to explain the acquisition of pronouns, as well as personal reference terms in general. Different predictions are derived from these theories regarding the order of acquisition of pronouns, children's performance in different speech roles, and the production of reversal errors.

The first theory, which can be called the "person-referring" theory (Clark, 1978), maintains that in Stage 1 children use pronouns as if they were proper names, with first-person pronouns referring to the adults (I = adult), and second-person pronouns referring to the child (you = child). According to this theory, children should misuse pronouns when they are the speaker, and, consequently, produce reversals. In contrast, it is expected that children should correctly understand the pronouns they hear as addressee. In Stage 2, children already use pronouns as adults do, shifting pronouns according to the role that the children occupy in the conversation (I = speaker; you = addressee). Clark softened her theory by saying that the majority of children do not go through the first step, that is some children use the role shifting hypothesis from the beginning. However, the data do not fit her theory, since reversals are scarce, not widespread, and coexist with correct use of pronouns. In addition, it is not at all clear that first-person pronouns are used before they are understood, or that *I* is used earlier than *you*.

The second theory, the "person in speech role referring theory" (Charney, 1980), suggests that pronouns refer to the same person (the children) but only as long as the children occupy a particular speech role. That is to say, when children are the speaker, then *I* is the correct form to refer to them; however, when children are the addressee, *you* is the correct form. This theory predicts that children will use first-person pronouns before they understand them correctly, and that first-person pronouns will be used earlier than second-person pronouns when the child is the speaker. The theory also predicts that second-person pronouns will be understood before they can be used correctly by the children and earlier than first-person pronouns when the child is the addressee. In addition, children will misunderstand first-person pronouns when they are being addressed, but they will not make reversal errors. After this stage, children become aware of the reciprocity of speech roles. Once again, available data do not entirely support the predictions of this theory (Chiat, 1986).

The third theory maintains that children, as a rule, will not have problems in understanding the role-shifting characteristics of pronouns and personal reference terms. According to this "speech role referring" theory, pronoun reversals seldom occur, and only a few children produce a few instances of reversal errors (Chiat, 1983, 1986; Dale & Crain-Thoreson, 1993; Shum et al., 1992). However, a few researchers have tried to explain why reversals are produced in certain cases. In this regard, different explanations have been given.

Chiat (1983, 1986) proposed that pronoun-reversing children correctly produce pronouns according to the speech role shift, but they also produce other pronouns wrongly following a "shifting perspective". The shifting perspective, a separate non-adult function, occurs when the child uses a pronoun in a way that would be appropriate if the addressee were speaking. That is to say, pronoun reversals take place because the child speaks from the addressee's perspective. They also reflect certain adult uses of pronouns which take a second or third person's perspective on speech roles, such as referring to self, impersonally or generally, from the second person or third person perspective (Chiat, 1986). Therefore, pronoun reversal occurs only in limited contexts, where the child is adopting speech roles from another's perspective.

Oshima-Takane (1992; Oshima-Takane & Benaroya, 1989) suggested that a failure to take note of pronouns in speech addressed to another person is a major reason why children, particularly children with autism, show pronominal errors, especially second-person pronoun errors. A similar idea was proposed by Urwin (1984a) in relation to blind children. She commented that the restricted use of pronouns in Suzanne (a blind girl she studied) was related to the girl's restricted access to surrounding context and, as a consequence, to the lack of opportunity to comment on others. Furthermore, it is logical to suggest that blind children have fewer opportunities to experience pronouns (specially second-person pronouns) than sighted children have (Pérez-Pereira, 1999), if we take into account that mothers address a greater number of directives and questions to their blind children than do sighted children's mothers (Conti-Ramsden & Pérez-Pereira, 1997; Kekelis & Andersen, 1984; Moore & McConachie, 1994; Pérez-Pereira & Conti-Ramsden, submitted). Therefore, restricted linguistic experience with pronouns as well as restricted experience with others' actions, possessions, and characteristics, may result in greater difficulties in learning personal reference terms.

Dale and Crain-Thoreson (1993) found that out of the thirty 20-month-old sighted children studied, 57% produced at least one pronoun reversal out of samples of 250–300 utterances. After analysing the instances of reversals, Dale and Crain-Thoreson found that reversals are more likely to occur in relatively complex phrases with two semantically reversible noun predicates, and in imitations of others' utterances. They also found that children who produce reversals tend to have a pronominal style, in contrast to non-reversers who tend to have a nominal style. Another feature of reversers is that they may be precocious children who adopt a risk taking approach to language acquisition, using pronouns—and other forms in the process of being learned—more frequently than more conservative language learning children. In addition, second person forms are produced more abundantly by reversers than by non-reversers. From these findings Dale and Crain-Thoreson conclude that reversals reveal a failure to perform a deictic shift which is more likely to happen when children's psycholinguistic processing abilities are overloaded.

Acquisition and use of personal reference terms by blind children

Concerning the acquisition of personal reference in blind children, the majority of the studies carried out until very recently (Andersen et al., 1984; Dunlea, 1989; Farrell et al., 1990; Fraiberg & Adelson, 1973; McGinnis, 1981; McGuire & Meyers, 1971) have suggested that blind children have many problems in acquiring personal reference terms. In providing explanations for these problems, two views can be discerned in the field.

The first view is clearly influenced by research with children with autism. As is well known, children with autism are considered to begin to use personal reference terms late, as well as to produce a relatively high percentage of reversals (Frith, 1989; Happé, 1994; Hobson, 1993a; Lord & Paul, 1997; Tager-Flusberg, 1994b). Some researchers have suggested that blind children show the same problems with personal reference terms, as well as other symptoms, as do children with autism, and have pointed to some similarities between blind children and children with autism. Fay (1973; Fay & Schuler, 1980) alluded to the echolalic speech of both groups of children as the factor responsible for the high number of pronoun reversals. Going further, Hobson (Brown et al., 1997;[14] Hobson, 1993a, 1993b; Hobson et al., 1997; Lee, Hobson & Chiat, 1994;) proposed that problems with pronouns are caused by a deficient development of a theory of mind (knowledge of mental processes of self and others). According to Hobson, lack of vision deprives blind children of information concerning the expression of emotions and others' attitudes, affecting the development of psychological perspective-taking and the concept of self, which is crucial for the development of a theory of mind (Brown et al., 1997; Hobson, 1993b; Hobson et al., 1997).

The second perspective compares blind children with sighted children, paying special attention to the way in which visual impairment affects blind children's cognitive and personal development. According to some authors, the lack of visual information negatively affects conceptual development, which in turn affects the acquisition of personal reference terms.

Probably, one of the most influential proposals has been that of Fraiberg and Adelson (1973, 1977). This proposal states that, because of lack of visual information, blind children have many problems in developing a body image, which is an essential component of self-representation or self-awareness (Zazzó, 1948). This deficient representation of self has effects not only on the late and wrong use of pronouns by blind children, but also on their late use of symbolic play (after 4;6). Thus, the use of pronouns reveals how children represent themselves in language. In a different vein, Warren (1984, 1994) considered that spatial knowledge and extralinguistic referential information is limited in blind children, and this, in turn, produces problems with the comprehension and production of deictic terms, such as spatial deictics and personal deictics. Similarly, Loveland (1984), affirmed that correct comprehension and use of *I/you* pronouns is related to the understanding of different points of view in sighted children. Thus, Loveland's research has important implications for the case of blind children, since it states that there is "a clear link between the child's growing understanding of the visual/spatial relations among persons and the child's emerging ability to refer to persons" (p. 555). Other authors (Andersen et al., 1984, 1993; Dunlea, 1989) have proposed that problems with pronouns are one manifestation of a more general problem with deixis, and are related to a general lack of a "perspective-taking" ability. This means that blind children have difficulties in adopting a definite perspective in relation to the role they occupy in conversation.

What is of interest is that all these explanatory views of blind children's use of personal reference terms are based on results provided by investigations with serious methodological flaws. It is important to point out that most investigations have based their interpretations on a few examples and anecdotal results and not on detailed quantitative and qualitative data analyses. Thus, Fraiberg and Adelson (1973, 1977) affirmed that blind children do not begin to use *non-syncretic I* until they are between 2;11 and 4;10, that is to say, later than sighted children do. In addition, they reported that blind children produced pronoun reversals frequently until these ages. Non-syncretic or analysed uses of pronouns occur when pronominal forms are used productively in new combinations. These non-syncretic uses of first-person personal pronouns differ from formulaic or unanalysed, *syncretic I*, used in verb forms of need or want (*I want milk*). The first instances of *syncretic I*, such as *I wanna*, appear about 2;0 to 2;6, in blind children, similarly to sighted children. However, Fraiberg and Adelson (1973, 1977) offer as evidence only a few examples and anecdotal observations. There is no doubt that these observations are based on wide clinical experience, but more rigorous analysis of language samples needs to be done before general conclusions are reached.

Similarly, Andersen et al. (1984) affirm that blind children learn personal reference terms late and deficiently, because of a problem with reversibility. This affects children's inability to shift perspective depending on the speech role they occupy, and to understand the shifting reference of pronouns. Andersen et al. (1984, p. 656) state that "a recurrent finding among developmental studies of the blind is that these children have difficulty mastering the pronoun system". But these authors again offer only a few examples of inappropriate pronoun use by the blind children they studied. No quantitative analysis of pronoun production and pronoun reversals has been provided.

Dunlea (1989) considered that the use of stereotypic speech contributes to the misuse of pronouns in blind children, and offered a few examples of pronoun reversals in stereotyped phrases. She affirmed that "almost all" of Lisa's self references occur as *you* or proper name, and that approximately 75 per cent of Teddy's self references involved pronominal errors. None the less, Dunlea did not provide any quantitative data on pronoun use for the two blind children in her study. In the individualized probe to measure first- and second-person pronouns, especially possessive pronouns, Dunlea found that Lisa and Teddy interpreted *your* correctly, but responded to *my* as if it referred to themselves in 70% of their responses. This result suggests that blind children may fail to understand pronominal deixis. Therefore, Dunlea suggests that blind children show a failure to understand the reciprocity encoded in pronominal deixis, and that lack of visual information negatively affects the grasping of speech roles.

Peters (1987) also reports that Seth, the blind child she studied, usually referred to himself as *you*, and she comments that this kind of reversal problem is typical of blind children, although not limited to them. A few reversals with *you* persisted until the child was 33 months old; however, he used *I* correctly from 24 months of age. Interestingly, Peters comments that most of the misuses of *you* occurred in formulaic or imitated phrases, in which the child repeated offers by his father as if they were requests for himself (*Do you wanna cookie?* meaning *I want a cookie*). In her opinion, this fact reveals that Seth had not fully analysed these phrases into their morphological parts. Peters also does not offer any quantitative data on Seth's pronouns use and the contexts in which pronouns were used.

The only study that offers quantitative results, to our knowledge, was carried out by McGinnis (1981). Although the author did not offer raw data, she provides significance levels for a Mann–Whitney U test used to compare the feature categories she analysed in a group of six blind children and six sighted children, ranging in age from 3;5 to 5;0. One of the categories analysed was "personal reference mistakes (*I* confusions)", in which the blind children made a significantly higher number of confusions ($P > .002$) than the sighted children. One possible limitation of McGinnis' data, is that these results were based on a small language corpus: a one-hour transcription of each blind children's language and half an hour of output per sighted child.

These studies have created a widespread belief, among the authors interested in blind children's language development, that pronoun reversals and late acquisition of pronouns are typical of blind children. This belief is clearly reflected in general descriptions of language development in blind children (Freeman & Blockberger, 1987; Warren, 1984, 1994; Webster & Roe, 1998). However, recent studies with more rigorous analysis performed on larger corpora (Pérez-Pereira, 1999), and classic studies such as that of Maxfield (1936), indicate that this widespread belief is not entirely appropriate. For example, Maxfield in her classic study with eight blind children around 40 to 68 months of age, did not report any remarkable use of pronouns by the children, which suggests that at least some of the cases of pronoun usage were normal.

The work of Pérez-Pereira (1999) deserves special attention, since it is the first study which includes quantitative and qualitative data on the use of personal reference terms, obtained from a sample of three totally blind Spanish children, one partially blind child, and one sighted girl. In addition, the sighted girl was the twin sister of one of the blind children. One important advantage of this study was the large corpus used for the analysis: 12 one-hour transcriptions recorded every month over a year for each child. In addition, the participation of one sighted subject and one partially blind subject allowed for interesting comparisons. Child 1 (partially sighted) was recorded between 1;2,7 and 2;1,5; Child 2 (blind) between 1;10,19 and 2;10,24; Child 3 (blind) between 2;4,15 and 3;5,27; and Child 4 (blind) and Child 5 (sighted) were recorded between the ages of 2;5,28 and 3;6,12.

The results indicate that the first forms to appear are first and second forms of personal pronouns (*me*—"me", *yo*—"I", *tu*—"you", *te*—"to you", *a mi*—"to me"), even before the children were 2 years old. First-person possessive pronoun forms (*mio*—"mine") to claim possession in a formulaic way were also used very early. Third-person personal pronouns (including enclitic forms) appear shortly after, between 2;0 to 2;8. First- and second-person forms of possessive adjectives and second- and third-person forms of possessive pronouns are first used between 2;1 and 3;6. In general, plural forms such as *nuestro*—"ours", *vuestro*—"yours" were very rare in the data, and never occurred before 2;6. Other personal reference forms do not appear in children's speech in such a predictable and regular way.

The important fact is that no delay in the time of emergence of personal reference forms was evident, if we compare blind children to the sighted or the partially sighted child, or to other sighted children studied by others (Chiat, 1986; Hernández-Pina, 1984; Pérez-Pereira et al., 1996; Shum et al., 1992). In addition, the blind children used personal reference forms, especially first- and second-person forms, with very high frequency. These findings challenge former claims about blind children's productive use of pronouns (Adelson & Fraiberg, 1977; Dunlea, 1989; Ferrel et al., 1990; Warren, 1994).

Even more important are the analyses performed on the correctness of use of personal reference terms. First- and second-person pronouns were classified regarding their use as correct, reversed, or other errors.[15] Figure 7 depicts the results found over time (Pérez-Pereira, 1999), which indicate that the use of pronoun reversals is not a general characteristic of blind children's language. Only one of the three totally blind children (Child 3) can be classified as a strong reverser, whereas the other two (Child 2 and Child 4) hardly produced any reversals. As much as 41.2% of the total number of first- and second-person personal reference forms produced by Child 3 were reversal errors, Child 2 and Child 4 only produced 4.4% and 1.5%, respectively. In addition, the older the children were (especially Children 2 and 4), the less likely they are to produce reversals. However, this

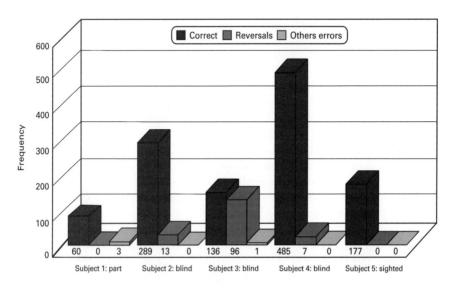

FIG. 7   Use of first and second-person pronouns.

developmental pattern does not fit the results for Child 3, since his reversals do not decrease over time.

Nearly all the reversals were produced when the children used first- and second-person pronouns and adjectives. Only 2 out of a total of 118 reversal errors were found when the children used third-person forms. This result contradicts McGuire and Meyers (1971) who reported that a high percentage of reversals involved third-person forms.

Pérez-Pereira (1999) also analysed the contexts in which reversal errors were produced (see Table 5.1, adapted from Pérez-Pereira, 1999). He found that the blind children who produced few reversals made the majority of the errors in inmediate imitations of others' previous pronouns (53.8% and 62.5%, for Child 2 and Child 4, respectively). However the reverser Child 3 only produced 29.9% of the reversals in such contexts. This means that, contrary to other authors' accounts (Dale & Crain-Thoreson, 1993; Dunlea, 1989; Peters, 1987) imitation can not explain the majority of the reversals produced by the blind children studied. This limited role of imitation in pronoun reversals is in tune with Peters' finding (personal communication) that Seth's pattern of reference to himself looked nothing like his father's pattern of referring to him (Seth), suggesting that Seth is far from using his father's language to refer to himself. As Table 5.1 shows, Child 3 produced a high number of reversal errors in utterances: (1) as if he were directing or describing his behaviour, the same as another person would do as an eyewitness (5.1%); (2) as if he were addressing himself in a general or impersonal way (9.3%); (3) answering a question (14.4%); (4) describing other's actions or intentions (25.8%); or (5) reproducing the speech he heard in a given situation (formula) (9.3%).

As Pérez-Pereira (1999) states, these contexts show the difficulties the child had in adopting a definite perspective for describing interchanges between people. Child

TABLE 5.1

Type of reversal errors produced by the children

Category	Child 2 (Blind)	Child 3 (Blind)	Child 4 (Blind)
1 Personal	3 (23,1)	5 (5,1)	0
2 General	0	9 (9,3)	0
3 Answer	0	14 (14,4)	0
4 Formula	0	9 (9,3)	0
5 Imitation	7 (53,8)	29 (29,9)	5 (62,5)
6 Request	1 (7,7)	2** (2,1)	1 (12,5)
7 Description	1 (7,7)	25 (25,8)	0
8 Other	1 (7,7)	4* (4,1)	2* (12,5)
Total	13	97	8

Percentages given in parenthesis.

*One of them a third-person form instead of a first-person form.

**There were six more instances of REQ which were produced after an adult's model and, thus, were counted as IMI.

3 had a real difficulty in adopting other's perspective, and in clearly separating his own point of view from that of his partner when he answered a question or described other's actions or intentions, as the following examples show:

1 *ya te deja montar Jesús*—"Jesus already let you ride on" instead of *ya me deja montar Jesús*—"Jesus already let me ride on" (3;0,4).

2 *Tu amiga*— "Your friend" instead of *Mi amiga*—"My friend" (answering to the question *¿Y quién es Lidia?*—"Who is Lidia?") (3;1,28).

The errors produced when the child referred to himself in an impersonal or general way also revealed a problem in adopting a definite point of view, as example 3 shows:

3 *Despues no te queda*—"Later on, nothing remains for you" instead of *Despues no me queda*—"Later on, nothing remains for me" (sucking a sweet) (3;5,27).

In addition, the errors Child 3 produced in formulae show that he can not shift perspective:

4 *Te ayuda mami*—"Mommy will help you", an utterance usually used by his mother, instead of *Mami, ¿me ayudas?* "Mommy will you help me?' (3;5,27).

These data seem to be in agreement with proposals from other researchers (Andersen et al., 1984, 1993; Chiat, 1986) concerning the difficulties in shifting perspective. However, this explanation only accounted for less than 60% of Child 3's reversal errors, and only a minimal proportion of the other blind children's errors. Thus, we should bear in mind that alluding to shifting perspective as an explanation is not enough, it is just a way of putting a name to a phenomenon not fully understood. Moreover, other studies have reported similar findings with sighted children. For example, Brigaudiot, Danon-Boileau, and Morgenstern (1996) reported that one French child used forms such as *tu*—"you", *il*—"he" or proper names as self-reference terms in narratives of events, but not in discourse, between 2;3 and 2;8. According to these researchers this happened because, on the one hand the child was using an auditory memory mode, that is to say, he was reproducing the type of utterance the mother had told him many times in similar circumstances. On the other hand, by using these types of forms, the child was keeping a distance from the characters in question and, thus, did not use first-person pronouns in narratives. Similarly, Chiat (1986) has suggested that sighted children produce reversals when they represent the addressee's perspective by using the pronoun that would be appropriate if the addressee were speaking (perspective shifting). Sometimes this use is like the adult's impersonal use of second- and third-person pronouns ("you cannot do it like this"). In addition, we should not forget that blind children have limited experience with the use of personal reference terms addressed to another person, as well as restricted access to surrounding context. These circumstances may add difficulties to the blind children's task of learning the pronominal system.

As Pérez-Pereira (1999) suggests, there appears to be no single explanation for the reversal errors produced by blind children. It is most likely that a number of factors combine to produce the patterns of errors that have been observed in different studies. What seems to be clear from his data is that pronoun reversal cannot be considered a general feature of all the blind children.

Individual differences among blind children are noticeable, as has already been discussed. In this connection, the idea that the production of pronoun reversals by blind children is related to problems in the development of a theory of mind and in ego development (Fraiberg & Adelson, 1973, 1977; Hobson, 1993a, 1993b; Hobson et al., 1997), seems to be misplaced (Pérez-Pereira, 1999). It is certainly true that a proportion of blind children (approximately 25%) show some features of autism spectrum disorders. Nevertheless, these children also have general developmental delays (Pérez-Pereira & Castro, 1994), many of them do not use language until very late (if at all), and their characteristics cannot be generalized to all blind children (see also Chapter 3). Of the remaining blind children, approximately 30% may be reversers. Therefore, it cannot be said that blind children learn pronouns late, nor that they use them rarely, and incorrectly with the most common error being reversals.

PRAGMATIC DEVELOPMENT

In this section we will review how blind children use language in order to make statements, to ask questions, to request, and so on, that is to say, how children convey the illocutionary force of speech (Austin, 1962; Searle, 1969). The expression of communicative intents by young language learners is probably the most widely studied topic in pragmatic development. Other topics related to pragmatic development, such as the acquisition of conversational skills, will be touched upon in a separate section.

There is evidence to believe that blind children may use language for purposes that are different than those of sighted children (Ninio & Snow, 1996). However, few studies have been carried out involving the pragmatic development of blind children: there is the longitudinal study with six children under 2;6 by Dunlea (1989); there is the study of two twin children between 2;5 and 3;5 by Pérez-Pereira and Castro (1992), and the follow up study of the same twins until they reached 5;5 (Castro & Pérez-Pereira, 1996; Pérez-Pereira & Castro, 1997); there is the sequential longitudinal study with four blind children between 1;10 and 3;5 (Pérez-Pereira & Castro, 1994); and, finally, there is the cross-sectional study on the acquisition of questions by blind, visually impaired, and sighted children between 4;0 and 10;0 (Erin, 1986).

Dunlea (1989) studied six children: two were totally blind, two were partially sighted, and two had normal vision. In this longitudinal study, the children were between 0;10 to 2;1 (Teddy, blind), 1;3 to 2;7 (Lisa, blind), 1;0 to 2;4 (Julie, partially sighted), 1;4 to 1;8 (Lydia, partially sighted), 1;5 to 2;0 (Brett, sighted), and 1;0 to 1;6 (Bonnie, sighted), at the beginning and the end of the study respectively. Children's speech samples were recorded approximately every month. Dunlea (1989) analysed the proportion of children's utterances produced with communicative intention (illocutionary force: IF) in relation to those that did not have IF and the utterances with probable IF. She found that the number of utterances containing illocutionary force increased steadily once the MLU of the children's utterances went beyond 1.02 and 1.64 (depending on the subject), which she called the "communicative threshold". Prior to that threshold the percentage of non-communicative utterances was greater that 50%, for all the children. After this point, the blind children (Teddy and Lisa) had a lower proportion of utterances without illocutionary force (39.3% and 33.4%, respectively) than the other children (45.9%, 64.6%, and 49.4% for Julie, Lydia, and Brett, the sighted one, respectively). Bonnie, the other sighted child, never reached the communicative threshold. This shows that blind children seem to use language to keep in touch with their parents and other people to a higher extent than the other partially sighted and sighted children, who can rely on other visual resources.

The blind children as well as Julie, who had only a small amount of vision, were more likely to produce non-interactive language when they produced utterances without illocutionary force. These utterances, moreover, also lacked discourse maintaining functions, and probably represented the emergence of verbal play strategies, which seem to replace object play for blind children (Dunlea, 1989; Kitzinger, 1984; Urwin, 1984a).

Regarding the order of emergence of illocutionary acts studied by Dunlea (1989; see Table 5.2), there seemed to be no remarkable difference between the children studied. Recall that Dunlea considered that a particular morpheme had been acquired by a child if it was used four times in a session. Applying the same criterion to illocutionary acts, she found that blind, as well as sighted and partially sighted children, acquired the illocutionary acts following the same pattern. The following hierarchy for the sequence of acquisition was found to be common to all the children in spite of their differences regarding vision: Identifications/ Descriptions>Requests>Assertions>Responses>Questions. This indicates that there is an progressive expansion in the number of illocutionary acts that children exploit. Dunlea also found that the two children with lower levels of language (that is, Julie, visually impaired and Bonnie, sighted) used non-verbal resources (such as movements) to participate in routines and to make requests. In addition, these two preverbal children showed a few differences: whereas the sighted child used more offering and attention-drawing gestures (pointing, showing, etc.), the partially blind girl persistently used vocal-getting behaviours, such as fussing and vocalizing. The absence of conventional communicative gestures in blind children was also

TABLE 5.2

List of pragmatic categories used by Dunlea (1989)

Request:
  object
  routine
  action
Question
Attention getting/calling
Social routine
Protest/refusal/rejection/denial
Identification/description
Elicited identification
Assertion
Response
Routine
Draw attention
Offer/show
Unspecifiable illocutionary force
No illocutionary force

---

observed in this study and has been generally observed by other scholars (Pérez-Pereira & Castro, 1995; Preisler, 1991; Rowland, 1983; Urwin, 1978, 1984a) Thus, this absence of conventional gestures seems to be a common feature of totally blind children. Interestingly, Dunlea (1989) suggests that the use of vocalizations to get attention is an adaptive strategy of blind children to open communication with other people.

In spite of finding a "remarkably similar" overall pattern of development for the blind and the sighted children, Dunlea (1989) also observed a few differences in their pragmatic development. The principal differences were: (1) Attention getting emerges prior to or contiguous with assertion in blind children's language, as a means to obtain the hearer's attention in an explicit way. Sighted children have at their disposal visual information about hearer's behaviour which makes attention getting speech acts unnecessary. In fact these were absent in the speech of the two sighted children. (2) Offer/show expressions were exploited by the sighted children, but were absent in the two totally blind children and appeared only twice in Julie's records (visually impaired).

In addition to the order of emergence, Dunlea (1989) analysed the relative frequency of use of the different verbal illocutionary acts.[16] She observed that blind children used Requests to a greater extent than sighted children.[17] Requests were used over 20% of the time by the blind children, and around 16% of the time by the sighted children. To a lesser extent, blind children used attention getting verbal expressions more frequently than sighted children. A similar trend was also found in relation to the use of verbal routines, and protests/refusals/rejections. In contrast, sighted children used assertions to a greater extent and more persistently than blind children, and a similar pattern was found for offering/showing. Again, it seems logical that blind children would be more dependent on others to obtain objects out of reach, whereas sighted children are able to talk about the external state of affairs and share attention with other people more easily, thanks to the visual information available to them.

Dunlea (1989) did not observe any other clear pattern of use of illocutionary acts in her sample, neither did she observe any relationship between the type of utterance (such as spontaneous language, reiteration, imitation, babbling, conventionalised gestures, etc.) and the use of illocutionary force. Dunlea's conclusion (p. 159) is that "the role of visual information is much less dramatic with respect to the use of illocutionary force than with respect to the development of more purely semantic constructs, and many areas where differences were observed point to adaptive strategies on the part of the blind children". Unfortunately, Dunlea did not undertake any statistical analyses to make comparisons between the children in her studies, which makes most of her conclusions tentative (McCune, 1991).

Pérez-Pereira and Castro (1992) studied two fraternal twin girls from the age of 2;5 until they were 3;5. One child was blind, and the other was sighted. The categories listed in Table 5.3 were used to analyse one-hour speech samples, which were recorded approximately every month, in their family environment. This category system was based on that of Dore (1977, 1978), with a few modifications.

These researchers found some differences between the two children, regarding the percentages of use of pragmatic categories, although they were living in the same family context. The blind child tended to use self-oriented language instead of externally oriented language. She used the categories referring to the description of her own action or her own intentions to do an action, or the expression of her wishes (personal action, determination, internal reports) to a significantly higher extent than her sighted sister. This suggests that her own activities must constitute a very important source of experience to the blind girl. Interestingly, Pérez-Pereira and Castro (1992) suggested that the use of language in relation to the performance of her own action may indicate that the blind girl could also use language to self-regulate and plan her ongoing or imminent actions. Probably, the blind child used language with this self-regulatory function (Luria, 1979; Vygotsky, 1986) as a way of compensating for her lack of visual information about her ongoing actions and as a driving function for the perception of external reality.

The following is an example of the blind girl's use of Personal category to regulate her own action:

Example 1: Sandra (blind twin girl) uses language to direct her own ongoing action.

Sandra, at 3;3,13, is playing with cubes to fit in.

S: *Aquí* (trying to fit in two pieces)—"Here"
S: *A ver*—"Let's see"
S: *Yo estoy haciendo una torre*—"I am building a tower"

TABLE 5.3

Pragmatic categories used by the children (percentages)

	Age 1;10 to 2;1		Age 2;5 to 3;0			Age 3;0 to 3;5	
Categories	Child 1	Child 2	Child 3	Child 2	Child 4	Child 3	Child 4
Personal (total)	7.14	6.31	15.54	17.20	10.21	9.08	15.45
action	1.32	0.00	2.21	2.24	3.30	2.09	6.67
determination/intention	1.45	0.52	1.42	4.40	2.04	1.47	3.52
refusal	3.83	4.21	10.22	9.41	2.20	4.30	4.23
protest	0.52	1.57	1.68	1.20	2.67	1.20	0.94
Request (total)	6.34	6.84	9.64	4.08	10.22	3.62	11.26
action	6.34	6.84	9.64	4.08	10.22	3.62	11.17
permission	0.00	0.00	0.00	0.00	0.00	0.00	0.09
Offering	0.66	0.00	0.10	0.40	2.67	0.05	1.88
Attention/showing	1.98	1.40	0.00	0.68	4.40	0.36	2.25
Description (total)	31.61	12.63	8.01	12.05	10.37	16.22	11.27
identification	18.12	8.94	8.37	6.33	5.97	7.02	4.93
events	5.42	1.57	4.95	3.56	2.67	3.88	4.65
properties	2.77	0.70	2.10	1.16	0.63	2.52	0.89
location	5.02	1.40	1.31	1.36	0.79	2.57	0.75
time	0.26	0.00	1.26	0.08	0.31	0.05	0.05
Statements (total)	2.77	0.70	2.90	4.52	7.55	4.46	8.02
rules	0.52	0.00	0.26	0.64	0.47	1.63	0.47
evaluations	0.79	0.00	0.00	0.24	1.10	0.21	0.56
inner states	1.05	0.52	1.95	3.00	5.35	1.94	6.38
attributions	0.39	0.17	0.42	0.28	0.63	0.10	0.38
explanations	0.00	0.00	0.26	0.36	0.00	0.58	0.23
Acknowledgements (total)	2.24	0.52	4.69	4.96	1.72	12.33	1.65
acceptances	1.19	0.17	0.58	2.40	0.31	3.63	0.38
approval/agreement	0.00	0.17	2.26	0.64	1.10	5.30	0.89
disapproval/disagreement	1.05	0.17	1.84	1.92	0.31	3.36	0.38
Performatives (total)	0.13	0.17	0.10	0.28	0.10	0.36	1.27
jokes	0.00	0.00	0.00	0.00	0.16	0.00	0.00
claims	0.13	0.00	0.00	0.08	0.47	0.15	0.52
warnings	0.00	0.00	0.00	0.08	0.16	0.00	0.66
teases	0.00	0.17	0.10	0.12	0.31	0.20	0.09
promises	0.00	0.00	0.00	0.00	0.00	0.00	0.00
Organizational devices (total)	3.70	2.45	9.38	4.24	18.40	3.51	10.00
returns	0.92	0.17	4.90	0.72	1.89	0.47	0.94
boundary markers	0.39	0.00	0.37	1.36	0.79	0.37	1.27
speaker selection	0.00	0.00	0.00	0.00	0.00	0.00	0.00
politeness markers	0.13	0.00	0.21	0.68	0.00	0.21	0.00
accompaniments	1.58	0.35	0.79	0.84	1.57	1.47	1.08
calls/vocatives	0.66	1.92	3.10	0.64	14.15	0.90	6.71
Questions	1.32	2.45	1.26	2.00	3.77	3.57	8.40
Responses	12.03	15.78	12.06	15.30	8.49	13.64	7.65
Repetition/imitation	19.04	34.21	17.07	19.63	3.77	20.90	5.73
Elicited identification	5.42	1.22	1.00	1.28	3.93	3.52	0.89
Routines	2.38	6.84	3.11	7.05	11.79	2.57	6.71
Exclamations	1.32	2.63	0.73	3.48	2.04	0.41	1.55
Unclassified	1.58	5.61	2.58	2.28	5.97	3.94	7.75
Double coded	0.34	0.24	1.84	0.22	6.44	1.04	1.74
Total number of utterances	756	570	1898	2496	636	1905	2130

117

S: *Espera*—"Wait"

S: *Espera Miguel que estoy haciendo una torre*—"Wait Miguel that I am building a tower"

S: *Miguel espera que estoy metiendo el grande*— "Miguel wait that I am putting in the big one"

In addition, Sandra was able to use language with reference to locations of objects and actions, qualities of objects, and the description of external events (properties, locations, descriptions).

These findings are not in line with Dunlea's statement that young blind children do not use language with these functions (Andersen et al., 1984, 1993; Dunlea, 1984, 1989). Sandra's use of language to offer, show or draw another's attention was lower than that of her sighted sister. This finding, however, is in agreement with the results of Dunlea's research (Dunlea, 1989), as well as with the results obtained by other researchers who studied the use of prelinguistic communicative resources by blind children (Preisler, 1991; Rowland, 1984; Urwin, 1978, 1984a). Another differential characteristic of the blind child was her higher use of routines and repetitions/imitations in comparison to her sighted sister. Pérez-Pereira and Castro (1992) suggested that the use of these functions is related to the Gestalt style of language acquisition, the children learning whole phrases or formulas for specific contexts and activities (see Peters, 1977, 1983). Moreover, the use of routines allows the child to participate in social interactions and play routines with other people, and to participate in stimulating activities. The twin sister's mother seemed to be sensitive to the usefulness of routines to create situations in which the child could participate. These situations of play (such as clapping one's hands, etc.) involved acoustic and kinetic stimulation very appropriate for the blind child, and favoured blind child's participation in enjoying activities (Castro & Pérez-Pereira, 1996; see also Peters, 1994 for a similar argument). Finally, the blind child also used calls or vocatives more abundantly than her sister. These vocatives had the function of attracting a listener's attention and of being certain of having secured it (Dunlea, 1989; Mulford, 1983), but also they functioned to get information about the presence and location of other people in the immediate environment, which probably gave her a sense of personal security (Maxfield, 1936). Sighted children can fulfil these functions by using eye contact and gaze. By contrast to Dunlea's (1989) report, Pérez-Pereira and Castro (1992) did not find differences in the use of requests between the blind child and her sighted sister. This contrast may be due not only to individual differences, but also to differences between the coding systems used by the two researchers, and, possibly, to the fact that the observations of the children were done in different settings.

The sighted child showed a higher tendency towards using language in relation to external reality as compared to her blind twin sister. For example, she used language to identify and describe the properties and locations of external objects to a greater extent than her twin sister. She also used devices for drawing the listener's attention and for offering objects more frequently than her blind sister. This indicated a higher sensitivity, as well as behavioural adequacy, to the presence of other people on the part of the sighted girl. Similarly, she gave explanations about external affairs more frequently than her blind sister, in keeping with the greater external orientation of her language.

The study of the pragmatic functions of these twin sisters' language was later expanded to the age of 5;4 (see Castro & Pérez-Pereira, 1996 for a full account, and Pérez-Pereira & Castro, 1997 for a shorter report). In order to compare results, the overall span of time was divided into six periods, 5 or 6 months each, the first period from 2;5 to 2;11, the second from 3;1 to 3;5, the third from 3;6 to 3;11, the fourth from 4;1 to 4;5, the fifth from 4;6 to 4;11, and the sixth one from 5;0 to 5;4. This allowed the authors to study the children's development after 3;5, and to find out whether the blind child approximated her speech functions to those of her sighted sister as age increased.

First, it was found that the blind child used the personal category (particularly personal action and determination), as well as internal reports, to a significantly higher extent than her sighted sister during the period 2;5 to 3;5. However, the differences decreased as the children grew older, in such a way that at the end of the period studied both children performed similarly (below 8%). This seemed to indicate that the blind child, when older than 5 years of age, no longer needed any more external language to regulate her actions and maintain her goals as she carried out an action. This developmental trend is possibly due to the internalization of speech (Luria, 1979), and parallels that observed in sighted children (Barrett, 1989), albeit at a slower pace. In any case, the results indicate that the blind child seemed to use this self-centred speech over a longer period of time than sighted children (Castro & Pérez-Pereira, 1996).

Second, Pérez-Pereira and Castro (1997; Castro & Pérez-Pereira, 1996) found that, although differences in the use of calls/vocative between the blind and the sighted child reached significance throughout the period studied (2;5 to 5;4), the percentage of use of calls and vocatives by the blind child declined greatly as she grew older, this percentage decreasing from 14% between 2;5 and 2;11 years to around 4% to 5% after 3;6. This fact possibly implies that the blind girl discovered other means to know whether other people were in the room, or to attract their attention.

Third, the blind child used significantly fewer instances of offering, and attention/showing than her sighted twin sister throughout the period studied. As the authors commented in an earlier work (Pérez-Pereira & Castro, 1992), this finding indicated that sighted children's language is more oriented towards external reality. These results with offering and attention/showing are in keeping with the significantly higher use of descriptions (properties and locations in particular) by the sighted child compared to her blind sister. However, what seems to be certain is that the blind child was able to talk about external objects and events, which puts into question the radical assertion of Andersen et al. (1984, 1993) and Dunlea (1989) that blind children are unable to describe external reality. For instance, her use of description ranged from 10.37% at the beginning of the study (period from 2;5 to 2;11) to 18.31% during the last period studied (5;0 to 5;4). Although the children studied by Andersen et al. (1984, 1993) and Dunlea (1989) were younger than the blind child studied by Pérez-Pereira and Castro (1997; Castro & Pérez-Pereira, 1996), and a possibility exists that the use of descriptions appears after 2;5 in blind children, the percentage of descriptions that Pérez-Pereira and Castro's blind subject used was stable and high enough to argue that she must have been using descriptions before 2;5.

Fourth, it was found that the blind child used imitations/repetitions, and routines, to a significantly higher extent than her sighted sister through the observation period. This strengthens the idea that the blind child's style is closer to a Gestalt type than that of her sister. However, both categories followed different patterns. Although routines showed a continuous decrease in both children, its percentage declining from 11.79% at the beginning to 2.70% at the end for the blind child, and from 3.56% to 0.08% for the sighted child, imitations/repetitions showed a constant increase in the speech of both children as they grew older. The percentage of repetitions/imitations grew from 3.77% at the beginning of the study to around 14% after 3;6 in the blind child, and from 2.61% to over 6% to 11% after 4;1 (reaching a peak of 13.08% during the period 3;6 to 3;11 years), in the sighted child.

Fifth, it was observed (Castro & Pérez-Pereira, 1996; Pérez-Pereira & Castro, 1997) that the sighted girl used statements more frequently than the blind girl after 4;1, rules and explanations being responsible for the observed difference. However, the blind girl used statements more frequently than her sighted sister from 2;5 to 3;5, although the difference was due, in this case, to the higher frequency of internal reports produced by the blind child.

Finally, both children showed a sharp increase in the use of questions after 3;1, maintaining a stable percentage later (between 8.5% and 13.5% approximately, for both girls) (Castro & Pérez-Pereira, 1996; Pérez-Pereira & Castro, 1997).

Pérez-Pereira and Castro (1994) also compared the development of pragmatic functions in the language of three totally blind children (with slight perception of strong light at best) and one visually impaired child. The visually impaired child (Subject 1) was considered legally blind—he had 20/200 vision. This visually impaired child made excellent use of his residual vision. The other three blind children were two girls (Subjects 2 and 4) and one boy (Subject 3), blind due to retinopathy of prematurity (retrolental fibroplasia). One of the girls was the twin sister already studied (see Pérez-Pereira & Castro, 1994 for details). The comparative analyses were done on the age periods where there were data for at least two subjects. Subjects 1 and 2 were studied between 1;10 and 2;1, Subjects 2, 3, and 4 were studied between 2;5 and 3;0, and Subjects 3 and 4 were studied between 3;0 to 3;5, approximately. Table 5.3 shows the results obtained.

The possibility of comparing the results of other blind children to those of the twin girl are specially interesting, since the authors have already compared this blind girl to her sighted twin sister. The comparison between the visually impaired child and the blind child of the same age also afford possible interesting contrasts.

Concerning the comparison between the visually impaired boy (Subject 1) and the Subject 2 blind girl during the period from 1;10 to 2;1, Pérez-Pereira and Castro (1994) found the following remarkable results: In the first place, although the percentage of offering was very low for both children as compared to the results obtained with the other older subjects, the visually impaired child used a significantly higher proportion of this pragmatic function than Subject 2. It was also found that the visually impaired child used many more descriptions (specially, identifications, properties, and localizations) than Subject 2 (31.6% against 12.6%). This result is even more striking if we take into account that Subject 2 produced a relatively high proportion of descriptions when we compare her results with those of the blind twin girl (Subject 4) during the period from 2;0 to 3;0. This indicates a common finding: that totally blind children seem to use descriptions of external objects and events to a lesser extent than those children who can access some degree of visual information. This is obviously due to the fact that they have restricted access to visual information about objects, actions, and events. On the other hand, the blind Subject 2 used calls/vocatives, repetition/imitation, and routines significantly more often than the visually impaired boy, thus confirming the earlier results of Pérez-Pereira and Castro (1992, 1997; Castro & Pérez-Pereira, 1996) when comparing the twin sisters. However, no significant differences were found in the use of offering and attention/showing by Subjects 1 and 2, although the visually impaired child used these functions to a slightly greater extent.

The results obtained by Pérez-Pereira and Castro (1994), coincide with those obtained by other authors (Andersen et al., 1984, 1993; Castro & Pérez-Pereira, 1996; Dunlea, 1989; Pérez-Pereira & Castro, 1992, 1997; Urwin, 1984a). The results confirm that lack of offering/showing is a typical feature of blind children in general, in spite of the fact that the twin girl (Subject 4) produced a significantly higher proportion of offering/showing acts than the other blind children. The same can be said of repetitions/imitations, which were produced by the other blind children to a significantly greater extent than by Subject 4. This fact strengthens the idea that imitations and repetitions (without any predominant additional pragmatic function) are a characteristic of blind children's language, since the blind Subject 4 already produced repetitions/imitations more frequently than her sighted twin sister. The use of language with a personal function seems to be another characteristic of blind children, as the percentage of this function is similar in Subject 4 and the other blind children of the same age.

However, the present results also indicate some individual differences among the blind children. The most remarkable was the greater use of refusals by Subjects 2 and 3 in comparison to Subject 4. The refusal of another's proposal seemed to be a function which was used repeatedly by a number of blind children, and may be related to an oppositional attitude on the part of some blind children. This is coincidental with the relatively high percentage of disapproval/disagreement in Subjects 2 and 3. Other individual differences found between blind children concerned the use of calls/vocatives, acknowledgements, routines, responses, and questions (for details see Pérez-Pereira & Castro, 1994).

Regarding questions, a few scholars have suggested that blind children use this speech act more frequently than their sighted peers, with the functions of gathering information, keeping social contact, and maintaining conversational control (Burlingham, 1961; Kekelis & Andersen, 1984). Maxfield (1936) observed that blind children used questions more often than sighted children, and, what was more important, that blind children showed a different developmental pattern in the use of questions. Whereas the use of questions decreased in the sighted children as they grew older, the opposite was the case for the blind children. Interestingly, similar proportions of use of questions by blind children (about 25–30%) have also been reported by different researchers studying blind children without additional disabilities (Maxfield, 1936; Mulford, 1983), although children with additional mental handicap seldom use questions (Rogow, 1981a).

With the aim of looking in depth at the use of questions by blind children, Erin (1986) carried out a study on the frequency of their use by one group of blind children, another group of visually impaired children, and a third group of sighted children. Each group was composed of 12 subjects between the ages of 4;0 to 10;0, making a total of 36 subjects. In addition, the total number of children was split into three different age groups: Group I: children between 4;2 and 5;6; Group II: children between 6;0 and 7;7, and Group III: children between 9;4 and 10;7, with 12 children each group. Speech samples were obtained in a situation in which the children had to explore different household items contained in a box with a circular opening in one of its sides. The children were asked to reach in the box and remove the objects one at a time. The conversations between the children and the experimenter were recorded until more than 100 utterances were produced by each child. The analysis of the frequency of questions was performed on a sample of 100 utterances per child, after the experimenter discarded the first 10 utterances produced by each child. In addition to the frequency of questions, Erin also analysed the type of questions, using the following categories: yes/no questions, Wh- questions, clarification questions, requests for action, permission requests, rhetorical questions, and tag questions.

Using an ANOVA analysis, Erin found a significant effect of age and degree of vision. No significant interaction between these factors was found. There was also a significant difference between the youngest Group I (24.08% of questions out of the total number of utterances) and the oldest group III (11.25%) for all visual conditions. (Group II's percentage of questions was 18.7). The group of blind children obtained an overall proportion of questions of 26.5, the visually impaired of 19.58, and the sighted group an average of 7.92 questions per 100 utterances. As a group, sighted children produced significantly fewer questions than the blind and visually impaired groups.

Regarding the type of questions, Erin (1986) found that Wh- questions was the most frequently used type of questions in all the three groups of children, with the blind and the visually impaired groups producing the highest percentages (49 and 48.6, respectively, v. 36.9 in the sighted group). According to Erin's interpretation, the children use Wh- questions to obtain information about the environment, and this function is more relevant for children with limited or no vision, who cannot perceive many aspects of the external world. Wh- questions for blind children are a unique way of finding out about reality in many circumstances, and we argue they play an important compensatory role in blind children's development. The use of Wh- questions shows a regular decrease with age, which was especially pronounced in the sighted group. Yes/no questions, with 27.4%, were the second most frequently used type of question. They were also more frequently used by the visually impaired and the blind children (in this order) than by the sighted group. In contrast to Wh- questions, yes/no questions were more abundantly used by the oldest group. The function they serve is that of confirming guesses about objects. Another interesting difference between the sighted group and the blind and visually impaired groups concerned the use of rhetorical questions, which do not have an informative purpose, but a social purpose. Rhetorical questions are more frequently used by sighted children, probably because they are not used to gather information. Finally, the children who used action requests were mostly blind or visually impaired. In any case, the percentage of use of this type of question was very low (under 3% at most). It is thought that the children deprived of vision may have used this type of question as a way of asking for assistance to get something.

Consequently, Erin's research (Erin, 1986) indicates that information gathering is the main function of questions for visually impaired and blind children in particular. However, the situation in which the speech samples were recorded was not a natural one, and favoured the use of questions, Wh- questions and yes/no questions in particular, by the blind children. This is because they were in an unfamiliar situation, and were presented with new objects, about which they could not get much information without the help of vision. Thus, they are compelled to ask questions to the adult about their characteristics, and to confirm their guesses. Furthermore, the data collection procedure was not the same for all the children, because whereas the blind and visually impaired children received individual instructions, the sighted children received instructions in a large-group setting. Possibly, these unequal circumstances affected children's willingness to initiate conversation and to ask questions. It seems reasonable to suppose that the procedure used by Erin magnified the use of questions in the blind children. In fact, no other naturalistic longitudinal study has found such a high percentage of question use in blind children, nor such large differences in use of questions between blind and sighted children. For instance, the four blind and visually impaired children in Dunlea's (1989) study reached scores ranging between 8.9% of questions and 4.7%. Pérez-Pereira and Castro (1997; Castro & Pérez-Pereira, 1996) reported a steady increase in the use of questions by their blind subject between 3.77% (before 3 years of age) and 13.56% (after 5 years of age), and similar results for the sighted sister. The blind twin girl produced the highest percentage of questions as compared to other blind children (Pérez-Pereira & Castro, 1994).

Finally, we turn to the use of spatial deictic terms. Mills (1993) reports the results of a study by Mulford in which three blind children showed a delay in the acquisition of spatial deictic terms *(this, that, here, there)* compared with sighted children. The blind children were still making errors at 6 years of age in contrast to sighted children. This is probably due to their problems with shifting spatial reference. Mulford observed that these spatial deictic terms were also more scarce and used without clarifying gestures. In addition, the blind children started to use proximal terms *(this, here)* before distal terms *(that, there)*, whereas this order was not followed by sighted children. Nevertheless, Pérez-Pereira (1999) found that there were no differences between blind and sighted Spanish children in the use of spatial adverbs and demonstratives, all of them using distal terms later, and infrequently.

Summarizing the main results of the studies we have reviewed, it seems that blind children do not differ greatly from sighted children in relation to the percentage of use of pragmatic functions in their speech, either regarding the order of acquisition or first uses of the different functions. Nevertheless, some differences exist, which are connected to the adaptive strategies that blind children put into practice, and, in other cases, to their limited access to information about external reality. Blind children use those functions related to the description of objects and external events (description) and the social perception of others (attention/showing, offering) to a lesser extent then sighted children, although they are able to use these functions. On the other hand, blind children appear to use language related to an ongoing action or their determination to perform an action with higher frequency than sighted children. The use of speech related to their own actions may on many occasions have a self-regulatory function. Several authors found that blind children used many requests for action (Dunlea, 1989; Erin, 1986). Even though this is not a general feature of blind children's language, it is logical that blind children may use requests more frequently than their sighted peers, since they may need help to get objects, for instance, that are out of reach. In this case, the lack of visual information may have an effect on the functions of speech, especially at an early age. In this connection, the frequent use of questions by blind and visually impaired children could also indicate the need for help that blind children have in order to compensate for their limited access to information about reality. Another feature of blind children's language is the lower use of responses as compared to sighted children, until 5 years of age, but not later. This points to a lower sensitivity to social interchanges. Finally, the majority of the studies found that blind children use imitations, repetitions, and routines to a higher extent than sighted children. This finding, will be analysed in depth in the following section. Nevertheless, what the results of Pérez-Pereira and Castro's study show is that, in spite of initial differences between blind and sighted children's use of language, in the long run, by 5 years of age, both groups of children use language to the same extent and to fulfil similar functions.

VERBAL ROUTINES AND IMITATIVE SPEECH: A WAY INTO LANGUAGE ANALYSIS

It has been widely reported that blind children tend to use many formulae and imitations in their speech (Dunlea, 1989; Keeler, 1957; Kitzinger, 1984; Pérez-Pereira, 1994; Pérez-Pereira & Castro, 1992, 1997; Peters, 1987, 1994; Urwin, 1978, 1984a, 1984b). These productions have also been called verbal routines, formulaic expressions, or stereotypic speech. Stereotypic speech is defined as chunks of maternal speech that are associated with a particular context and which are reproduced by children. These are assumed to be imitated chunks or phrases, unanalysed units of language for the child, which are used in specific contexts, and their meaning is attached to these contexts (Dunlea, 1989). Generally speaking, this type of stereotypic speech, verbal routines, or whatever name we use share a common pattern with imitations of others' utterances, and repetitions of previous utterances produced by the child. All of them are modelled speech, or, to say the same thing with different words, a type of speech that copies a model.

However, markedly different interpretations of these productions have been put forward by scholars. On the one hand, there are those authors who conceive formulaic speech as a negative feature of language without any progressive function for language development. On the other hand, there are those scholars who conceive verbal routines and stereotypic speech to be a tool children use for promoting cognitive development, social interaction, and understanding.

The first standpoint was first stated by psychoanalytically oriented scholars (Burlingham, 1961, 1964, 1965; Nagera & Colonna, 1965; Wills, 1979), who described language routines and stereotypic speech as *parroting*, characterized by the use of non-meaningful words or "speaking without understanding". In a similar vein, other authors considered the high use of imitations by blind children to be a defective feature of their language, or as a symptom of pathological language, and concluded that there existed a similarity between the language of blind children and that of children with autism (Brown et al., 1997; Fay, 1973; Hobson, 1993a; Hobson et al., 1997). These authors often use the label of *echolalia* to name this imitative speech.

Recent studies specifically focused on the acquisition of language by blind children carried out by Dunlea (1989), as well as Andersen and colleagues (Andersen et al., 1984, 1993; Miecznikowski & Andersen, 1986), adopted a similar view. These researchers pointed out that blind children use stereotypic speech more often than sighted children, although their production is not exclusive to blind children. In their opinion, although the chunks children imitate are used in specific contexts at first, later on they may also be extended to new contexts. As we have indicated, another assumed feature of stereotypic speech is their unanalysed nature.

However, these scholars (Andersen et al., 1984, 1993; Dunlea, 1989; Miecznikowski & Andersen, 1986) believe that these unanalysed chunks are subsequently analysed into their constituents. Thus, these authors appear to suggest that there is a normal evolution from stereotypic speech to analysed language, although, in contrast with sighted children, blind children do not begin to segment a phrase until a few weeks after a phrase is adopted. In spite of this, these authors do not see any progressive role or useful function in the use of stereotypic speech for blind children. In the first place, and contrary to other authors' suggestion (Castro & Pérez-Pereira, 1996; Pérez-Pereira & Castro, 1992, 1997; Peters, 1994), the use of these phrases in relation to the ongoing activity of the children is not considered to have any self-regulatory function by these scholars, since these phrases rarely anticipate the activity, but are considered to be part of the activity itself (Dunlea, 1989, p. 81). In addition, it is believed that the use of stereotypic speech contributes to the misuse of pronouns, because children do not introduce the deictic shifts into the imitated chunks (Andersen et al., 1984, 1993; Dunlea, 1989). However, in spite of this statement, no quantitative data for this correlation has been provided.

In contrast, Peters (1994) maintains that stereotypic speech is useful for an understanding of the world and social situations. Studying the developing language of one visually impaired child (Seth) in interaction with his father, between 20 and 30 months of age, Peters observed a high dependence on highly contextualized language. Seth's formulae were used before he had analysed their components, and were produced in order to participate and promote social interactions with his father. Peters, analysing the speech of the father, observed that his language was finely tailored to specific situations with the intention of scaffolding Seth's developing abilities. Seth's father used language as a script of the activity to be performed in a given situation which acted as an eventcast. Through the use of this script-like language, the father: (1) highlighted culturally important aspects of the activity, (2) provided labels for the objects, attributes, and actions involved, and (3) modelled syntactic constructions appropriate for talking about events. In this way, Seth could identify the situation and participate in the ongoing routine activity. Similarly, Kitzinger (1984) and Urwin (1984a, 1984b) pointed out that blind children use verbal routines to participate in social interactions.

As this script-like language was specific to certain activities or social routines (mealtimes, building blocks towers, bathtime, etc.), every script was distinctive in vocabulary used, formulaic expressions, and even syntactic constructions. This linguistic compartmentalization initially produces an isolation of the contexts experienced. In addition, the lack of constant visual input collaborated in this isolation of contexts, which in turn produced difficulties in the generalization of language across contexts for the blind child. Nevertheless, Seth was able to generalize beyond the immediate script, although he did not do that with a high frequency. For instance, Peters (1994) indicates that Seth, who had learnt to use the formula "knock it down" in the context of tower building interactions, used this formula in the context of ball retrieval when a ball had landed on the top of a fan, simultaneously using the same tool (a big cardboard mailing tube) to reach for the objects in both situations. Other examples include the use of *on* and *off* in a variety of situations: turning the tape recorder on or off, turning a tap on or off, and having his clothes put on or off. These observations are in tune with those of Norgate et al. (1997) regarding the generalization of verbal routines and words by blind children.

Thus, Seth used a given formulaic expression nearly every time he identified a situation as corresponding to the modelled one. In addition, he learnt to produce this stereotypic type of speech for planning and directing his own activity (see also Kitzinger, 1984 for a similar suggestion). Thus, language served not only the function of promoting social interaction between Seth and his father, but also a cognitive function. As Peters (1994, p. 199) stated, "the lack of a visual channel thus rendered him more dependent on speech, both as a source of information about the world and as a means of social interaction".

Obviously, the use of formulaic expressions depended heavily on Seth's capacity to imitate and memorize his father's speech, which sometimes gave place to temporary uses of formulae, which made sense within the contexts, but were syntactically deviant (see Wilson & Peters, 1988 in particular).

In addition to the functions that the use of imitations and formulaic speech serve for cognitive and social development, they also serve an important basis for language development, since they form part of a strategy to analyse language. As Peters (1977, 1983) convincingly argued, not all children have the same style in learning and using language. Some children rely heavily on the use of imitation to reproduce chunks of other's speech longer than a word from the beginning of their language development. According to her, these are whole phrases not yet analysed, which, eventually, will be analysed and separated into their constituent parts. However, when unanalysed (or partially analysed), they allow the child to participate in social interactions and activities with others, as we have already seen. This strategy was named a holistic or Gestalt strategy by Peters (1977, 1983). Peters reported data on a blind child's language who tended to rely heavily on the use of this type of Gestalt style strategy, which she called "use first, analyse later" (Peters, 1987).

The effects of modelled speech for the analysis and use of language was also the topic of a study by Pérez-Pereira (1994). This author carried out a comparative study of the development of use of imitations, repetitions, and routines by one blind child and her sighted twin sister from 2;5 to 3;5. In this study, it was found that those productions, particularly imitations and repetitions, were used by both children to maintain the ongoing conversation and to execute speech acts. For instance, imitations and self-repetitions were used to fulfil different pragmatic and conversational functions, such as to request, to choose among several alternatives, to forbid, to insist on a request, to repeat an offering, or to attract a listener's attention, among the pragmatic functions, and to agree with what had just been

TABLE 5.4

Some examples of the conversational and pragmatic uses of imitations
and repetitions by one blind child and her sighted sister
(taken from Pérez-Pereira, 1994)

To ask:

SC: *Que ten (tiene)* ("What does she have?")
I: *Pecas* ("Freckles")
SC: *¿Pecas?* ("Freckles?")
I: *Si* ("Yes")
SC: *¿Por qué tiene pecas?* ("Why does she have freckles?")

To confirm:

SC: *Tiralo eso* ("Throw it away that")
I: *Donde lo tiro, ¿en la basura?* ("Where shall I throw it, in the garbage can?")
SC: *Basura* ("Garbage")
I: *Muy bien* ("All right")

To forbid:

BC: *Andrea, no juegues* ("Andrea, you don't play")
BC: *No juegues* ("Don't play")
SC: *Caray!* ("Gosh!")
BC: *Que no juegues* ("That you don't play")
BC: *Tu no juegues* ("Oh, you don't play")
BC: *Oy, no juegues* ("Oh, you don't play")

To insist in a request.

SC: *Botón* ("Button")
I: *Umm?* ("Umm?")
SC: *Átame el botón* ("You tie the button")
I: *Si, espera un poco* ("Yes, wait a moment")
SC: *Átame el botón* ("You tie the button")
I: *A ver, vamos para allá* ("Let see, let's go over there")
SC: *Átame el botón* ("You tie the button")

To attract listener's attention.

SC: *Mira roto* ("Look, broken")
SC: *Mira roto* ("Look, broken")
SC: *Miguel está roto* ("Miguel, it is broken")

To repeat an offering:

BC: *Miguel toma* ("Miguel, take")
I: *¿Qué me das?* ("What do you give me?")
BC: *Toma el zumo* ("Have the juice")
BC: *Toma el zumo* ("Have the juice")
BC: *Miguel, toma el zumo* ("Miguel have the juice")
BC: *Venga, toma el zumo de agua* ("Come on, have the juice of water")

BC = blind child; SC = sighted child; I: interlocutor

said, to indicate shared attention, to make contributions, or to indicate comprehension, among the conversational functions. In Table 5.4 a few examples of these uses are shown (see Pérez-Pereira, 1994 and also Pérez-Pereira, 1991 for additional examples).

Similar functions of modelled speech (imitations, repetitions, and routines) have been found by other researchers studying sighted children (Casby, 1986; Keenan, 1977; McTear, 1978; Prizant, 1983; Réger, 1986; Snow, 1983). Kitzinger (1984) has suggested that the use of repetitions by one blind girl had the function of keeping social contact, insisting on a request, or clarifying her comments, as well as giving herself directions. In other cases, the children studied by Pérez-Pereira (1994) used routines to create a social situation, in a similar way to that reported by Peters (1994), as in the following example:

The sighted child is eating with a spoon at 2;11,7.

Child: *Por mami* ("For Mummy")
Mother: *Por quien quieras* ("For whoever you want").
Mother: *Por Raquel* ("For Raquel")
Child: *Por la abuela* ("For Granny")

In this situation, the verbal routine is used to create social interaction. In other situations, verbal routines were also used to initiate shared activity or social play. This is an interesting function that routines may serve. Furthermore, comparing the use of routines, imitations, and repetitions in the blind child and her sighted sister, Pérez-Pereira (1994) found that the blind child used a significantly greater percentage of routines than her sighted twin sister (7.91% v. 1.86%, respectively).

Therefore, Pérez-Pereira's (1994) findings are in agreement with Peters' (1994) proposal that modelled speech has the important function of promoting cognition and social interaction in blind children, and its use is an adaptive strategy that blind children use to avoid social isolation.

However, in addition to these functions, Pérez-Pereira (1994) found that the use of imitations, repetitions, and routines had an important role in analysing language. He observed that both twin sisters studied used many imitations and repetitions which were modified or expanded, that is to say, modelled productions on which the children introduced some changes, such as the substitution of a nominal predicate for a pronoun, or an expansion of the copied phrase with new elements. According to his interpretation, and coinciding with the proposals of other scholars (Kitzinger, 1984; Moerk, 1989; Peters, 1983; Pine & Lieven, 1993; Speidel, 1989), modified and expanded imitations and repetitions allowed the children to analyse language by segmenting and substituting some parts of the utterance, or expanding it. The following examples show how the blind girl copied an impersonal way of prohibition from her mother's previous utterance:

The sighted and the blind girls are having tea with their mother at 2;11,7.

Mother:	*Sandra no se mastica, te lo acabo de decir*
	("Sandra, you don't chew it, I've just told you").
Sighted child:	*¿Que no se qué?* ("You don't what?").
Sighted child:	*¿No se qué?* ("You don't what?").
	(A little while later)
Blind child:	*Andrea no se tiran las cosas* ("Andrea you don't throw things").

In this example, the blind girl is using a frame model (Name + you don't + verb predicate) copied from her mother's speech.

In other instances, the children progressively modified their expressions to convey their intention in a more explicit way. What is interesting is to observe how they are segmenting and substituting elements step by step, as in the two following examples:

Blind girl at 3;3,13.

Blind child:	Una trompeta cogí ("I got a trumpet").
Blind child:	Mira qué cogí ("Look what I got").
Blind child:	Mira lo que cogí ("Look it what I've got")

Blind girl at 2;11,7 is playing with a board for fitting animal shapes in.

Blind child:	*Poner el camello a mí* ("Me put the camel in").
Blind child:	*Lo ponemos aquí* ("We put it in here").
Blind child:	*Ponemos aquí el camello* ("We put the camel in here").

Pérez-Pereira (1994) found that Sandra used a significantly higher proportion of modified imitations and repetitions than her sighted twin sister Andrea (22.42% v. 12.16%). This result, again, seems to indicate that modelled speech forms part of a strategy for analysing language that is more prominent in the blind child than in her sighted sister.

Apart from giving a number of examples which show how children analyse language by using modified and expanded imitations and repetitions, Pérez-Pereira (1994) analysed whether the utterances containing imitations, repetitions, or routines (IRR speech) had a higher MLU than those which did not (referred to as productive utterances). The assumption under which this comparison was done was that if IRR speech promoted morphosyntactic development those utterances containing them should be longer, since the children could use the modelled utterance as a scaffold to build an utterance of greater complexity. The results showed that IRR utterances had significantly longer MLUs than productive utterances for both children, although the MLU measures of the blind child were always longer than the corresponding MLUs of her sighted sister.

It has been proposed that the use of imitations and repetitions reduces the memory load of blind children (Speidel, 1989; Speidel & Nelson, 1989) when speaking. This allows them to produce longer utterances by reducing their attention to those elements which are new or a modification of the frame model. Thus, Pérez-Pereira (1994) viewed the use of modelled utterances as a type of self-scaffolding. The use of a modelled frame allows children to produce more complex utterances, since they do not need to pay so much attention to the part of their utterance that is a copy of a previous one, and, in this way, can focus on the variations they introduce (modifications, expansions).

This author suggested, in tune with others (Peters, 1987, 1994) that the blind girl was more prone than her sighted sister to use a style of processing language, according to which whole utterances were subsequently analysed by means of the variations she introduced in the frame of the model utterance. Following Peters (1987, 1994), this strategy may be called "use first, analyse later", and seems to be typical of those children who show a Gestalt style of language acquisition. The children who show this style reproduce whole sentences and phrases previously uttered by an adult with a roughly similar intonation. However, the component parts of the modelled utterances are, at first, not used in other combinations, suggesting that the modelled utterances are still unanalysed. In this case, each whole utterance functions as if it were a word. Later on, the children are able to introduce changes on the formerly whole phrases, by segmenting their elements, and combining their components with other elements in other new combinations (Peters, 1977, 1983, 1995; Peters & Menn, 1993). This is exactly what the children studied by Pérez-Pereira (1994) and Peters (1987, 1994) seemed to do. Lieven, Pine, & Baldwin (1997; Pine & Lieven, 1993) have also documented that sighted children of the same age perform this kind of distributional analysis on positional patterns.

Therefore, those scholars (Leonard & Kaplan, 1977; Stine & Bohannon, 1983; Tager-Flusberg & Calkins, 1990) who have argued that imitation is merely an empty mechanism, with no utility for analysing language, seem to have under-appreciated its value. The same is true of those experts on blind children's language acquisition who have denied any positive value to repetitive and highly imitative speech (formulaic speech), such as Andersen et al. (1984, 1993) and Dunlea (1989). Accordingly, these authors deemed that blind children are less creative than sighted children in the process of language acquisition (Andersen et al., 1993). This position has been put into question by Pérez-Pereira's (1994) and Peters' (1987, 1994) accounts.

To summarize, formulaic speech seems to fulfil several important functions for blind children. First, it is useful to maintain conversational interchanges and to continue the conversational topic. Second, it allows children to express many pragmatic functions. Finally, it is a useful strategy that children adopt to analyse language, particularly those phrases or formulae which are at first unanalysed chunks. Their high reliance on modelled speech points to the fact that blind children are closer to the holistic or Gestalt style (Peters, 1983) of language acquisition, which is one end of the continuum of possible routes used by any child to acquire language. A number of authors have suggested that the capacity to retain long units of speech, which they eventually will analyse with a kind of verbal play, indicates that blind children pay more attention to language than sighted children, or are particularly sensitive to the formal properties of linguistic input (Pérez-Pereira, 1994; Pérez-Pereira & Castro, 1997; Peters, 1987, 1994). It seems logical that this be the case, since in the absence of visual information, language itself must be a highly relevant kind of experience, in addition to its relevance as a channel to get information about the world (McCune, 1991; Pérez-Pereira & Castro, 1997). Consequently, the idea that blind children have less creative language, seems to be the result of a relatively superficial analysis of certain features of their language, which yields to an underestimation of blind children's abilities.

BLIND CHILDREN'S LANGUAGE AND LANGUAGE ACQUISITION THEORIES

As Mills (1993) has stated, research on the language of blind children has seldom focused on theoretical questions about language acquisition, with a few exceptions (Landau & Gleitman, 1985). Nevertheless, from this research important implications may be drawn for theories of language acquisition. Children born blind and without any additional impairment can be considered a kind of natural experiment to test hypotheses about the role of visual information on the acquisition of language.

As we have already discussed, the predominant view on this issue affirms that, since visual information affects cognitive development, and this, in turn, influences language development, those children deprived of visual information will show problems or differences in language learning as compared to sighted children. Although the term *differences*, instead of *deficits* or *problems*, apparently involves the use of a non-pejorative word (Andersen et al., 1984, 1993; Dunlea, 1989), it is important to remind ourselves that this is not a neutral term, because its use is always surrounded with negative considerations about those features of blind children's language considered *different*. In reality these authors mean *not normal*, especially if we remember that they assume a single model for all children acquiring language (McCune, 1991).

The data considered so far on lexical acquisition and semantic development (including semantic relationships), cast doubt on the idea that blind children are unable to generalize the meanings of words to other instances of the same category, or that they can not use words to describe external reality, restricting the use of words to their own activity. The interpretations of blind children's semantic development offered by those cognitive-theory-based scholars, apart from being discredited in its radical formulation by other accounts, does not take into consideration some common characteristics of children's first words, such as their context-bound nature, the existence of interindividual variations, or the limited access that blind children have to the information about current state of external affairs. If these points are taken into consideration, it is possible to give a different, non-deficient, view of blind children's semantic development. The view that the meaning and use of words are severely affected by lack of vision can be overridden provided that we adopt a view more in tune with recent advances in semantic development, and show a wider more comprehensive view of blindness.

Other aspects of language development have also been considered to be affected (to a lesser degree) by the lack of vision. However, the results found by many researchers point to good development of morphology and syntax in blind children. In spite of certain claims on the lack of creativity of blind children's language, which can be observed in the alleged absence of over-regularization and stereotypic speech, it has been recently suggested that blind children's language is not lacking in creativity (Pérez-Pereira, 1994; Pérez-Pereira & Castro, 1997; Peters, 1987, 1994; Peters & Menn, 1993); on the contrary, blind children introduce many modifications and expansions on so considered stereotypic speech, and manifest as many over-regularizations as their sighted peers, which indicates their capacity for language analysis and creativity.

Therefore, if, as it has been shown, blind children can acquire a non-deficient language, there must be some mechanisms that compensate for the absence of visual information. In this regard, a number of authors (McCune, 1991; Pérez-Pereira, 1994; Pérez-Pereira & Castro, 1997; Peters, 1987; Pring, 1988) have proposed that blind children pay special attention to language, since linguistic input is relatively more salient to them than to sighted children. Certain features of blind children's language, such as the greater use of ready-made phrases or routines, and their greater reliance on modified imitations and repetitions, as compared to sighted children, support this idea. Their high use of routines, stereotypic speech, imitations, and repetitions (modelled speech), reveals that they may use verbal memory more fully than their sighted peers. Moreover, blind children use verbal play to a greater extent than their sighted peers, providing another piece of evidence for the idea that blind children pay particular attention to language. Overall, these arguments point to the fact that language is a specially interesting area of experience for blind children. Because blind children pay more attention to language than sighted children, and use certain processing strategies to a greater extent, they can compensate for their lack of visual experience in acquiring language. This compensatory view is compatible with other theories of language acquisition that consider that, in the task of learning language, children pay attention and process linguistic information that language itself provides (Gleitman, 1990; Karmiloff-Smith, 1992; Lieven, Pine & Baldwin, 1997; Maratsos, 1983). Language requires children's mental effort, and sets a formal problem space for them. Therefore, visual information about external objects and events is not the only input available to children in order to acquire language; linguistic information pays an important role in language acquisition as well, and, as is logical, blind children use this to learn language to a greater extent than non-visually impaired children.

One part of what is considered as language input consists of child-directed speech, or, to use a more traditional label, motherese. The results of some studies

(Dunlea & Andersen, 1992; Landau & Gleitman, 1985; Peters, 1994; Wilson & Peters, 1988) show that certain characteristics of the speech addressed to children may affect the acquisition process, by facilitating or not the acquisition of certain structures (such as verb-auxiliary constructions). Evidence in favour of this hypothesis is, however, weak, and more research is needed to arrive to firm conclusions. This is particularly so if we consider that new studies of verbal interaction between blind children and their mothers cast doubt on previous assumptions about the inadequate nature of language input to blind children. Earlier descriptions of mother's speech to blind children assumed that they used too many directives and too few descriptions; however, this account has been recently criticized by Conti-Ramsden and Pérez-Pereira (1997, in press; Pérez-Pereira & Conti-Ramsden, submitted). In Chapter 6 we review this topic in detail. Other authors (Mills, 1993) have suggested that the influence of verbal input is limited and related to features of a given language. For instance, the delay found in the use of verbal auxiliary by Anglo-American blind children possibly does not exist in Spanish-speaking children, as in Spanish these forms are used to a much lesser extent. Such considerations add to the complexity of the possible relationships between maternal speech and child language learning.

In addition to the former considerations, the analysis of modelled speech suggests that blind children are more prone to use a Gestalt or holistic strategy of language processing and acquisition. This does not mean that blind children are different from sighted children as a whole, but that the majority of them seem to be closer to one end of the continuum which goes from the analytic style to the Gestalt style. Obviously, there are sighted children who use the Gestalt strategy as well, although perhaps, not in as high a proportion as found in blind children. Thus, visual impairment seems to favour a certain type of language acquisition style, characterized by an initial, at least, holistic approach to processing language. Consequently, blind children are but an extreme case of existing individual differences in language acquisition. Thus, they are not a special case different from other children without visual impairment. As is logical, human beings exploit resources and mechanisms that they have at their disposal as a species. What seems to happen is that blind children use some of these mechanisms, those which are more adaptive to them, to a greater extent, as a way of compensating for their visual deficit. All this means that, contrary to a monolithic position, children may arrive at a similar endpoint following different routes to acquire language. The comparative study of pragmatic development in blind and sighted children strongly supports this conclusion.

However, language is also a privileged tool for acquiring knowledge about external reality and for participating in social interaction for the blind child. In this regard, language allows these children to compensate for their lack of information about reality and for their lack of visual clues in social interaction. Peters (1994) highlighted the intertwining of language development, on the one hand, and cognitive and social development, on the other. This intertwining is especially remarkable and adaptive in blind children. These considerations are in tune with Vygotskian ideas on language as a symbolic tool, and as an instrument to regulate one's own behaviour, as well as the interrelationship between developmental processes (Luria, 1979; Vygotsky, 1978, 1986).

Nevertheless, the defence of the previously mentioned intertwining does not deny the fact that there may be specifically linguistic mechanisms for acquiring language. Language relates to other areas of development, and the opposite is likely to be true as well, but this does not preclude that there may be domain-specific mechanisms intervening in the process of language acquisition.

As a way of building bridges between the sociocultural theory and the domain-specific mechanisms of language acquisition views, the idea that blind children use linguistic frames as a way of self-scaffolding seems to us extremely interesting. This self-scaffolding promotes language development (Pérez-Pereira, 1994). The use of these frames is particularly evident when children use imitations of others' previous utterances introducing modifications, as well as when they use repetitions of previous utterances spoken by themselves in which they introduce modifications gradually.

Apart from these broad theoretical implications, the study of blind children's language also lets us see the role of lack of visual information on more specific aspects of language acquisition. As an example, Mills (1993) suggested the possible importance of the perception of lip movements for the perception of speech sounds, which was discussed earlier in this chapter.

In conclusion, the study of blind children's language acquisition is not only a useful realm for clinicians, educators, and those interested in helping blind children, but also for interesting theoretical discussions and debates about the nature of language acquisition itself.

CHAPTER SIX

Parent–child conversational interaction with blind children

All children learning to talk acquire their conversational skills within the context of dialogue and, most commonly, within the context of caregiver–child dialogues (Gallaway & Richards, 1994). Thus, it is not surprising that much research has concentrated on examining the nature of mothers' dialogues with normal language learning children. It is also not surprising that researchers interested in atypical populations have addressed themselves to this area as well. Studies investigating the characteristics of mother–child dialogues with blind children have been few in number and methodologically too simplistic. The claim that the linguistic input to blind children is directive and controlling and lacks in description is no longer warranted. In addition, the characterization of conversations with blind children as asymmetrical and non-contingent, where blind children have very few initiations and are unable to sustain conversational interaction, is also brought into question.

Furthermore, it is argued that research on parent–child interaction with blind children is in need of reformulation. Such a reformulation involves looking more closely at possible processes involved in dialogue interaction in parent–blind-child dyads themselves, being particularly sensitive to the meaning and function of blind children's behaviours and that of their parents, and exploring the possible adaptive nature of interactive behaviours in dyads involving blind children.

This chapter therefore does not delve into the role of parental input for language development in either sighted or blind children, nor do we focus in particular on the issue of individual differences in parental interaction styles and individual differences in children (but see Gallaway & Richards, 1994; Lieven, 1997; Pine, Lieven, & Rowland, 1997; Slobin, Gerhardt, Kyratzis, & Guo, 1996).

GENERAL CHARACTERISTICS OF CONVERSATIONAL INTERACTIONS WITH BLIND CHILDREN

Conversational interactions with blind children have been characterized as being highly asymmetrical, with blind children rarely initiating dialogue or doing so to a lesser extent than sighted children (Kekelis & Andersen, 1984; Moore & McConachie, 1994). Furthermore, conversational interactions with blind children have been considered to be non-contingent, with blind children being unable to sustain dialogue around a particular topic and making more non-contingent contributions to conversations in general (Kekelis & Andersen, 1984; Moore & McConachie, 1994). None the less, more recent research has not replicated these findings. We now turn to the details of these investigations and possible explanations for the discrepant results.

Pérez-Pereira and Conti-Ramsden have recently carried out two longitudinal studies of blind children (Conti-Ramsden & Pérez-Pereira, in press; Pérez-Pereira & Conti-Ramsden, submitted). The first study examined children between the ages of 22–25 months and the second study investigated the development of children between the ages of 28 to 32 months (Period 1) and from 33 to 40 months (Period 2). Table 6.1 shows the age and mean length of utterance (MLU) of the children participating in the study; the subjects in these studies were a little older than those studied by Kekelis and Andersen (1984) and Moore and McConachie (1994). Table 6.2 presents the results of the study involving Period 1 and Period 2. It can be observed that there were no significant differences between the blind children and the sighted control child in the percentage of initiations.

Furthermore, these authors point out that there was variation across time for the same dyads in the percentage of initiations, thus, there was not a "constant" style across developmental time. This is a very important consideration in interpreting cross-sectional studies (i.e. Moore & McConachie, 1994), which by definition only have data available on a particular stage in children's development. Furthermore, these findings were replicated in the study involving the younger children at earlier stages of development (22–25 months; Conti-Ramsden & Pérez-Pereira, in press).

Insofar as the contingency of blind children's utterances is concerned, the aforementioned studies of Pérez-Pereira and Conti-Ramsden suggest that blind children are able to sustain and participate contingently in conversational interactions around a particular topic. They found that the mean length of blind children's contribution to conversational episodes around a particular topic was not shorter than those of the sighted child (see Table 6.2). Thus, it is clear that if blind children were producing non-contingent utterances, they would not be able to participate in such lengthy conversations as is evident in the data presented in Table 6.2. In addition, much like Kekelis and Prinz (1996), the studies of Pérez-Pereira and Conti-Ramsden found that in general the amount of non-contingent, breakdown interactive turns was very small for all the dyads participating in both their studies. Having said this, individual differences were noted (see for example,

TABLE 6.1

Age and MLU of the children participating in the study

	Period 1		Period 2	
	Age	*MLU*	*Age*	*MLU*
Alba	2;4,22	2.05		
	2;6,23	2.07		
	2;7,17	2.04		
	2;8,15	2.26		
	2;9,17	2.10		
	2;10,24	2.08		
Javi	2;4,15	2.04	3;0,2	2.81
	2;5,11	2.60	3;0,24	2.46
	2;7,2	2.55	3;1,28	2.53
	2;7,23	2.51	3;3,10	3.11
	2;8,14	2.39	3;4,24	3.02
	2;9,17	2.31		
	2;10,23	2.08		
Sandra	2;5,28	2.24	2;11,7	2.73
	2;8,10	2.52	3;1,2	3.37
	2;10,17	2.74	3;1,23	3.85
			3;2,13	3.50
			3;3,13	3.67
			3;4,8	3.61
Andrea	2;5,28	2.80	2;11,7	2.42
(sighted)	2;8,10	2.11	3;1,2	2.77
	2;10,17	2.37	3;1,23	2.98
			3;2,13	2.82
			3;3,13	2.04
			3;4,8	3.18

TABLE 6.2

Conversational characteristics of mother–child dialogues

	Alba 1 Blind	Javi 1 Blind	Sandra 1 Blind	Andrea 1 Sighted	Javi 2 Blind	Sandra 2 Blind	Andrea 2 Sighted
Who initiated conversations?							
Mother	55.5%	50.0%	48.9%	40.0%	58.4%	44.9%	38.8%
Child	44.5%	50.0%	51.1%	60.0%	41.6%	55.1%	61.2%
What was the mean length of turns per conversation around a particular topic?							
Mother	33.20	5.03	3.97	3.90	7.95	4.39	2.88
Child	19.23	2.44	3.08	3.90	3.68	3.44	2.48
Overall	52.43	7.47	7.15	7.80	11.63	7.83	5.36
What proportion of the conversational interaction was non-contingent?							
Mother	0.4%	6.1%	7.1%	3.6%	4.2%	2.5%	2.6%
Child	0.4%	6.3%	7.4%	8.1%	5.0%	5.8%	1.6%

Alba v. Javi and Sandra, Table 6.2), and overall all the mothers of the blind children had significantly greater number of non-contingent acts when interacting with their children than did the twins' mother when interacting with her sighted child at Period 1 (with the exception of Alba's mother) and at Period 2. A similar pattern was observed for Period 2 for the children but this pattern was not found to be statistically significant.

In addition, differences from Period 1 to Period 2 in the amount of non-contingent conversational breakdowns engaged in by the same dyad were found. These results suggest that blind children and their mothers in general engage in contingent conversational interaction most of the time with non-contingent utterances consisting of 1–14% of the dyadic interaction.

Furthermore, Pérez-Pereira and Conti-Ramsden (submitted) analysed a range of pragmatic functions in the conversational interactions between mothers and their blind versus sighted children at Period 1 and Period 2 (data presented in Tables 6.3 and 6.4). As far as similarities, all mothers used more directives and recasts than their children at Period 1 and Period 2. In addition, all mothers used more requests for clarification than their children at Period 2. In contrast, all children used more non-verbal behaviours and responsives than their mothers at Period 1 and Period 2 and there was a decrease in the use of children's non-verbal behaviours from Period 1 to Period 2. These findings are consistent with previous research documenting the inherent asymmetry that exists in conversational interaction between adults and young language learning children (Ninio & Snow, 1996).

TABLE 6.3

Pragmatic functions of communicative acts at period 1
(percentages of total number of communicative acts)

	Alba		Javi		Sandra		Andrea	
	MOT	CHI	MOT	CHI	MOT	CHI	MOT	CHI
Affirmatives	15.4	10.2	9.0	7.8	10.8	4.8	18.5	5.5
Change of topic	0.0	1.4	0.0	4.4	0.0	0.0	0.0	1.7
Description	3.9	4.6	3.8	5.7	8.6	11.2	7.0	14.0
Directives	21.4	0.2	30.2	2.2	34.7	5.9	22.2	5.2
Imitations	1.9	3.1	2.3	1.5	1.3	1.6	0.0	5.3
No responses	0.0	0.2	0.1	2.9	0.9	1.0	0.0	0.0
Non-verbal behaviours	0.0	20.1	0.0	16.1	0.0	7.6	5.5	14.0
Offers	1.0	0.7	1.7	0.0	0.0	1.1	1.8	3.5
Other	17.3	20.1	11.5	11.8	6.7	23.5	6.3	14.0
Performatives	1.2	0.7	0.9	0.2	0.9	0.0	0.0	0.0
Recasts	1.4	0.1	3.8	0.3	3.1	0.0	1.8	0.0
Regulation of action	0.1	2.5	0.1	2.7	0.0	0.0	0.0	0.0
Requests for clarification	3.1	0.2	2.7	6.0	2.3	3.2	7.4	0.0
Requests	29.3	4.7	22.5	5.5	16.7	2.7	22.2	33.3
Responsives	1.9	27.8	9.8	29.0	9.0	23.0	5.5	3.5
Routines	1.2	3.3	1.5	3.0	2.3	3.2	0.0	0.0
Vocatives	0.9	0.1	0.1	0.9	2.7	11.2	1.8	0.0

TABLE 6.4

Pragmatic functions of communicative acts at period 2
(percentages of total number of communicative acts)

	Javi		Sandra		Andrea	
	MOT	*CHI*	*MOT*	*CHI*	*MOT*	*CHI*
Affirmatives	14.9	13.9	8.4	13.7	16.5	6.1
Change of topic	0.0	3.4	0.0	1.4	0.0	0.2
Description	1.9	3.7	16.5	19.1	9.7	16.8
Directives	17.3	0.0	29.7	4.0	14.2	5.1
Imitations	3.5	2.8	1.1	0.9	1.8	1.0
No responses	0.0	1.5	0.5	1.0	0.2	0.5
Non-verbal behaviours	0.0	10.4	0.0	5.2	0.0	5.0
Offers	1.0	0.4	2.2	0.8	0.5	1.3
Other	13.4	8.4	8.6	9.5	8.1	10.2
Performatives	0.4	0.8	1.8	0.5	1.8	0.8
Recasts	3.5	0.2	1.1	0.0	1.8	0.0
Regulation of action	0.0	1.7	0.0	0.2	0.0	0.2
Requests for clarification	4.9	0.2	2.8	1.8	4.5	2.1
Requests	33.7	2.8	13.1	10.0	22.8	16.3
Responsives	5.3	40.7	10.6	27.7	10.5	27.2
Routines	0.1	8.5	2.1	2.7	7.1	5.9
Vocatives	0.1	0.6	1.5	1.5	0.5	1.3

Adults, on the one hand, scaffolded their children via the use of recasts and requests for clarifications and they also used directives with them to get things done. Children, on the other hand, used non-verbal behaviours communicatively more often than their parents and they undertook a responsive role more often than the adults in the two developmental periods studied. Furthermore, the reduction in the use of non-verbal behaviours by the children in this study gives support to Shatz's (1978) suggestion that "action responding" strategies are typical of very young children and decrease with increasing age.

In addition, like previous research (Kekelis & Andersen, 1984; Moore & McConachie, 1994), this study found that mothers used more directives with their blind children than with the sighted child at both Period 1 and Period 2. This finding was based on an examination of the proportions of maternal directives used. We argue later that such an analysis may be misleading and may disguise the more complex nature of the conversational function of directives in mother–child dialogues. In contrast, and unlike previous research (Kekelis & Andersen, 1984: Moore & McConachie, 1994; Mulford, 1988), we did not replicate previous findings on the use of descriptions. In this study, we found no differences in the use of descriptions by mothers of blind children when compared with the mother of the sighted child. Part of the explanation for the discrepancy of the finding may lie on the nature of the comparisons made by the different studies. Previous investigations have not included amongst their subjects control sighted children thus, comparisons have been usually made with data available from other already existing investigations. Such comparisons are problematic given the different methods, analyses, and contexts of different investigations. Thus, in the present study we are making comparisons of the same mother addressing her sighted versus her blind child and in this context, no differences in the use of descriptions were found.

To the contrary, on further analysis (discussed later), we found that mothers of blind children used significantly more descriptions within their directives than the mother of the sighted child at Period 1. Thus, we would argue that in Period 1, at early stages of language development and in contexts where mothers are directing their children, mothers of blind children made *more* use of descriptions of the environment that is visually unavailable to their conversational partners. Perhaps previous research has been too narrow in only counting "pure" descriptions in their analyses, thus failing to acknowledge the multifunctional nature of communicative interaction. It has been argued that descriptive verbal input should in principle help blind children organize and categorize information about their environment (Kekelis & Andersen, 1984). Consequently, the findings of the present investigation suggest that parents of blind children have developed an adaptive strategy in their use of descriptions within directives in the early stages of their children's linguistic development.

CHILD-DIRECTED SPEECH

Differences between child-directed speech and adult–adult speech are so well known and well documented in the literature that the terms "motherese", and more recently, "parentese", have been coined to refer to them as a cluster of co-occurring behaviours (Snow, 1994). One of the most prevalent questions in the area of interaction with blind children has been whether these children receive input which is similar to that received by normal language learners. That is, do parents of blind children provide parentese to their children like parents of young, normally developing children do? The results of these investigations have been both limited and somewhat controversial. None the less, it is evident that, if results are placed in a historical perspective, one can note an increasing awareness on the part of all researchers that the answer to this question may well be more complicated than was originally thought.

As was seen from Chapter 3, some research effort has gone towards understanding parent–child interaction with blind children at the early, prelinguistic stages of development. In contrast, there have been very few studies that have focused on the specific characteristics of child-directed speech to blind children. On the one hand, the majority of investigators have argued that parental speech to blind children is different from that of sighted children in that parents of blind children use more directives and less descriptions, are more controlling, and in general are less responsive (Behl, Akers, Boyce, & Taylor, 1996; Kekelis & Andersen, 1984; Moore & McConachie, 1994, 1995; Rowland, 1983). On the other hand, some investigators have failed to replicate these findings when a control group of sighted children was included in the studies in question. Thus, the finding of directives was not replicated by Kekelis and Prinz (1996) and the findings on lack of descriptions and lack of responsivity were not replicated by Pérez-Pereira & Conti-Ramsden (submitted) nor by Conti-Ramsden & Pérez-Pereira (in press).

What can account for these conflicting results? First, research with blind children has usually involved very small samples and often has not included sighted comparison groups. As a result much of the data available has been anecdotal and qualitative with little quantitative information give. Second, the analyses carried out have usually involved the contribution of one conversational partner (usually the mother). Little attention has been paid to the possible effect the child may have on the mother and of the possible conversational processes that may be taking place in dyadic interaction. Third, there has been great variation in the definition and approach to analysis of "directives" as well as "responsivity". For example, in the case of directives the criteria have ranged from syntactical information only (e.g. imperatives) to pragmatic functions (e.g. directives including indirect directives); thus, comparisons across studies has been difficult.

In the next two sections we will examine in detail the information available on parent–child interaction with blind children. These two headings subsume most of the issues around which the debate regarding parent–child interaction with blind children has taken place, namely, parental responsivity and parental directiveness.

PARENTAL RESPONSIVITY

Research with normal language learning children has documented the positive effects of responsivity, and more specifically semantic contingency on the development of language in young children (Nelson, 1981; Nelson, Denninger, Bonvillian, Kaplan, & Baker, 1984; Pine, 1994; Snow, Perlmann, & Nathan, 1987). It is natural therefore that some investigators interested in language development in blind children have examined this area in this population. On the one hand, studies have reported that mothers of blind children are less responsive vocally in play interaction contexts (Rogers & Puchalski, 1984), less responsive in general in interactions with their young blind infants between 11 and 32 months of age (Rowland, 1983, 1984), and tend to use more initiations than responses with their preverbal blind children (Moore & McConachie, 1995). Unfortunately, these investigations have varied greatly in the characteristics of the subjects studied. Thus, most of Rowland's subjects were not only blind but also severely developmentally delayed. Furthermore, these studies have tended to present mothers of blind children as a homogeneous group with a single "non-responsive" interactive style, rather than as individuals whose behaviour may vary considerably. Finally, these studies have suggested that the mothers' behaviours are a probable cause of or exacerbate their children's problems with language (for example, lack of responsivity in the blind children themselves as found by Rogers & Puchalski, 1984;

Rowland, 1983) without due consideration to the possible adaptive role of some of the maternal strategies used (for an example of an alternative explanation see Urwin, 1984a).

On the other hand, not all studies investigating this area have found mothers of blind children to be less responsive. Dote-Kwan (1995) for example identified that mother-responsive behaviours were positively related to visually impaired children's development, and interestingly, mothers of visually impaired children displayed a high percentage of repeats or rephrases (also referred to in the literature as expansions or recasts; Conti-Ramsden, 1990) of the children's communicative intents. This study also found that the mothers of visually impaired children presented a high percentage of responses and compliance with a very low percentage of ignoring and refusing their children's initiations and requests for help. The study of Dote-Kwan examined children between the ages of 20 and 36 months. The children in this study did not have any other handicapping conditions and this may explain the differences between the results of this study and those of Rowland (1983, 1984). Furthermore, Dote-Kwan used a larger sample of 18 visually impaired children in contrast to the very few cases studied by previous researchers. In the same vein, Pérez-Pereira and Conti-Ramsden (submitted) did not find any consistent differences between mothers of blind children and the mother of a sighted child in their use of responsives and recasts between 28 and 40 months of age. None the less, these authors found large individual differences among the three mother–blind-child dyads in what they refer to as the directivity–responsivity dimension. Once again, to characterize mothers of blind children as a homogeneous "non-responsive" group is both too simplistic and misleading. Similarly, Conti-Ramsden and Pérez-Pereira (in press), in their longitudinal study of three young infants between 22 and 25 months of age, found that the mother of the blind infant did not differ from the mother of a partially sighted child and the mother of a sighted child in her use of conversational responsives and use of recasts in dialogue. What these authors did find was that the mother of the blind infant spoke more to her infant than the other two mothers did. This finding lends support to the idea that for blind children language is extremely important as it creates a context for social interaction and learning (Pérez-Pereira, 1994; Pérez-Pereira & Castro, 1997; Peters, 1994). The mother in the study by Conti-Ramsden and Pérez-Pereira (in press) appeared to know this and to exploit the use of language as a way to share the world with her child.

PARENTAL DIRECTIVENESS

One of the most consistent themes in the literature on parent–child interaction with atypical language learners has been parents' directive style. This has been measured in different ways by different researchers, be it increased used of imperatives (Buium, Rynders, & Turnure, 1973), mands, that is, demands, commands, and requests (Marshall, Hegrenes, & Goldstein, 1973), or directive speech acts

(Conti-Ramsden, 1990; Conti-Ramsden & Friel-Patti, 1983). The argument put forth by some researchers has been that a highly directive parent tends to use language primarily to control the child's attention and behaviour, rather than using language as a reciprocal, communicative, and informational exchange. Thus, there has been a tendency to equate parental directiveness with parental intrusiveness and insensitivity (Pine, 1992). Such directive parental style has been found in studies involving a variety of atypical children including intellectually impaired children (Davies, Stroud, & Green, 1988), physically impaired children (Barrera & Vella, 1987; Hanzlik, 1989), hearing impaired children (Meadow, 1980) and specifically language impaired children (Bondurant, Romeo, & Kretschmer, 1983).

More recently, studies of parental directiveness have focused on blind children (Kekelis & Andersen, 1984; Moore & McConachie, 1994). It has become clearer that, although there are many great similarities between blind and sighted children's language development, there are also a number of important differences (Andersen et al., 1984; Dunlea, 1989). Consequently, the role of the input has come under scrutiny. Kekelis and Andersen (1984), for example, argue that the qualitative differences found in the language of blind children reflect the patterns of parental input language to these children. In their study, they examined input language directed to six children aged 1 to 3 years of whom two were blind, two were visually impaired, and two were sighted. They found that parents of the blind children provided a highly directive input (i.e. parents used more imperatives and fewer declaratives) and provided their children with very few descriptions (i.e. parents provided little information on the functions and attributes of objects, events, and people). These findings are interpreted negatively and it is suggested that such input "can impair children's development". Moore and McConachie (1994) replicated Kekelis and Andersen's results with a larger group of blind children (16 in total) at 18 months of age, although their language samples were considerably shorter (15 minutes in length). These authors also found increased directiveness and lack of descriptions in parental language to blind children. Preisler (1991) also noted similar parental input patterns in her anecdotal, descriptive case study of one blind infant. Thus, overall, the current state of our knowledge suggests there is a negative effect of parental speech on blind children's language development and that the characteristics of parental speech are maladaptive and perhaps detrimental to language learning. How warranted are these conclusions?

Recent research challenges these conclusions. For example, Kekelis and Prinz (1996) were unable to replicate the findings on maternal directives for two blind children aged 27–36 months in their longitudinal study. Kekelis and Prinz did not include descriptions in their analysis so no comparisons with previous studies in this area were possible. In Kekelis and Prinz's investigation, the two blind children studied did not receive more directives from their mothers than the comparison sighted children did. All the mothers used directives approximately 25% of the time in interaction with their young children. The authors call for further research to reconcile the discrepancy between their results and those of other studies but do not offer any possible explanations for why such differences may have been observed. Recent research may provide some clues as to possible reasons for such discrepant results. Pérez-Pereira and Conti-Ramsden (submitted) found that maternal use of directives varied with developmental time for both blind and sighted children, with maternal use of directives decreasing when children were in their late twos and early threes. Thus, it may be the case that maternal differences in the use of directives may be more evident at earlier stages of development.

The work of Pérez-Pereira and Conti-Ramsden is worth further discussion as these authors longitudinally examined the conversational characteristics of mother–blind-infant dyads between 22–25 months (Conti-Ramsden & Pérez-Pereira, in press) and between 28–40 months (Pérez-Pereira & Conti-Ramsden, submitted), with particular attention being given to the use of directives and descriptions. Interestingly, and unlike previous research (Kekelis & Andersen, 1984; Moore & McConachie, 1994; Mulford, 1988), these authors did not replicate previous findings on the use of descriptions in either of the two studies. The two investigations found no differences in the use of descriptions by the mothers of the blind children and the mother of the sighted children (see Tables 6.3 and 6.4). Part of the explanation for the discrepancy of the findings may lie in the nature of the comparisons made by the different studies. Previous investigations have not included amongst their subjects control sighted children; thus, comparisons have been usually made with data available from other already existing investigations. Such comparisons are problematic given the different methods, analyses, and contexts of different investigations. Methodologically, the Pérez-Pereira and Conti-Ramsden studies are more powerful in that they include as a control sighted infants of the same age and language stage, and in one of the studies, the sighted control child happened to be the twin sister of the blind child, thus providing a further control of the same mother addressing a blind versus a sighted offspring.

In addition, these authors found that simple proportional analysis of directives replicated previous findings that mothers of blind children tend to use more directives than mothers of sighted children. In order to further understand the possible role of directives in the conversations between mothers and their blind infants, two sets of further analyses were carried out by these authors: a qualitative analysis of the content of maternal directives use and a sequential analysis of maternal directives.

The qualitative analysis of the content of maternal directives attempted to ascertain whether maternal directives were multifunctional and, in addition to directing the child's behaviour, they performed other functions. Specifically, these authors examined the proportion of directive maternal utterances that contained descriptions. A directive with a description included descriptions of objects and events in the environment, information about location, or how, why, or when to do something. Examples of maternal directives containing descriptions included: "look at it with your nose to see what it smells like" or "first pick it up with your hand and then do not drop it until it is inside the container" or "put this hand out and search for it ... look for it with this hand". In the Pérez-Pereira and Conti-Ramsden (submitted) study, it was found that mothers of blind children used significantly more descriptions within their directives than mothers of sighted children at Period 1 (47% of directives contained descriptions for Alba, 25% for Javi, 37% for Sandra and 11% for Andrea the sighted child).

The same findings were evident in the Conti-Ramsden and Pérez-Pereira study with younger children (see Table 6.5). Thus, these authors argue that at early stages of language development and in contexts where mothers are directing their children, mothers of blind children made *significantly more* use of descriptions of the environment that is visually unavailable to their conversational partners. Perhaps previous research has been too narrow in only counting "pure" descriptions in their analyses thus failing to acknowledge the multifunctional nature of communicative interaction. It has been argued that descriptive verbal input should in principle help blind children organize and categorize information about their environment (Kekelis & Andersen, 1994). Consequently, the finding of Pérez-Pereira and Conti-Ramsden (submitted) and Conti-Ramsden and Pérez-Pereira (in press) suggest that parents of blind children have developed an adaptive strategy in their use of descriptions within directives in the early stages of their children's linguistic development.

As previously mentioned, the studies of Pérez-Pereira and Conti-Ramsden also examined dialogue sequences containing directives. Specifically, these authors examined what proportion of maternal directive utterances were followed by another maternal directive utterances. First, we calculated the proportion of maternal directive utterances that were followed by other maternal utterances (as opposed to child utterances or turns). Having calculated this proportion, we examined the percentage of those maternal following utterances that were also directives. We then multiplied both proportions to get what we called a maternal directives repetition index. The data for both studies are presented in Tables 6.6 and 6.7.

These studies found that maternal directives to blind children tended to occur in clusters within dialogue sequences. Thus, studies that count single occurrences of directives are unable to capture the role of such speech acts in dialogue. Mothers of blind children tended to sequentially elaborate or repeat the directives they used

TABLE 6.5

Proportion of directives that contained descriptions and 95% confidence intervals

Category	Time 1	Time 2	Time 3
Blind	43.3	64.4	47.3
	(38.4–48.4)	(59.8–69.1)	(43.1–51.5)
Sighted	9.1	16.0	11.1
	(5.5–12.7)	(11.5–20.5)	(6.7–15.6)
Partially sighted	13.1	14.7	18.4
	(8.9–17.6)	(10.5–18.8)	(15.9–21.9)

TABLE 6.6

Maternal Directives Repetition Index and 95% confidence intervals
(Conti-Ramsden & Pérez-Pereira, in press)

Category	Time 1	Time 2	Time 3
Blind	24.3	18.3	15.8
	(20.0–28.6)	(14.5–22.1)	(12.7–18.9)
Sighted	4.5	4.8	15.2
	(1.9–7.1)	(2.1–7.5)	(10.7–19.7)
Partially sighted	3.6	4.2	7.5
	(1.2–6.0)	(1.6–6.8)	(4.1–10.9)

TABLE 6.7

Maternal Directives Repetition Index and 95% confidence intervals
(Conti-Ramsden & Pérez-Pereira, submitted)

	Period 1	Period 2
Alba	31.9	
	(30.3–33.5)	
Javi	32.2	34.8
	(30.1–34.6)	(31.6–38.0)
Sandra	28.7	16.4
	(22.9–34.6)	(14.2–18.6)
Andrea (sighted)	11.1	10.4
	(2.7–19.5)	(7.3–13.5)

with their children. Why may this be the case? Without visual support for interaction, language acts as a tool for contact between mother and child and for creating contexts for dialogue. Mother–child dyads with blind children are thus more dependent on language for social interaction (Peters, 1987, 1994). Repeating or elaborating on directives provides a context for the blind child and allows the blind child to have access to information while preparing to respond. Thus, if we consider clusters of directives, it is not the case that mothers of blind children use more directives *per se*. Future research needs to take into consideration these and the previously discussed findings and investigate more deeply the complex role that directives and descriptions can play in dialogue between parents and their blind children.

CONCLUDING REMARKS

The findings discussed in the previous two sections suggest that monolithic analyses of directives, descriptions, and responsivity can be misleading as they treat potentially quite different forms of linguistic behaviour as if they were essentially equivalent. Pine (1992) has argued on similar lines in his study of sighted, normal children, and he, for example, distinguished between attentional directives and behavioural directives. It is essential that future research be more sensitive to the aforementioned differences in the use of directives, descriptions, and in the definitions of responsibility. If we can take the case of directives as an illustration, we find that so far, there has been a tendency to draw conclusions based on two implicit assumptions. First, there has been an assumption that directives are not conducive for language learning at any stage of development. Second, there has been an assumption that sighted and blind parent–child dyads function similarly in conversational interaction and thus, any differences found between these two groups of parents are likely to predict or exacerbate the blind child's language learning task in some way. Consequently, finding more directives in parental speech to blind children has been considered evidence enough to argue for a detrimental language learning environment for those children. What we need is careful analysis of the interaction between the child's perceptual and processing mechanisms and the speech to which he or she is actually being exposed. It may be the case that parental input may not be conducive for language learning in some parent–blind-child dyads. The point is we need to demonstrate this, we can not simply assume it. In other words, the exact relationship between particular aspects of parental language and blind children's language problems need to be specified. Thus, in the case of blind children we want to argue that descriptive information in directive contexts may be particularly important for the young language-learning child as such information can be crucial for the dyad to establish joint attention and participate in conversational interaction.

Finally, we want to emphasize that research with blind children is in need of reconceptualization. Parent–child interaction with blind children is a process that inherently involves different goals and most likely uses different routes to achieve them. Thus, researchers need to be more sensitive to the meaning of parental and blind children's behaviours. It is likely that what is apparently the same behaviour as that produced or experienced by a non-impaired child, in reality is a behaviour that may have a different function for the blind child or his or her parents. Such a possibility cautions against comparisons of blind children with sighted children without explanations of the processes involved in both groups of children. With this framework it should be possible to construct a clearer picture of the ways in which blind children participate in conversational interaction with their parents.

CHAPTER SEVEN

Ideas on intervention with blind children

The purpose of this chapter is to attempt to relate some of the information presented so far to considerations of intervention with blind children and their families. In this sense, this chapter is aimed at readers who are interested in working with blind children and their families. The content of the chapter focuses very much on practical matters and as such it is rather different to previous chapters in the book. Before delving into the details concerning this chapter, we want to provide a brief summary of what the book has achieved so far with the view to provide some grounding for future research.

Throughout the book we have tried to emphasize the relevance of research on special populations for theories of development pointing out that future theoretical research needs to take seriously the task of accounting for individual differences and the existence of multiple developmental pathways that lead to similar outcomes. The book has provided a critical review of the literature on early development in blind children with a particular focus on topics related to language and the development of social-interactive skills. We argue strongly that we need to reconsider the widely held belief that blind children's early language and communicative skills are deficient relative to those of sighted children. We propose that blind children's behaviours that have traditionally been viewed as "maladaptive" may in reality provide the blind child with alternative pathways and strategies for language and communication. In this sense, future research needs to continue to consider blind children's development in its own right, needs to continue to emphasize the functional significance of particular behaviours in blind children, and needs to continue to document and examine the positive role language plays as a cognitive and social tool in the development of blind children.

THE CASE FOR INTERVENTION

From previous chapters it has become clear that the population of blind children is highly heterogeneous. Within the spectrum of legal blindness (visual loss of 80% or more in Spain, or 20/200 in the USA), there exist large differences in degree of residual vision from children whose eyes have no functional use at all, to those who have (with stimulation) significant use of residual vision and behave much more like sighted children. Blindness can be the only handicap a child experiences or it may be one of a number of related handicaps that co-occur in a particular child. Furthermore, the aetiology of blindness is very variable and can be manifested prenatally, perinatally, or postnatally and, in the latter case, can occur at different stages during childhood. All these considerations make it difficult to talk about blind children as a group and to make generalizations. Thus, it is important to make it clear that although in this chapter we will attempt to draw some general guidelines, it is essential that intervention with blind children be highly individualized, paying particular attention to the characteristics of the child, the family, and the interaction between them. Furthermore, the importance of a multidisciplinary approach needs to be emphasized. Given the heterogeneity of the population of blind children and the high incidence of related handicaps, such an approach is essential for the success of any intervention. There is one further caveat. The guidelines offered in this chapter are likely to be most relevant for congenitally blind children who have total blindness or only minimal light perception. We think this is justified, as congenital blindness is the most frequent type of blindness in the first five years of life (Garwood, 1983; Walker et al., 1992).

We have argued that language can have a compensatory effect in the development of blind children. The relationship between different developmental psychological processes such as language, cognition and social interaction, underline the importance that language can have for the blind child (Peters, 1994). Language can provide blind children with a tool to access information about the world and social interaction, which would not be possible without it. None the less, we need to remember that there are a number of developmental milestones the child needs to have reached that form the basis for oral language learning. These milestones tend to develop in the first two years of life and many of them have to do with using vision and the information vision affords to understand the characteristics of people, objects, and events/actions. Therefore, it can not be emphasized enough that intervention with blind children should begin as early as possible to avoid developmental delays that may hinder later development and language learning. In these early years, the role of parents in the child's development is crucial; thus, any intervention programme must involve parents and take their views, expectations, ideas, and worries into consideration (Pérez-Pereira, 1998). In many cases intervention will mean bringing about some changes in the parents' ideas and expectations about their blind children. Intervention programmes should be based on our understanding of how blind children develop and on a detailed examination of where the blind child in question is developmentally, so that intervention can be fine-tuned to the level the child is at, and thus work within what Vygotsky (1986) would call the child's zone of proximal development. It is also important to reinstate our earlier argument that blind children do not simply follow a slower version of "normal" development. The idea that there is a universal pathway to development independent from individual characteristics and circumstances is simply erroneous. Blind children often use different mechanisms for learning about the world around them and for learning language. As such, blind children can provide us with an interesting case in learning how individual characteristics and environmental variables can lead to particular outcomes and such knowledge can be usefully applied in intervention.

There are usually three groups of children who are likely to need early intervention (Guralnick, 1997; Guralnick & Bennett, 1987). First, those children that live in high-risk, socially deprived situations including poverty, low socio-economic status, single-parent families, adolescent mothers, parents with drug or alcohol problems, etc. Second, children that are biologically at a high risk, that is, premature children, low birth-weight babies, babies with complicated perinatal histories such as anoxia, etc. Third, children with developmental delays and handicaps, of which blind children are a subset. Table 7.1 presents the types of developmental difficulties found in this third category and the incidence figures (taken from Guralnick & Bennett, 1987). An examination of Table 7.1 and the previously mentioned considerations shows that blind children are only a minority group in relation to other children who require early intervention. None the less, we would like to emphasize how important early intervention is for blind children and in the following sections we hope to provide details that support this assertion.

THE BIRTH OF A BLIND CHILD:
IDEAS, EXPECTATIONS, AND REACTIONS OF PARENTS

One of the most painful experiences parents can go through is having children who have any sort of problem that affects their development. In the case of blind children,

TABLE 7.1

Types of developmental delays/handicaps
and incidence figures

Type of delay/handicap	Incidence
Mental retardation	2–3%
Motor delays (cerebral palsy, spina bifida, muscular dystrophy)	1/400
Speech and language delays	5–7%
Autism	1/2000
Sensory problems:	
deafness	1/1000
blindness	1/2500–3000
deaf/blind	5% of the two figures above

parents may discover that their child has no vision under a variety of circumstances and at different developmental stages. These factors affect the way parents react to the diagnosis of blindness, the way parents care for the child, and the way the child develops.

Interestingly, not all blind children are diagnosed as such at birth or shortly thereafter. It is not uncommon for blind children to be a number of months old before parents and health visitors/doctors realize that they are blind, unless they have an obvious lesion (such as anophthalmia or cataracts). This delay adds to the difficulties of blind children as intervention is not available to them during this time. The majority of blind children are diagnosed around 2 to 3 months of age, when it is possible to observe that they do not have typical reactions to people (they do not smile in face-to-face interaction with their mothers) nor to objects (they do not visually track an interesting, moving object). The problem is compounded if diagnosis is delayed to 5 or 6 months of age, when sighted children are already attempting to grasp objects and control their environment.

Some parents have negative reactions to the diagnosis of blindness in their children, with adverse consequences for the child's development (Pérez-Pereira, 1998). In some cases, there is a total denial of the problem by the parents that is often related to a delay in seeking help, which in turn results in the diagnosis being obvious only considerably later. Many parents who are denying their child's problems, will "shop around", seeking for second, third, or fourth medical opinions hoping that they will find someone who will tell them that their child is not blind or that what is wrong with their child is curable. This stage of looking for different opinions can last for months and during this time the blind child is not receiving adequate attention and care. This type of psychological reaction to "bad news" is not uncommon; it is only sensible to confirm any diagnosis that has deep and difficult consequences. But, in this case, we are talking about behaviours that go beyond what is expected of the majority of people and it is this exaggerated reaction that can have a negative impact on the blind child's development.

In other cases, parents feel responsible and guilty for the child's blindness, even in cases when they have been told that the particular behaviour in question (for example, having worked up until the birth, having had drinks at a particular event) had nothing to do with their child's difficulty. Parents who blame themselves for their child's problem can experience anxiety, which can in some cases lead to severe depression. It is also possible for parents to reject the child, leading in some cases to neglect and abuse of the blind child. But, it is not necessary for this type of reaction to be very strong for there to be adverse consequences. Parents may simply appear undisturbed by their children's handicap and uninterested in their care, development, and education.

Yet another type of reaction involves overprotecting the child. Parents are very cautious with the blind child, so much so, that the child is not given opportunities to explore objects, try new things, or develop autonomy in such activities as feeding, washing, personal care, and exploring the environment. More often than not, the majority of parents do not know what to do with a blind child. Information for parents is not always readily available and parents are not always aware of where to go for assessment and help. Furthermore, many parents have to interact with their blind children without guidance, pretty much on a trial-and-error basis. This situation leads to insecurity and lack of confidence in the part of the parents on how to interact with their blind children.

We now turn to circumstances that can make more pronounced the possible negative consequences of the birth of a blind child. If there is marital conflict, unemployment, lack of time and/or resources, the birth of a blind child can exacerbate the aforementioned existing difficulties. In the same vein, first-time, inexperienced parents may not have enough knowledge of parenting to react adequately or constructively when confronted with the challenges of having a blind child (Holden, 1988). Contrastively, experienced parents who have had other children, can draw from their experience of parenting to develop strategies to adapt and cope with their blind child. Rarely do experienced parents who have other healthy children blame themselves for their child's blindness.

Parental education is another factor that can influence the development of blind children. Parents encourage certain types of activities in their children based on their beliefs of what their children are capable of doing at a particular age (Goodnow & Collins, 1990; Miller, 1988) and what they think the role of the parent is in the child's development. A number of studies carried out in Spain suggest that parents with higher levels of education are better able to promote development in their children than parents with lower levels of education (Palacios, 1987, 1990; Triana, 1991). In the case of blind children, there is no reason not to believe that parental education will have an effect on these children's overall development. None the less, the effect of parental education level on blind children's development has not been carefully investigated and we must be cautious in drawing premature conclusions.

Finally, parental interactive style can also exert an influence on the development of blind children. Parental sensitivity to the demands of their young infant and parental predictability are essential ingredients for a secure attachment between parent and infant. This secure attachment then forms the basis for later development (Schaffer, 1984, 1996). In the case of blind children, the ability of the parents to be able to interpret the reactions of their blind children and their ability to respond adequately to their children's needs and intentions have added importance given the fact that blind children's behaviours are less transparent than those of sighted infants. It is important to note that what parents know about development of children is usually based on typical behaviours of sighted infants. Consequently, parents of blind children need to adapt their behaviours to the new situation created by the blind child where there is little overt, clear feedback from the blind child to the parents.

It is precisely for these reasons that early assessment and intervention play such an important role in the development of blind children.

INTERVENTION FOR DEVELOPMENT:
PRINCIPLES AND THE ROLE OF PARENTS

In the first years of life, children are able to develop and learn a number of basic skills and relationships which will form the basis for later development. Any difficulties at this early stage can have serious consequences for later successful development. The difficulties blind children experience are usually related and rooted in what they experience in the first few years of life. We thus reiterate that it is very important that intervention begins as early as possible with blind children. But, what makes for successful intervention? What are the principles upon which early intervention programmes should be based?

First, early intervention should be about preventing and anticipating possible difficulties and challenges for the blind child. It is useful to intervene before delays in particular areas of development are obvious. Unfortunately, in reality most intervention is about dealing with specific delays in the blind child that are already in existence. Second, early intervention should be based on a careful evaluation of the child's development in different areas. This will provide information about the child's developmental profile and underline specific areas of difficulty. The Reynell–Zinkin scales (Reynell, 1979) for children between 0–5 years of age and the Leonhardt scales (1992) for children between 0–2 years are both very useful instruments for the assessment of blind children's development. It probably has become obvious to the reader of this book that blind children face challenges and delays in particular areas of development and we will return to these in the next section.

Consequently, before developing an intervention programme, it is necessary to carefully analyse all the information available on the child's history and development. This will include information from medical records, family circumstances including how the parents feel about their child and the handicap of blindness, and details of the child's performance. In the same vein, in order to plan for intervention, it is important to have knowledge of the child's physical environment and of the child's interactive experience (essentially parents and family when the children are young) that may not be conducive for the child's development. In order to make this judgement, it is often necessary to obtain information on family history: how did the parents discover their child was blind, what they did, what their reaction was, what are their ideas and attitudes towards the child now. This information is essential if we are to modify possible parental behaviours such as rejection, overprotection, denial, guilt, and anxiety, which may prevent parents from developing a positive interactive style with their blind child.

Another important first step in the development of an intervention programme involves the need of parents to have appropriate knowledge about the patterns of development of blind children (Guralnick, 1997). Such information is essential for the parents to develop a sense of "what is normal for blind children". As mentioned before, parents' knowledge about development is based on sighted children and this knowledge is not easily translated into what one should expect of blind children. In addition, parents are often nervous and worried about interacting with their blind children. This lack of knowledge and fine-tuning between parents and their blind children can lead to interactions that are not sensitive enough to the blind child's needs. Thus, parents may not be able to respond appropriately to their child's subtle initiations (overall excitement and shaking of limbs) or responses (being still and quiet). It is therefore essential that an intervention programme should include parental education where typical interactive situations are examined, where examples are provided of how to initiate, respond to, and understand the intentions of their blind children, and where the role of parents in the overall development of their children is discussed. It is important to underline to parents the importance of learning how to interpret correctly the intentions of their blind children (Rowland, 1984; Sostek, 1991; Urwin, 1984a). Furthermore, the situation previously described can lead to parents lacking confidence and developing a sense of inability to cope with their blind children (Joffee, 1988). It has been argued that lack of knowledge about child development in terms of needs and stages of development tends to be associated with less effective parenting strategies (Schlesinger, 1987). Consequently, an intervention programme should have as one of its main objectives not only to provide information but also to promote self-confidence in parents of blind children.

But, at the end of the day, intervention is about promoting development in the blind child. This is conceptualized as providing the child with opportunities to engage in activities that children can do with the help of parents/educators, but can not yet do on their own. This is Vygotsky's (1986) Zone of Proximal Development (ZPD) where mediated social-intentional activity can foster and enhance the child's level of functioning. But, before one can develop activities in the ZPD, it is important to know what the actual level of development the child has, as one is intrinsically related to the other. For this, and as discussed earlier, we need a detailed assessment of the child's abilities, which oftentimes requires gathering information from a number of areas and involving a number of professionals (for example, doctors, psychologists, speech-language therapists, educators). Thus, the specialist intervening with the blind child needs to be part of a multidisciplinary team and have knowledge in most key areas of development (Olson, 1987).

The specialist intervening with the blind child also needs to have a very close and continued relationship with parents, especially in early intervention. Parents spend a great deal of their time with their children and therefore they can be seen as intervention agents in this process. Parents benefit from receiving concrete, detailed programmes containing activities that they can engage in with their children. It is important for these programmes to be evaluated regularly by the specialist with the parents so that changes to the programme can be brought about when necessary.

BLIND CHILDREN'S DEVELOPMENT:
AREAS OF PARTICULAR DIFFICULTY

Although there are large individual differences in the development of blind children (Pérez-Pereira & Castro, 1994; Warren, 1994), there are areas of development that appear to be particularly challenging for them. Table 7.2 presents a summary of the major areas of difficulty experienced by blind children (taken from Pérez-Pereira, 1998). These have been discussed in detail in previous chapters. These areas of difficulty usually form part of any intervention programme with blind children. Sostek (1991) for example, argues that an intervention programme with blind children should include work on motor development, sensory and emotional development, cognitive development, communication and language, personal and daily living activities to develop autonomy and independence, as well as mobility and orientation. We now turn to suggest some general guidelines for intervention with blind children. These will complement our discussion from the previous section.

An intervention programme should involve information and help for parents to be able to interpret their blind children's behaviours. Blind children's behaviours may be subtle and easily missed by parents or misinterpreted. In general, parents need help first to interpret blind children's facial and other expressions, and later, any alternative signals or signs blind children may use to share their intentions. The key is to take blind children's behaviours as meaningful and communicative. Thus, cycles of interaction can be established between parents and their blind infants. Given the importance of vocalizations in the development of language, it is essential that parents learn early on to respond consistently to their blind children's vocalizations. For example, parents may be able to imitate their children's vocalizations, or respond with another, different vocalization after the child has finished his or her turn so that turn taking is clear and reciprocal (see Rowland, 1984 for further suggestions). In this way parents will be able to engage their infants in interaction, will stimulate the child's vocalizations, and will develop turn-taking routines that can form the basis for later dialogue. Smiles should also be treated in this way, as communicative behaviours and consistent responses will help the blind infant to use the smile appropriately. Similarly, parents need to be able to interpret blind children's responses involving becoming still and quiet. These behaviours should be interpreted as the child being interested in what is going on, in paying attention, and listening. They should not be interpreted as lack of responsiveness or indifference. It is also important for parents to be aware that blind children may well develop manual gestures, body postures, and facial expressions which are idiosyncratic to the child but which have communicative value. It is important for parents to be able to read the context in which these idiosyncratic behaviours occur so that parents can respond consistently and appropriately. In this way, cycles of interaction are reinforced and not broken (Tronick, Als, & Brazelton, 1977). Fraiberg (1977) also had a number of ideas about fostering better parent–child interaction and attachment amongst blind infants. Fraiberg, for

TABLE 7.2

The development of blind children: Areas of particular difficulty

Motor	Cognitive	Social Interaction	Personal	Language
General motor development	Object permanence	Reaction of stillness	Problem of social isolation	Tendency to imitate and to repeat (echolalia)
Orientation to the external environment	Other sensorimotor concepts such as means–end, causality, etc.	Non-contingent use of smile and vocalizations	Stereotypic behaviours	Excessive use of vocatives
Reaching and grasping objects	Spatial representations	Does not understand reactions, actions and expressions from adults	Social autonomy: problems with feeding, washing, dressing, moving by themselves	Egocentric use of talk
Hand coordination	Knowledge and use of objects	Low social responsivity		Problems referring to external objects and events
Sound-hand coordination	Relationships between objects (in, on, under, at the side of)	Joint attention	Physical and personal image	Some children reverse personal names and pronouns
Crawling	Exploration of the environment	Difficulty establishing cycles of interaction, social games, routines (regularity and anticipation)	Understanding social situations	Topic maintenance problems
Walking	Social understanding.	Absence of typical communicative gestures such as offering, requesting, pointing, etc	Relationships with peers	Behaviours and facial expressions which are not adequate to the communicative context
Balance	Conservation and other logical operations		Social norms	
Self-initiated mobility				
Movement in space and movement around the environment				

example, suggested that blind infants should be encouraged to explore manually their mother's face.

It is important that an intervention programme provides parents with alternative strategies for interacting with their blind children. It is not enough for parents to understand their children's behaviours, it is important for parents to go out of their way to foster social interaction with their blind children. Urwin (1984a) noted that parents used vocalizations in the form of successive imitations, alternation of sounds, and "dialogues" at a distance with their children. She also found that behaviours with strong physical contact and movement such as tickling and balancing the child were both pleasurable and could develop as games and routines with clear turn-taking characteristics. These alternative routes to interaction are not always discovered spontaneously by parents of blind children; thus, an intervention programme can play an important role in suggesting such strategies and fostering them.

In summary, it is important for parents and their blind infants to develop social routines together, involving a clear format that allows for the child to participate socially; where children can take turns, vocalize, and begin to use their first words. Such contexts provide the foundation for a secure attachment and the functional basis for communication.

As far as motor development is concerned, it is important to note that blind children have particular problems in this area due to the lack of visual feedback (see also Chapter 2). Thus, blind children and their parents need to participate in activities that help the children develop and reach normal motor milestones such as head control, rolling over, sitting up, crawling, walking, and so on. In addition, strategies to encourage exploration of objects and the environment need to be developed. Fraiberg (1971) suggests that blind children need to learn to put their hands together in the midline, a prerequisite for the manipulation of objects with both hands. Thus, one can encourage blind infants to put both hands around their feeding bottle, play pat-a-cake, and offer objects in the child's midline. Toy frames are available that have a number of hanging objects which the child can reach to play with either standing or sitting (or even lying down if appropriate). There are also objects that require the child to use both hands in order to operate them. For example, objects with a lever that needs to be pulled down for something else to happen, containers that can be held and filled, an object that can be pulled apart only with both hands. The child should be encouraged to develop an upright position, either sitting, or standing, as this position strengthens the muscles that support the head and the trunk as well as their legs and arms, preparing them for crawling and later walking. Thus, the child needs to discover that the upright position is interesting and the use of objects, play frames, or play mats with different sensory and auditory experiences can provide an incentive for the child to remain in the upright position. Parents should actively encourage children to crawl and later to walk, as blind children will most certainly feel unsure as they can not see where they are going. Talking to children while they attempt to become more mobile and offering them objects that are just outside their reach can both help to encourage the child to develop motorically, especially crawling. As far as walking is concerned, blind children have no models of people walking as they can not see how other people do it, but also they are not able to see where they are going, which makes it a difficult milestone to reach for many children. A couple of ideas to help blind children walk include putting the children's feet on top of the adults' feet and walking with them in that way and/or putting a string across a room from point A to B and guiding blind children to hold on to the rope while they take their first steps (Lowenfeld, 1971).

Other authors have suggested the need for early physical intervention to help blind children's knee and hip extensors' strength (Wyatt, & Ng, 1997), in combination with a diet to avoid fat. Similarly, Warren (1994) has suggested the usefulness of physical exercise for blind children in order to avoid delays in motor development. These ideas are in agreement with other authors' suggestions to improve physical fitness and muscular strength in blind children (Janowski & Evans, 1981; Seelye, 1983).

It is also important for blind children to be able to orient themselves around their environment. Thus, it is important for furniture not to be moved regularly. Also, it is helpful to have objects that make a characteristic noise in particular areas of the house, for example, a clock. In this way, they become points of reference for children to orient themselves. It is also useful for parents to always enter and exit rooms by the same way, and actively put landmarks such as specific toys or objects in each room, so that the child can easily identify each one of them (Joffee, 1988).

As far as cognitive development is concerned, many authors underline the need to have adequate sensory stimulation for blind infants, to avoid isolation, and to provide the context from which meaning derives (Olson, 1987; Sostek, 1991). This is particularly relevant for children who have residual vision which needs to be used as much as possible. In the case of totally blind children, sensory stimulation will include the auditory, olfactory, tactual, and taste channels. For example, in the case of touch, the child should explore objects of different sizes, textures, shapes, etc. Similarly, in terms of audition, children should be exposed to objects that make different noises so that they can recognize the objects by the sound they make. In all activities it is important to provide children with the opportunity to experience and perceive the objects in question by a number of different channels (touching it, smelling it, hearing what sound it makes). This fosters the integration of information for the purpose of object identification. From early on language should be used to accompany social activities of this kind, so that blind children begin to realize that objects and activities have names in language.

Another area of interest in cognitive development in blind children has been the development of object permanence, causality, and conservation. For object permanence, it is thought that situations that allow the child to search for an object by its sound are particularly useful. Thus, Fraiberg (1971) suggests the use of a board or table, which is put in front of the blind child, who is sitting down. On top of this board or table different objects are placed that make different noises and feel different to the touch. This activity allows the child to explore the objects and search for them. It is also possible for the adult to ask the child to find a particular object. Olson (1987) further suggests that objects that continue to vibrate, move, or make a sound after the child pushes them or hits them, can help the child understand the notion of causality. He also suggests that materials such as plasticine, which allow different shapes to be made out of the same material, can help the child develop and understand the concept of conservation. The more typical use of containers to be filled with rice, beans, or water can also be used with blind children for experience with the notion of conservation. Other devices such as the "little room" (Nielsen, 1991) have also been useful to facilitate understanding of spatial relationships and object permanence in congenitally blind infants between 5 and 19 months of age.

In terms of personal and social development and exploration of the environment, it is essential that parents do not develop an overprotective attitude towards their blind children. Parents need to be advised to let the children experiment with their environment. Thus, children need to try to move, crawl, and walk, first in a reduced, safe space such as on a mat or carpet, and then gradually to move further out to the whole room, the house, and outside. It may be necessary to re-arrange the home to remove dangerous objects or pieces of furniture that may be in the child's way and limit the possibilities for exploration. It will also be important for parents to actively teach their blind children everyday personal care such as feeding, dressing, and washing. Blind children can not learn by observation nor by visual imitation, so self-help skills need to be taught.

Lack of visual information also has repercussions for language learning, as we have discussed in previous chapters. For the child to realize the nature of the articulatory movements involved in speech, it is useful if parents make contact between their mouths and their children's skin, for example, their face or head. This should be done both when the parent is talking but also when the parent is silent, so that blind children can learn the difference. In addition, blind children should be encourage to explore manually the parents' lips, mouth, and neck, while they are talking, so again children can relate speech with mouth–tongue movements and phonation. It is useful if the parent can imitate children's first sounds and help them to feel the sound by touching the parents' phonatory apparatus.

When the child moves on to articulate first words, parents can use both imitations and recasts, where the parent expands what the child has just said, to engage in dialogue with their children. It is important to provide blind children with a context for interaction and activities, but it is important not to have a constant running commentary describing everything going on—selectivity and periods of silence are also important to reflect and think through an experience (Rowland, 1984). For example, if one can hear voices approaching it may be useful to tell the child who is coming, or if particular noises of machinery, trucks, or other objects are apparent, it may be useful to describe them. As the child explores an object, the parent can describe its physical characteristics and its function, and thus go beyond mere labelling (Kekelis & Andersen, 1984). In addition, the use of songs, rhymes, and stories provide useful formats for engaging with the child, also at a distance. For example, one can take turns at singing a song; the mother can be in the kitchen while the blind child can be in the playroom, but they are in contact via the song. These formats allow for both turn taking and role reversal, which may help blind children understand speaker–listener roles in language, especially with respect to the correct use of personal pronouns (Rogow, 1981). Questions can also clarify the speaker–listener roles in conversation: "What do I have on my head?" followed by "what do you have on your head?" force the blind child to experience the differences in perspective when participating in dialogue (Evans & Johnson, 1988).

The previous discussion on activities related to intervention only provide a very basic sketch of possible suggestions. A detailed programme has to take into consideration the individual characteristics of the child and needs to have concrete relevance to the child's total situation. In that sense, intervention with blind children should be highly individualized.

HOW EFFECTIVE IS EARLY INTERVENTION?

In a review article, White, Taylor, and Moss (1992) argue that, due to the lack of well-controlled experimental evidence on parental involvement on early intervention, it is impossible to conclude that parental involvement makes early intervention more effective. Unfortunately, White et al. did not include intervention with blind children in their study. This situation is characteristic of work with blind children. There is a dearth of research in most areas of functioning of blind children and intervention is no exception (Davidson & Harrison, 1997). Thus, there are a handful of studies that involve early intervention with blind children, none of which allow for firm conclusions about the effectiveness of early intervention. Some of the problems are methodological in nature. Thus, most of the intervention studies have included small numbers of blind children posing difficulties of generalizability from a small, heterogeneous group to the general population. In addition, the intervention programmes all have their own framework, time-involvement, and objectives, which make comparisons across programmes difficult. Furthermore, very few studies include a control group, where blind children are not provided with intervention, as this is deemed unethical—it is difficult to leave out a child from an intervention programme that has anticipated positive outcomes. Ideally studies should include control groups of sighted children as well as blind children.

Consequently, the design of most intervention studies with blind children involve assessment before and after the intervention programme. Most studies report positive gains after participation in an intervention programme. Olson (1987) reviewed a number of intervention studies with blind children. Table 7.3

TABLE 7.3

Analysis of three intervention programmes with young blind children (based on Olsen, 1987)

Authors	Objectives	Intervention Details	Parents	Subjects	Design	Results
Adelson & Fraiberg (1974)	Hand–sound coordination	Bi-monthly visits to the home and monthly video recordings until 2 years of age	Initial observation followed by guidance to parents	10 blind children aged 1–8 months	Post-intervention comparisons with norms for sighted children and with other blind children	Better results for the blind children in the intervention vs. control conditions
Bregani et al. (1981)	Multidisciplinary team. To help parents with play and learning activities. To reduce emotional problems	Weekly one-hour visits for one year	Direct work with parents	8 blind children aged 8–24 months	Pre-test and post-test	Reduction of stereotypic behaviours: advances in motor and language development
Fraiberg (1977)	Guidance for parent–child interaction	Bi-monthly visits to the child's home	Assessment and guidance to parents	10 blind children	Pre-test and post-test	Progress more like that of sighted children for measures of attachment, cognitive, motor, and language development

presents in summary form the results of these. It is clear that the three intervention programmes gave a great deal of importance to assessment and guidance to parents. They all had positive results for the children. Tables 7.4 and 7.5 further illustrate some of the effects of early intervention on blind children from studies that involved both a control group of blind children without intervention, and a control group of sighted children. Table 7.4 concentrates on motor development, whereas Table 7.5 details the development of object permanence. These data suggest that children who were able to participate in an early intervention programme had better outcomes than children who did not (Fraiberg, 1977). The blind children who were involved in intervention were more like sighted children than those who did not participate in intervention.

In conclusion, although the data available on the effectiveness of early intervention are very meagre, what is available is positive and should encourage us to foster the implementation of early intervention with blind children as well as detailed studies that evaluate such intervention. Early intervention programmes should involve detailed assessment of blind children's development and their familial context, should involve parents, should promote activities that are just ahead of what children can do by themselves, should involve multidisciplinary consultations, and should involve regular monitoring of progress that allows for

TABLE 7.4

Comparison of motor development in blind children with and without intervention
(Pérez-Pereira & Castro, 1994)

| Behaviour | Blind Children | | Sighted children |
	Intervention	Non-intervention	
Sitting alone for a few seconds	6.8	12	8 months
Turning over	7.3	12	7 months
Sitting alone (stable)	8.0	12	9 months
Support themselves on hands and knees	9.3	–	10 months
A few steps being held by both hands	10.8	18	11 months
A few steps holding on to furniture	–	18	12 months
Standing up alone	11.0	23	10 months
Walk a few steps alone	15.3	30	13 months
Walk across a room walking	19.3	36	15 months

TABLE 7.5

Comparison between blind children with and without intervention
with reference to object permanence, in months

Study	Subjects	Stage III	Stage IV	Stage V
Piaget, 1937	3 sighted children	4–8	8–12	12–18
Fraiberg, 1977	10 blind children with intervention	6-8	9	>10
Bigelow, 1986	5 blind children without-intervention	20.5	20.8	22.6
Rogers & Puchalsky, 1988	11 blind + 9 visually-impaired children without intervention	16–17	19	20–22

adjustments and changes to be made to the programme. We cannot emphasize enough the importance of a positive, regular, and informative relationship between specialists and parents so that parents can be provided with detailed suggestions for activities to engage in with their blind children. Progress can then be evaluated regularly, feedback given, and encouragement provided. This close relationship between parents and specialists will continue throughout the preschool years and will have added importance when the blind child is integrated in the regular classroom (Odom et al., 1996; Webster & Roe, 1998).

Notes

[1] Nevertheless, the use of blindfolded sighted controls is not free of problems in tasks that demand gathering information through manual exploration. Manual exploration by blindfolded children is incomplete, the information they gather is limited, and their performance in these tasks is generally worse than that of their sighted or blind agemates.

[2] The mean age of acquisition in months is given, followed by the difference in relation to the mean age of acquisition in the sighted children studied by Bayley (1969).

[3] These two children, who were prematurely born, suffered from physical problems with their tendons. This circumstance prevented them from walking normally, and for this reason they had to be operated upon.

[4] Other authors (Als, Tronick, & Brazelton, 1980; Bower, 1974) have reported an earlier appearance of this behaviour (around 5 months of age), although evidence is based on occasional observations.

[5] For instance, Rogers and Puchalski (1988) used the following task to test the achievement of Stage 4: The examiner placed a small object in his or her own hand and allowed the child to feel the object there. Then, still with the child's hand on the object in the adult's hand, the adult's hand moved under a washcloth placed on the floor. The adult then removed the child's hand from under the cloth, leaving the object under the cloth, and removed his or her hand from the cloth. The adult had the child feel the adult's hand to realize that the object was no longer there, and then the adult encouraged the child to find the object. To pass the item the child must then search and retrieve the object from under the washcloth.

[6] See Reynell (1979) for a description of the abilities involved in every scale.

[7] The BDI is an inventory designed for non-impaired children that assesses five domains of development: Personal-Social, Adaptive, Motor, Communication, and Cognitive.

[8] Coinciding with Landau's (1991) findings, other authors have also found that congenitally blind children show difficulties in locating objects in their original position in a 90° rotation task (Bower, 1989).

[9] Topological space involves relationships of proximity or closeness, order or spatial sequence, continuity and shape. Euclidean or metric space is mainly based on the concept of distance between objects, and implies a general system of spatial organization based on coordinate axes. This requires the conservation of angles, straight lines, curves and distances.

[10] In event representation the information of the temporal sequence of actions in a familiar event or everyday situation is organized in a coherent way (Nelson, 1986). This type of representation appears very early in the development of children, probably before they form conceptual representations of the world. In this familiar and regular situation, the first words, such as *down,* produced by a child when he pulls down a tower made of cubes, form part of the sequences of actions that occur in the situation, but the words do not have a conceptual status yet. The child does not use the word *down* in other circumstances (for instance, when an object falls down or is dropped). The use of the word is contextualised. On the other hand, prototypical representation occurs when the children are in the process of forming a concept or a categorical representation (Rosch, 1973, 1978). The children do not form a category in its full, adult form from the beginning. They start to fill in a category with some prototypes or best examples of this category, and later they include other instances of this category based on their familiar resemblance with the prototype. Thus, at the beginning, children may be using a word only with the prototypes, but not with other examples of the category. For instance, this happens when a child uses the word *table* with a canonical example of a table made of wood and with four legs, but not with other instances of table, such as a triangular table made of iron and glass.

[11] Maxfield (1936) found the coefficient of egocentricity by dividing the number of sentences with self as subject by those sentences with another person or persons and things as subject.

[12] In spite of this, Webster and Roe (1998, p. 91) affirmed that few significant delays in syntactic development "cannot be explained in terms of differences in exposure, i.e. the language being used around the child".

[13] These were the eight most prevalent semantic relationships produced by children speaking different languages: Agent + Action; Action + Object; Agent + Object; Action + Locative; Entity + Locative; Possessor + Possession; Attribute + Entity; and Demonstrative + Entity. It was estimated that they account for over 75% of children's two-word speech (Brown, 1973).

[14] However, from a methodological point of view, Hobson and colleagues' evidence (Brown et al., 1997) is rather weak, since the instruments they employed are not appropiate for use with blind children. For instance, they used the WISC test to measure blind children's intelligence and to form the groups.

[15] Pérez-Pereira (1999) did not find any developmental pattern similar to that found in *ego-anchored children* by Budwig (1990). These children, initially, used forms such as *my* or *me* for *I* in utterances with a high degree of agentivity. In fact, no uses of Spanish equivalent forms of *my* or *me* instead of *I* were observed.

[16] However, as McCune (1991) pointed out, reporting throughout Dunlea's (1989) text is in terms of proportions of categories, often omitting total frequency from tables, which constitutes a methodological pitfall.

[17] Regarding requests, Urwin (1978) found that the first requests expressed in early language by blind children are requests for an action related to the self, with request for objects beginning a little later, at 20 months.

References

Adelson, E., & Fraiberg, S. (1974). Gross motor development in infants blind from birth. *Child Development, 45*, 114–126.

Aguirre, C. (1995). *La adquisición de las categorías gramaticales en español*. Unpublished doctoral Dissertation. Universidad Autónoma de Madrid, Spain.

Ainsworth, M., Bell, S., & Stayton, D. (1974). Infant–mother attachment and social development: "Socialization" as a product of reciprocal responsiveness to signals. In M.P Richards (Ed.), *The integration of a child into a social world* (pp. 99–135). Cambridge, UK: Cambridge University Press.

Als, H., Tronick, E., & Brazelton, T.B. (1980a). Affective reciprocity and the development of autonomy: The study of a blind infant. *Journal of the American Academy of Child Psychiatry, 19*, 22–40.

Als, H., Tronick, E., & Brazelton, T.B. (1980b). Stages of early behavioral organization: The study of a sighted infant and a blind infant in interaction with their mothers. In T.M. Field (Ed.), *High risk infants and children, adult and peer interaction* (pp. 181–204). New York: Academic Press.

Alvira, F. (1988). *Ceguera y sociedad*. Madrid, Spain: ONCE.

Andersen, E.S., Dunlea, A., & Kekelis, L. (1984). Blind children's language: Resolving some differences. *Journal of Child Language, 11*, 645–664.

Andersen, E.S., Dunlea, A., & Kekelis, L.S. (1993). The impact of input: Language acquisition in the visually impaired. *First Language, 13*, 23–49.

Andersen, E.S., & Kekelis, L. (1986). The role of sibling input in the language socialization of younger blind children. In J. Connor-Linton, C.J. Hall, & M. McGinnis (Eds.), *Southern California occassional papers in linguistics: Vol. 11. Social and cognitive perspectives on language* (pp. 141–156). Los Angeles: University of Southern California.

Aparici, M., Capdevila, M., Serra, M., & Serrat, E. (1996). Adquisición y desarrollo de la sintaxis: La oración compuesta. In M. Pérez-Pereira (Ed.), *Estudios sobre la adquisición del castellano, catalán, euskera y gallego* (pp. 207–216). Santiago de Compostela, Spain: Publicaciones de la Universidad de Santiago de Compostela.

Austin, J.L. (1962). *How to do things with words*. Oxford, UK: Clarendon.

Baldwin, D.A. (1995). Understanding the link between joint attention and language. In C. Moore & P.J. Dunham (Eds.), *Joint attention: Its origins and role in development* (pp. 53–66). Hillsdale, NJ: Lawrence Erlbaum Associates Inc.

169

Baldwin, V. (1993). Population demographics. In J.W. Reiman & P.A. Johnson (Eds.), *Proceedings of the National Symposium on Children and Youth who are deaf-blind* (pp. 53–66). New York: Teaching Research Publications.

Baron-Cohen, S. (1987). Autism and symbolic play. *British Journal of Developmental Psychology, 5,* 139–148.

Baron-Cohen, S. (1989). Perceptual role-taking and protodeclarative pointing in autism. *British Journal of Developmental Psychology, 7,* 113–127.

Baron-Cohen, S. (1991a). Precursors to a theory of mind: Understanding attention. In A. Whiten (Ed.), *Natural theories of mind: Evolution, development, and simulation of everyday mindreading* (pp. 233–251). Oxford, UK: Blackwell.

Baron-Cohen, S. (1991b). The theory of mind deficit in autism: How specific is it? *British Journal of Developmental Psychology, 9,* 301–314.

Baron-Cohen, S. (1995). *Mindblindness: An essay on autism and theory of mind.* Cambridge, MA: MIT Press.

Baron-Cohen, S., Leslie, A.M., & Frith, U. (1985). Does the autistic child have a theory of mind? *Cognition, 21,* 37–46.

Barrera, M., & Vella, D. (1987). Disabled and nondisabled infants' interactions with their mothers. *American Journal of Occupational Therapy, 41,* 168–172.

Barrett, M. (1983). The early acquisition and development of meaning of action-related words. In T.B. Seiler & W. Wannenmacher (Eds.), *Concept development and the development of word meaning* (pp. 191–209). Berlin, Germany: Springer-Verlag.

Barrett, M. (1986). Early semantic representation and early word-usage. In S.A. Kuczaj & M.D. Barrett (eds.), *The development of word meaning* (pp. 39–68). New York: Springer-Verlag.

Barrett, M. (1989). Early language development. In A. Slater & G. Bremner (Eds.), *Infant development* (pp. 211–241). Hove, UK: Lawrence Erlbaum Associates Ltd.

Barrett, M. (1995). Early lexical development. In P. Fletcher & B. MacWhinney (Eds.), *The handbook of child language* (pp. 362–392). Oxford, UK: Blackwell.

Barrett, M., Harris, M., & Chasin, J. (1991). Early lexical development, and maternal speech: A comparison of children's initial and subsequent uses of words. *Journal of Child Language, 18,* 21–34.

Bartsch, K., & Wellman, H.M. (1989). Young children's attribution of action to beliefs and desires. *Child Development, 60,* 946–964.

Bates, E., Camaioni, L., & Volterra, V. (1975). The acquisition of performatives prior to speech. *Merrill-Palmer Quarterly, 21,* 205–226.

Bateson, M.C. (1979). The epigenesis of conversational interaction: A personal account of research development. In M. Bullowa (Ed.), *Before speech: The beginning of interpersonal communication* (pp. 63–77). Cambridge, UK: Cambridge University Press.

Bayley, N. (1969). *Bayley scales of infant development.* New York: Psychological Corporation.

Behl, D.D., Akers, A.F., Boyce, G.C., & Taylor, M.J. (1996). Do mothers interact differently with children who are visually impaired? *Journal of Visual Impairment and Blindness, 90,* 501–511.

Benveniste, E. (1974). La estructura de los pronombres. In E. Benveniste, *Problemas de lingüística general.* México, Mexico: Siglo XXI Editores.

Bigelow, A., & Bryan, A. (1982, June). *The understanding of spatial prepositions "in", "on", and "under" in blind and sighted preschool children.* Paper presented at the conference of the *Canadian Psychological Association.* Montreal, Canada.

Bigelow, A.E. (1983). Development of the use of sound in the search behavior of infants. *Developmental Psychology, 19,* 317–321.

Bigelow, A.E. (1986). The development of reaching in blind children. *British Journal of Developmental Psychology, 4,* 355–366.

Bigelow, A.E. (1987). Early words of blind children. *Journal of Child Language, 14,* 47–56.

Bigelow, A.E. (1988). Blind children's concepts of how people see. *Journal of Visual Impairment and Blindness, 82,* 65–68.

Bigelow, A.E. (1990). Relationships between the development of language and thought in young blind children. *Journal of Visual Impairment and Blindness, 15,* 414–419.

Bigelow, A.E. (1991a). Spatial mapping of familiar locations in blind children. *Journal of Visual Impairment and Blindness, 85,* 113–117.

Bigelow, A.E. (1991b). The effects of distance and intervening obstacles on visual inference in blind and sighted children. *International Journal of Behavioral Development, 14,* 273–283.

Bigelow, A.E. (1992a). Blind children's ability to predict what another sees. *Journal of Visual Impairment and Blindness, 86,* 181–184.

Bigelow, A.E. (1992b). Locomotion and search behavior in blind infants. *Infant Behavior and Development, 15,* 179–189.

Bigelow, A.E. (1995). The effect of blindness on the early development of the self. In P. Rochat (Ed.), *The self in infancy: Theory and research* (pp. 327–347). Amsterdam: Elsevier.

Bigelow, A.E. (1996). Blind and sighted children's spatial knowledge of their home environments. *International Journal of Behavioral Development, 19,* 797–816

Bigelow, A.E. (1997, April). *The development of joint attention in blind infants.* Paper presented at the conference of the Society for Research in Child Development, Washington DC.

Blank, H.R. (1975). Reflections on the special senses in relation to the development of affect with special emphasis on blindness. *Journal of the American Psychoanalytical Association, 23,* 32–50.

Blass, T., Freedman, N., & Steingart, I. (1974). Body movement and verbal encoding in the congenitally blind. *Perceptual and Motor Skills, 39,* 279–293.

Bloom, L., Lightbown, P., & Hood, L. (1975). Structure and variation in child language. *Monographs of the Society for Research in Child Development, 40* (2, Serial No. 160).

Bloom, P. (1993). Overview: Controversies in language acquisition. In P. Bloom (Ed.), *Language acquisition: Core readings* (pp. 5–48). New York: Harvester Wheatsheaf.

Bloom, P. (1994). Possible names: The role of syntax-semantics mapping in the acquisition of nominals. In L. Gleitman & B. Landau (Eds.), *The acquisition of the lexicon* (pp. 297–329). Cambridge, MA: MIT Press.

Bondurant, J.L., Romeo, D.J., & Kretschmer, R. (1983). Language behaviors of mothers of children with normal and delayed language. *Language, Speech and Hearing Services in Schools, 14,* 233–242.

Bower, T.G.R. (1974). *Development in infancy.* San Francisco: Freeman.

Bower, T.G.R. (1977). *The perceptual world of the child.* London: Open Books.

Bower, T.G.R. (1989). *The rational infant: Learning in infancy.* New York: Freeman.

Bowerman, M. (1978).The acquisition of word meaning: An investigation into some current conflicts. In N. Waterson & C. Snow (Eds.), *The development of communication: Social and pragmatic factors in language acquisition* (pp. 263–287). London: Wiley.

Bowerman, M. (1982). Reorganizational processes in lexical and syntactic development. In E. Wanner & L.R. Gleitman (Eds.), *Language acquisition: The state of the art* (pp. 319–346). Cambridge, UK: Cambridge University Press.

Bregani, P., Cepellini, C., Cerebalini, R., Contini, G., Damascellini, A., Livingstone, J.B., Premoli, M., & Rocca, A. (1981). Blind children: Prevention of emotional disturbances by early intervention with parents and child. *Courier, 31,* 256–262.

Brieland, D.M. (1950). A comparative study of the speech of blind and sighted children. *Speech Monographs, 17,* 99–103.

Brigaudiot, M., Danon-Boileau, L., & Morgenstern, A. (1996, July). *Selfwords in discourse and narratives.* Paper presented at the 7th international congress for the study of child language, Istanbul, Turkey.

Brown, R. (1973). *A first language.* Cambridge, MA: Harvard University Press.

Brown, R., Hobson, R.P., Lee, A., & Stevenson, J. (1997). Are there "autistic-like" features in congenitally blind children? *Journal of Child Psychology and Psychiatry, 38,* 693–703.

Bruner, J.S. (1978). Learning how to do things with words. In J.S. Bruner & A. Garton (Eds.), *Human growth and development: The Wolfson lectures* (pp. 62–84). Oxford, UK: Clarendon Press.

Bruner, J.S. (1982). Formats of language acquisition. *American Journal of Semiotics, 1,* 1–16.

Bruner, J.S. (1983). *Child's talk: Learning to use language.* New York: Norton.

Budwig, N. (1990). A functional approach to the acquisition of personal pronouns. In G. Conti–Ramsden & C.E. Snow (Eds.), *Children's language: Vol. 7* (pp. 121–146). Hillsdale, NJ: Lawrence Erlbaum Associates Inc.

Buium, N., Rynders, J., & Turnure, J. (1973). Early maternal linguistic environment of normal and nonnormal language–learning children. In *Proceedings of the 81st annual convention of the American Psychological Association* (pp. 79–80). Washington, DC: American Psychological Association.

Burlingham, D. (1961). Some notes on the development of the blind. *The Psychoanalytic Study of the Child, 16,* 121–145.

Burlingham, D. (1964). Hearing and its role in the development of the blind. *The Psychoanalytic Study of the Child, 19,* 95–112.

Burlingham, D. (1965). Some problems of ego development in blind children. *The Psychoanalytic Study of the Child, 20,* 194–208.

Butterworth, J. (1991). The ontogeny and phylogeny of joint visual attention. In A. Whiten (Ed.), *Natural theories of mind: Evolution, development, and simulation of everyday mindreading* (pp. 223–232). Oxford, UK: Blackwell.

Campos, J.J., & Stenberg, C.R. (1981). Perception, appraisal, and emotion: The onset of social referencing. In M. Lamb & L.R. Sherrod (Eds.), *Infant social cognition: Empirical and theoretical considerations* (pp. 273–314). Hillsdale, NJ: Lawrence Erlbaum Associates Inc.

Caputo, D. (1973). Cause ed effetti del verbalismo nei non vedenti. *L'Educacione dei Minorati della Viste, 4,* 18–23.

Carpenter, M., Nagell, K., & Tomasello, M. (1998). Social cognition: joint attention and communicative competence from 9 to 15 months of age. *Monographs of the Society for Research in Child Development, 63* (4, serial no. 255).

Carreiras, M., & Codina, B. (1992). Spatial cognition of the blind and sighted visual and amodal hypotheses. *Cahiers de Psychologie Cognitive, 12,* 51–78.

Casby, M.W. (1986) A pragmatic perspective of repetition in child language. *Journal of Psycholinguistic Research, 15*(2), 127–140.

Cassidy, K.W. (1998). Preschoolers' use of desires to solve theory of mind problems in a pretense context. *Developmental Psychology, 34,* 503–511.

Castro, J., & Pérez-Pereira, M. (1996). Funciones comunicativas del lenguaje de niños ciegos y videntes [Communicative functions of the language of blind and sighted children]. *Infancia y Aprendizaje, 74,* 139–154.

Charney, R. (1980). Speech roles and the development of personal pronouns. *Journal of Child Language, 7,* 509–528.

Chess, S. (1971). Autism in children with congenital rubella. *Journal of Autism and Childhood Schizophrenia, 1,* 33–47.

Chiat, S. (1983). If I were you and I were me: The analysis of pronouns in a pronoun-reversing child. *Journal of Child Language, 9,* 359–379.

Chiat, S. (1986). Personal pronouns. In P. Fletcher & M. Garman (Eds.), *Language acquisition (2nd ed.)* (pp. 339–355). Cambridge, UK: Cambridge University Press.

Civelli, E.M. (1983). Verbalism in young blind children. *Journal of Visual Impairment and Blindness, 77,* 61–63.

Clark, E.V. (1978). From gesture to word: On the natural history of deixis in language acquisition. In J.S. Bruner & A. Garton (Eds.), *Human growth and development* (pp. 85–120). Oxford, UK: Oxford University Press.

Clifton, R.K., Rochat, P., Litovsky, R.Y., & Perris, E.E. (1991). Object representation guides infant's reaching in the dark. *Journal of Experimental Psychology: Human Perception and Performance, 17,* 323–329.

Conti-Ramsden, G. (1990). Maternal recasts and other contingent replies to language-impaired children. *Journal of Speech and Hearing Disorders, 55,* 262–274.

Conti-Ramsden, G., & Friel-Patti, S. (1983). Mothers' discourse adjustments to language-impaired and non-language impaired chidlren. *Journal of Speech and Hearing Disorders, 48,* 360–367.

Conti-Ramsden, G., & Pérez-Pereira, M. (1997). *Verbal interaction between blind children and their mothers.* Paper presented at the 7th European conference on developmental psychology, Rennes, France.

Conti-Ramsden, G., & Pérez-Pereira, M. (in press). Conversational interactions between mothers and their infants: The case of congenital blindness. *Journal of Visual Impairment and Blindness.*

Cromer, R.F. (1973). Conservation by the congenitally blind. *British Journal of Psychology, 64,* 241–250.

Cromer, R.F. (1991). *Language and thought in normal and handicapped children.* Oxford, UK: Blackwell.

Curcio, F. (1978). Sensorimotor functioning and communication in mute autistic children. *Journal of Autism and Childhood Schizophrenia, 8,* 281–292.

Curson, A. (1979). The blind nursery school child. *Psychoanalytical Study of the Child, 34,* 51–83.

Cutsford, T.D. (1951). *The blind in school and society.* New York: American Foundation for the Blind.

Dale, P., & Crain-Thoreson, C. (1993). Pronoun reversals: Who, when and why? *Journal of Child Language, 20,* 573–589.

Davidson, P., & Harrison, G. (1997). The effectiveness of early intervention for children with visual impairments. In M.J. Guralnick (Ed.), *The effectiveness of early intervention* (pp. 483–495). Baltimore: Paul H. Brookes.

Davies, H., Stroud, A., & Green, L. (1988). Maternal language environment of children with intellectual impairment. *American Journal of Mental Retardation, 93,* 144–153.

Davison, M. (1990). [Review of *Language and experience: Evidence from the blind child* by B. Landau and L.R. Gleitman]. *Linguistic, 25,* 384–386.

Dawson, G., Hill, D., Spencer, A., Galpert, L., & Watson, L. (1990). Affective exchanges between young autistic children and their mothers. *Journal of Abnormal Child Psychology, 18,* 335–345.

Dawson, G., & Osterling, J. (1997). Early intervention in autism. In M.J. Guralnick (Ed.), *The effectiveness of early intervention* (pp. 307–326). Baltimore: Paul H. Brookes.

Dekker, R., Drenth, P.J.D., & Zaal, J.N. (1991). Results of the intelligence test for visually impaired children (ITVIC). *Journal of Visual Impairment and Blindness, 85,* 261–267.

Demott, R.M. (1972). Verbalism and affective meaning for blind, severely visually impaired, and normally sighted children. *New Outlook for the Blind, 66,* 1–8.

Dimcovic, N., & Tobin, M.J. (1995). The use of language in simple classification tasks by children who are blind. *Journal of Visual Impairment and Blindness, 89,* 448–459.

Dodd, B. (1979). Lip reading in infants: Attention to speech presented in and out of synchrony. *Cognitive Psychology, 11,* 478–484.

Dodd, B. (1983). The visual and auditory modalities in phonological acquisition. In A.E. Mills (Ed.), *Language acquisition in the blind child: Normal and deficient* (pp. 57–61). London, UK: Croom Helm.

Dodds, A.G., Howarth, C.I., & Carter, D.C. (1982). The mental maps of the blind: The role of previous experience. *Journal of Visual Impairment and Blindness, 76,* 5–12.

Dokecki, P.R. (1966). Verbalism and the blind: A critical review of the concept and the literature. *Exceptional Children, 32,* 525–530.

Dore, J. (1977). "On Them Sheriff": A pragmatic analysis of children's responses to questions. In S. Ervin-Tripp & C. Mitchel-Kernan (Eds.), *Child's discourse* (pp. 139–163). New York: Academic Press.

Dore, J. (1978). Variation in preschool children's conversational performances. In K. Nelson (Ed.), *Children's language: Vol. 1* (pp. 397–444). New York: Gardner Press.

Dote-Kwan, J. (1995). Impact of mothers' interactions on the development of their young visually impaired children. *Journal of Visual Impairment and Blindness, 89,* 46–58.

Dromi, E. (1987). *Early lexical development.* New York: Cambridge University Press.

Dunham, P.J., & Moore, C. (1995). Current themes in research in joint attention. In C. Moore & P.J. Dunham (Eds.), *Joint attention: its origins and role in development* (pp. 15–28). Hillsdale, NJ: Lawrence Erlbaum Associates Inc.

Dunlea, A. (1984). The relation between concept formation and semantic roles: Some evidence from the blind. In L. Feagans, C. Garvey, & R. Golinkoff (Eds.), *The origins and growth of communication* (pp. 224–243). Norwood, NJ: Ablex.

Dunlea, A. (1989). *Vision and the emergence of meaning: Blind and sighted children's early language.* Cambridge, UK: Cambridge University Press.

Dunlea, A., & Andersen, E.S. (1992). The emergence process: Conceptual and linguistic influences on morphological development. *First Language, 12,* 95–115.

Easton, R.D., & Bentzen, B.L. (1987). Memory for verbally presented routes: A comparison of strategies used by blind and sighted people. *Journal of Visual Impairment and Blindness, 81,* 100–105.

Elman, J.L., Bates, E.A., Johnson, M.H., Karmiloff-Smith, A., Parisi, D., & Plunkett, K. (1996). *Rethinking innateness: A connectionist perspective on development.* Cambridge, MA: MIT Press.

Elonen, A.S., & Cain, A.C. (1964). Diagnostic evaluation and treatment of deviant blind children. *American Journal of Orthopsychiatry, 34,* 625–633.

Erin, J.N. (1986). Frequencies and types of questions in the language of visually impaired children. *Journal of Visual Impairment and Blindness, 80,* 670–674.

Evans, C.J., & Johnson, C.J. (1988). Training pragmatic language skills through alternate strategies with a blind multiply handicapped child. *Journal of Visual Impairment and Blindness, 82,* 109–112.

Farrell, K.A., Trief, E., Dietz, S.J., Bonner, M.A., Cruz, D., Ford, E., & Stratton, J.M. (1990). Visually Impaired Infants Research Consortium (VIIRC): First-year results. *Journal of Visual Impairment and Blindness, 84,* 404–410.

Fay, W.H. (1973). On the echolalia of the blind and the autistic child. *Journal of Speech and Hearing Disorders, 38,* 478–488.

Fay, W.H., & Schuler, A.L. (1980). *Emerging language in autistic children.* London: Arnold.

Ferguson, R., & Buultjens, M. (1995). The play behaviour of young blind children and its relationships to developmental stages. *British Journal of Visual Impairment, 13,* 100–107.

Flavell, J.H. (1988). The development of children's knowledge about the mind: From cognitive connections to mental representations. In J. Astington, P. Harris, & D. Olson (Eds.), *Developing theories of mind* (pp. 244–267). New York: Cambridge University Press.

Fletcher, J.E. (1981). Spatial representation in blind children 2: Effects of task variations. *Journal of Visual Impairment and Blindness, 75,* 1–3.

Forján, M., García, S., & Pérez-Pereira, M. (1995). Análise do primeiro léxico producido por nenos galegos. [Analysis of the first lexicon produced by Galician-speaking children]. *Cadernos de Lingua, 11,* 83–101.

Fraiberg, S. (1968). Parallel and divergent patterns in blind and sighted infants. *The Psychoanalytic Study of the Clind, 23,* 264–306.

Fraiberg, S. (1971). Intervention in infancy: A program for blind infants. *Journal of the American Academy of Child Psychiatry, 10,* 381–405.

Fraiberg, S. (1977). *Insights from the blind.* London, UK: Souvenir Press.

Fraiberg, S., & Adelson, E. (1973). Self-representation in language and play: Observations of blind children. *Psychoanalysis Quarterly, 42,* 539–562.

Fraiberg, S., & Adelson, E. (1977). Self-representation in language and play. In S. Fraiberg (Ed.), *Insights from the blind* (pp. 248–270). London: Souvenir Press.

Freedman, D.A., Fox-Colenda, B.J., Margileth, D.A., & Miller, D.H. (1969). The development of the use of sound as a guide to affective and cognitive behavior: A two-phase model. *Child Development, 40,* 1099–1105.

Freeman, R., & Blockberger, S. (1987). Language development and sensory disorder: Visual and hearing impairments. In W. Yule & M. Rutter (Eds.), *Language development and disorders* (pp. 234–247). Oxford, UK: Blackwell.

Frith, U. (1989). *Autism: Explaining the enigma.* Oxford, UK: Blackwell.

Gallaway, C., & Richards, B.J. (1994). *Input and interaction in language acquisition.* Cambridge, UK: Cambridge University Press.

Garwood, S. (1983). *Educating young handicapped children: A developmental approach* (2nd ed.). Rockville, MD: Aspen.

Gassier, J. (1983*). Manual del desarrollo psicomotor del niño. [Handbook of psychomotor development of the child*]. Barcelona, Spain: Toray-Masson.

Gesell, A., & Amatruda, C.S. (1946). *Developmental diagnosis.* New York: Harper & Row.

Gillman, A.E.. & Goddard, D.R. (1974). The 20-year outcome of blind children 2 years old and younger: A preliminary survey. *New Outlook for the Blind, 68,* 1–7.

Gleitman, L.R. (1990). The structural sources of verb meanings. *Language Acquisition, 1,* 3–55.

Gombert, J.E. (1992). *Metalinguistic development.* Hemel Hempstead, UK: Harvester Wheatsheaf.

Gómez, J.C. (1991). Visual behavior as a window for reading the minds of others in primates. In A. Whiten (Ed.), *Natural theories of mind: Evolution, development, and simulation of everyday mindreading* (pp. 195–207). Oxford, UK: Blackwell.

Gómez, J.C., Sarriá, E., & Tamarit, J. (1993). The comparative study of early communication and theories of mind: Ontogeny, phylogeny, and pathology. In S. Baron-Cohen, H. Tager-Flusberg, & D. Cohen (Eds.), *Understanding other minds: Perspectives from autism* (pp. 397–426). Oxford, UK: Oxford University Press.

Goodnow, J.J., & Collins, W.A. (1990). *Development according to parents: The nature, sources and consequences of parents' ideas.* Hillsdale, NJ: Lawrence Erlbaum Associates Inc.

Gottesman, M. (1971). A comparative study of Piaget's developmental schema of sighted children with that of a group of blind children. *Child Development, 42,* 573–580.

Gottesman, M. (1973). Conservation development in blind children. *Child Development, 44,* 824–827.

Gottesman, M. (1976). Stage development of blind children: A Piagetian view. *New Outlook for the Blind, 70,* 94–100

Green, M.R., & Schecter, D.E. (1957). Autistic and symbiotic disorders in three blind children. *Psychiatric Quarterly, 31,* 628–646.

Grice, H.P. (1957). Meaning. *Philosophical Review, 66,* 377–388.

Groenveld, M., & Jan, J.E. (1992). Intelligence profiles of low vision and blind children. *Journal of Visual Impairment and Blindness, 86,* 68–71.

Guralnick, M.J. (1997). Second-generation research in the field of early intervention. In M.J. Guralnick (Ed.), *The effectiveness of early intervention* (pp. 3–20). Baltimore: Paul H. Brookes.

Guralnick, M.J., & Bennett, F.C. (1987). A framework for early intervention. In M.J. Guralnick & F.C. Bennett (Eds.), *The effectiveness of early intervention for at risk and handicapped children* (pp. 3–29). Orlando, FL: Academic Press.

Haith, M.M. (1980*). Rules that babies look by.* Hillsdale, NJ: Lawrence Erlbaum Associates Inc.

Hanzlik, J. (1989). Interactions between mothers and their infants with developmental disabilities: analysis and review. *Physical and Occupational Therapy in Paediatrics, 9,* 33–47.

Happé, F. (1994). *Autism: An introduction to psychological theory.* London: UCL Press.

Harley, R.K. (1963). *Verbalism among blind children: An investigation and analysis.* New York: American Foundation for the Blind.

Harper, F.W. (1978). Gestures of the blind. *Education of the Visually Handicapped,* Spring, *10,* 14–20.

Hartlage, L.C. (1976). Development of spatial concepts in visually deprived children. *Perceptual and Motor Skills, 42,* 255–258.

Hatton, D.D., Bailey, D.B., Burchinal, M.R., & Ferrell, K.A. (1997). Developmental curves of preschool children with vision impairments. *Child Development, 68,* 788–806.

Hatwell, Y. (1966). *Privation sensorielle et intelligence.* Paris: Presses Universitaires de France.

Hayes, S. P. (1942). Alternative scales for the mental measurement of the visually handicapped. *Outlook for the Blind, 42,* 225–230.

Hayes, S.P. (1950). Measuring the intelligence of the blind. In P.A. Zah (Ed.), *Blindness* (pp. 141–173). Princeton, NJ: Princeton University Press.

Helbrügge, T., Lajosi, F., Menara, D., Schanberger, R., & Rautenstrauch, T. (1980*). Diagnostico funcional del desarrollo durante el primer año de vida* [Functional assessment of development during the first year of life]. Alcoy, Spain: Marfil.

Hermelin, B., & O'Connor, N. (1970). *Psychological experiments with autistic children.* Oxford, UK: Pergamon Press.

Hernández-Pina, F. (1984). *Teorías sociopsicolingüísticas y su aplicación a la adquisición del español como lengua materna.* Madrid, Spain: Siglo XXI de España.

Hiroto, D.S., & Seligman, M.E.P. (1975). Generality of learned helplessness in man. *Journal of Personality and Social Psychology, 31,* 311–327.

Hobson, R.P. (1990). On acquiring knowledge about people and the capacity to pretend: A response to Leslie. *Psychological Review, 97,* 114–121.

Hobson, R.P. (1993a). *Autism and the development of mind.* Hillsdale, NJ: Lawrence Erlbaum Associates Inc.

Hobson, R.P. (1993b). Through feeling and sight to self and symbol. In U. Neisser (Ed.), *Ecological and interpersonal knowledge of self* (pp. 254–279). Cambridge, UK: Cambridge University Press.

Hobson, R.P., Brown, R., Minter, M. E., & Lee, A. (1997). "Autism" revisited: The case of congenital blindness. In V. Lewis & G.M. Collis (Eds.), *Blindness and psychological development in young children* (pp. 99–115). Leicester, UK: British Psychological Society Books.

Hoff-Ginsberg, E. (1992). How should frequency input be measured? *First Language, 12,* 233–244.

Holden, G.W. (1988). Adults' thinking about a child-rearing problem: Effects of experience, parental status and gender. *Child Development, 59,* 1623–1632.

Hornik, R., Risenhoover, N., & Gunnar, M. (1987). The effects of maternal positive, neutral, and negative affective communications on infant responses to new toys. *Child Development, 58,* 937–944.

Huertas, J.A., & Ochaita, E. (1992). The externalization of spatial representation by blind persons. *Journal of Visual Impairment and Blindness, 86,* 398–402.

Huttenlocher, J., Haight, W., Bryk, A., Seltzer, M., & Lyons, T. (1991). Early vocabulary growth: Relation to language input and gender. *Developmental Psychology, 27,* 236–248.

Iverson, J.M. (1998). Gesture when there is no visual model. In J.M. Iverson & S. Goldin-Meadow (Eds.), *The nature and functions of gesture in children's communication* (pp. 89–100). San Francisco: Jossey-Bass.

Iverson, J.M. (in press). How to get to the cafeteria: Gesture and speech in blind and sighted children's spatial descriptions. *Developmental Psychology.*

Iverson, J.M., & Goldin-Meadow, S. (1997). What's communication got to do with it? Gesture in congenitally blind children. *Developmental Psychology, 33,* 453–467.

Iverson, J.M., & Goldin-Meadow, S. (1998). Why people gesture when they speak. *Nature, 396,* 228.

Iverson, J.M., Tencer, H.L., & Goldin-Meadow, S. (1998, April). Prelinguistic communication in congenitally blind children. Poster presented at the 11th International conference on infant studies, Atlanta, GA: USA.

Jakobson, R. (1968). *Child language, aphasia, and phonological universals.* The Hague, The Netherlands: Mouton.

Jan, J.E., Freeman, R.D. & Scott, E.P. (1977). *Visual impairment in children and adolescents.* New York: Grune & Stratton.

Janowski, L., & Evans, J. (1981). The exercise capacity of blind children. *Journal of Visual Impairment and Blindness, 75,* 248–281.

Joffee, E. (1988). A home-based orientation and mobility program for infants and toddlers. *Journal of Visual Impairment and Blindness, 82,* 282–285.

Jones, U., & Prior, M. (1985). Motor imitation abilities and neurological signs in autistic children. *Journal of Autism and Developmental Disorders, 15,* 37–49.

Jure, R., Rapin, I., & Tuchman, R.F. (1991). Hearing impaired autistic children. *Developmental Medicine and Child Neurology, 33,* 1062–1072.

Jusczyk, P.W. (1997). *The discovery of spoken language.* Cambridge, MA: MIT Press.

Karmiloff-Smith, A. (1992). *Beyond modularity: A developmental perspective on cognitive science.* Cambridge, MA: MIT Press.

Kaye, K. (1982). *The mental and social life of babies: How parents create persons.* London, UK: Methuen.

Keeler, W.R. (1957). Autistic patterns and defective communication in blind children with retrolental fibroplasia. In P.H. Hoch & J. Zubin (Eds.), *Psychopathology of communication* (pp. 64–83). New York: Grune & Stratton.

Keenan, E.O. (1977). Making it last: repetition in children's discourse. In S. Ervin-Tripp & C. Mitchell-Kernan (Eds.), *Child discourse* (pp. 125–138). New York: Academic.

Kekelis, L.S., & Andersen, E.S. (1984). Family communication styles and language development. *Journal of Visual Impairment and Blindness, 78,* 54–65.

Kekelis, L.S., & Prinz, P.M. (1996). Blind and sighted children with their mothers: The development of discourse skills. *Journal of Visual Impairment and Blindness, 90,* 423–434.

Kephart, J.G., Kephart, C.P., & Schwartz, G.C. (1974). A journey into the world of the blind child. *Exceptional Children, 40,* 421–427.

Kitzinger, M. (1984). The role of repeated and echoed utterances in communication with a blind child. *British Journal of Disorders of Communication, 19,* 135–146.

Kuhl, P.K., & Meltzoff, A.N. (1982). The bimodal perception of speech in infancy. *Science, 190,* 69–72.

Lamb, M.E. & Easterbrooks, M.A. (1981). Individual differences in parental sensitivity: Origins, components, and consequences. In M.E. Lamb & L.R. Sherrod (Eds.), *Infant social cognition: Empirical and theoretical considerations* (pp. 127–153). Hillsdale, NJ: Lawrence Erlbaum Associates Inc.

Landau, B. (1983). Blind children's language is not "meaningless". In A.E. Mills (Ed.), *Language acquisition in the blind child: Normal and deficient* (pp. 62–76). London: Croom Helm.

Landau, B. (1991). Knowledge and its expression in the blind child. In D. Keating & H. Rosen (Eds.), *Constructivist perspectives on developmental psychopathology and atypical development* (pp. 173–192). Hillsdale, NJ: Lawrence Erlbaum Associates Inc.

Landau, B. (1997). Language and experience in blind children: retrospective and prospective. In V. Lewis & G.M. Collis (Eds.), *Blindness and psychological development in young children* (pp. 9–28). Leicester, UK: British Psychological Society.

Landau, B., & Gleitman, L.R. (1985). *Language and experience: Evidence from the blind child.* Cambridge, MA: Harvard University Press.

Landau, B., Spelke, E., & Gleitman, H. (1984). Spatial knowledge in a young blind child. *Cognition, 16,* 225–260.

Lee, A., Hobson, R.P., & Chiat, S. (1994). I, you, me and autism: An experimental study. *Journal of Autism and Developmental Disorders, 24,* 155–176.

Leonard, L.B. (1998). *Children with specific language impairment.* Cambridge, MA: MIT Press.

Leonard, L.B., & Kaplan, L. (1977) A note on imitation and lexical acquisition. *Journal of Child Language, 3,* 449–455.

Leonhardt, M. (1992). *Escala Leonhardt: Escala de desarrollo de niños ciegos de 0–2 años.* Barcelona, Spain: ONCE.

Leslie, A. (1987). Pretense and representation: The origins of theory of mind. *Psychological Review, 94,* 412–426.

Levinson, S.C. (1983). *Pragmatics.* Cambridge, UK: Cambridge University Press.

Lewis, V., & Collis, G.M. (Eds.). (1997a). *Blindness and psychological development in young children.* Leicester, UK: British Psychological Society.

Lewis, V., & Collis, G.M. (1997b). Methodological and theoretical issues associated with the study of children with visual impairment. In V. Lewis & G.M. Collis (Eds.), *Blindness and psychological development in young children* (pp. 1–8), Leicester, UK: British Psychological Society.

Lieven, E. (1997). Variation in cross-linguistic context. In D. Slobin (Ed.), *The crosslinguistic study of language acquisition, Vol. 5* (pp. 199–263). Hillsdale, NJ: Lawrence Erlbaum Associates Inc.

Lieven, E.V.M., Pine, J.M., & Baldwin, G. (1997). Lexically based learning and early grammatical development. *Journal of Child Language, 24,* 187–219.

Lord, C., & Paul, R. (1997). Language and communication in autism. In D.J. Cohen & F.R. Volkmar (Eds.), *Handbook of autism and pervasive developmental disorders* (2nd ed.). New York: Wiley.

Loveland, K.A. (1991). Social affordances and interaction: II. Autism and the affordances of the human environment. *Ecological Psychology, 3,* 335–349.

Loveland, K.A. (1993). Autism, affordances, and the self. In U. Neisser (Ed.), *The perceived self: Ecological and interpersonal sources of self-knowledge.* Cambridge, UK: Cambridge University Press.

Loveland, K.A. (1984). Learning about points of view: Spatial perspective and the acquisition of "I/you". *Journal of Child Language, 11,* 535–556.

Loveland, K.A., McEvoy, R., Tunali, B., & Kelley, M. (1990). Narrative story telling in autism and Down syndrome. *British Journal of Developmental Psychology, 8,* 9–23.

Lowenfeld, B. (1971). *Our blind children: Growing and learning with them.* Springfield, IL: Charles C. Thomas.

Luria, A.R. (1979). *The making of mind: A personal account of Soviet Psychology.* Cambridge, MA: Harvard University Press.

Lyons, J. (1977). *Semantics.* Cambridge, UK: Cambridge University Press.

MacNamara, J. (1972). Cognitive bases of language learning in infants. *Psychological Review, 79,* 1–13.

Maratsos, M. (1983). Some current issues in the study of the acquisition of Grammar. In P.H. Mussen (Ed.), *Handbook of child psychology. Vol. 3* (pp. 707–786). New York: Wiley.

Marshall, N., Hegrenes, J., & Goldstein, S. (1973). Verbal interactions: Mothers and their retarded children versus mothers and their nonretarded children. *American Journal of Mental Deficiency, 77,* 415–419.

Maxfield, K.E. (1936). The spoken language of the blind preschool child: A study of method. *Archives of Psychology,* 201.

McAlpine, L.M., & Moore, C.L. (1995). The development of social understanding in children with visual impairments. *Journal of Visual Impairment and Blindness, 89,* 349–358.

McConachie, H. (1990). Early language development and severe visual impairment. *Child: Care, Health and Development, 16,* 55–61.

McConachie, H.R., & Moore, V. (1994). Early expressive language of severely visually impaired children. *Developmental Medicine and Child Neurology, 36,* 230–240.

McCune, L. (1991). [Review of *Vision and the emergence of meaning: Blind and sighted children's early language* by Anne Dunlea]. *Language and Speech, 34,* 97–103.

McGinnis, A.R. (1981) Functional linguistic strategies of blind children. *Journal of Visual Impairment and Blindness, 75,* 210–214.

McGuire, L.L. (1969). *Psycho-dynamic development problems in the congenitally blind child.* San Diego, CA: University of Southern California.

McGuire, L.L., & Meyers, C.E. (1971). Early personality in the congenitally blind child. *New Outlook for the Blind, 65,* 137–143.

McGurk, H., & MacDonald, J. (1976). Hearing lips and seeing voices. *Nature, 264,* 746–748.

McTear, M.F. (1978). Repetition in child language: Imitation or creation? In R.N. Campbell & P.T. Smith (Eds.), *Recent advances in the psychology of language: Language development and mother-child interaction*. New York: Plenum.

Meadow, K.P. (1980). *Deafness and child development*. Berkeley, CA: University of California Press.

Meltzoff, A.N. (1988). Infant imitation after a 1-week delay: Long term memory for novel acts and multiple stimuli. *Developmental Psychology, 24,* 470–476.

Meltzoff, A.N., & Moore, M.K. (1993). Why faces are special to infants— On connecting the attraction of faces and infants' ability for imitation and cross-modal processing. In B. de Boysson-Bardies, S. de Schonen, P. Jusczyc, P. McNeilage, & J. Morton (Eds.), *Developmental neurocognition: Speech and face processing in the first year of life* (pp. 211–225). Dordrecht, The Netherlands: Kluwer.

Menn, L., & Stoel-Gammon, C. (1995). Phonological development. In P. Fletcher & B. MacWhinney (Eds.), *The handbook of child language* (pp. 335–359). Oxford, UK: Blackwell.

Messer, D.J. (1994). *The development of communication: From social interaction to language*. Chichester, UK: John Wiley & Sons.

Miecznikowski, A., & Andersen, E. (1986). From formulaic to analysed speech: Two systems or one? In J. Connor–Linton, C.J. Hall, & M. McGinnis (Eds.), *Perspectives on language. Southern California Occasional Papers in Linguistics: Vol. 11: Social and cognitive* (pp. 181–202). Los Angeles: University of Southern California.

Miletic, G. (1995). Perspective taking: Knowledge of level 1 and level 2 rules by congenitally blind, low vision, and sighted children. *Journal of Visual Impairment and Blindness, 89,* 514–523.

Millar, S. (1988). Models of sensory deprivation: The nature/nurture dichotomy and spatial representation in the blind. *International Journal of Behavioral Development, 11,* 69–87.

Millar, S. (1994). *Understanding and representing space: Theory and evidence from studies with blind and sighted children*. Oxford, UK: Oxford University Press.

Miller, S.A. (1987). *Developmental research methods*. Englewood Cliffs, NJ: Prentice-Hall.

Miller, S.A. (1988). Parent's beliefs about children's cognitive development. *Child Development, 59,* 259–285.

Mills, A.E. (1983). Acquisition of speech sounds in the visually-handicapped child. In A.E. Mills (Ed.), *Language acquisition in the blind child: Normal and deficient* (pp. 46–56). London: Croom Helm.

Mills, A.E. (1987a). [Review of *Language and experience* by B. Landau & L.R. Gleitman]. *Journal of Child Language, 14,* 397–402.

Mills, A.E. (1987b). The development of phonology in the blind child. In B. Dodd & R. Campbell (Eds.), *Hearing by eye: The psychology of lip reading* (pp. 145–161). Hove, UK: Lawrence Erlbaum Associates Ltd.

Mills, A.E. (1993). Visual handicap. In D. Bishop & K. Mogford (Eds.), *Language development under exceptional circumstances* (pp. 150–164). Hove, UK: Lawrence Erlbaum Associates Ltd.

Minter, M., Hobson, R. P. & Bishop, M. (1998). Congenital visual impairment and theory of mind. *British Journal of Developmental Psychology*, 16, 183–196.

Moerk, E.L. (1989). The fuzzy set called "imitations". In G.E. Speidel & K.E. Nelson (Eds.), *The many faces of imitation in language learning* (pp. 277–303). Berlin, Germany: Springer-Verlag.

Mogford, K. (1993). Oral language acquisition in the prelinguistically deaf. In D. Bishop & K. Mogford (Eds.), *Language development in exceptional circumstances* (pp. 110–131). Hove, UK: Lawrence Erlbaum Associates Ltd.

Moore, V., & McConachie, H. (1994). Communication between blind children and severely visually impaired children and their parents. *British Journal of Developmental Psychology, 12,* 491–502.

Moore, V., & McConachie, H. (1995). How parents can help young visually-impaired children to communicate. *Health Visitor, 68,* 105–107.

Mulford, R. (1983). Referential development in blind children. In A.E. Mills (Ed.), *Language acquisition in the blind child: Normal and deficient* (pp. 89–107). London: Croom Helm.

Mulford, R. (1988). First words of the blind child. In M.D. Smith & J.L. Locke (Eds.), *The emergent lexicon: The child's development of a linguistic vocabulary* (pp. 293–338). New York: Academic Press.

Mundy, P., Sigman, M., Ungerer, J., & Sherman, T. (1986). Defining the social deficits of autism: The contribution of non-verbal communication measures. *Journal of Child Psychology and Psychiatry, 27,* 657–669.

Murray, L., & Trevarthen, C. (1985). Emotional regulation of interactions between two-month–olds and their mothers. In T.M. Field & N.A. Fox (Eds.), *Social perception in infants* (pp. 177–197). Norwood, NJ: Ablex.

Nagera, H., & Colonna, A.B. (1965). Aspects of the contribution of sight to ego and drive development: A comparison of the development of some blind and sighted children. *The Psychoanalytic Study of the Child, 20,* 267–287.

Neisser, U. (1991). Two perceptually given aspects of the self and their development. *Developmental Review, 11,* 197–209.

Neisser, U. (1993). The self perceived. In U. Neisser (Ed.), *The perceived self: Ecological and interpersonal sources of self-knowledge* (pp. 3–21). Cambridge, UK: Cambridge University Press.

Nelson, K. (1973). Structure and strategy in learning to talk. *Monographs of the Society for Research in Child Development, 38*(1–2) Serial No. 149.

Nelson, K. (1985). *Making sense: The acquisition of shared meaning.* New York: Academic Press.

Nelson, K. (Ed.). (1986). *Event knowledge: Structure and function in development.* Hillsdale, NJ: Lawrence Erlbaum Associates Inc.

Nelson, K.E. (1981). Toward a rare-event cognitive comparison theory of syntax acquisition: Insights from work with recasts. In P. Dale & D. Ingram (Eds.), *Child language: An international perspective* (pp. 229–240). Baltimore: University Park Press.

Nelson, K.E., Denninger, M.M., Bonvillian, J.D., Kaplan, B.J., & Baker, N.D. (1984). Maternal input adjustments and non-adjustments as related to children's linguistic advances and to language acquisition theories. In A.D. Pellegrini & T.D. Yawkey (Eds.), *The development of oral and written languages: Readings in developmental and applied linguistics* (pp. 31–56). New York: Ablex.

Newport, E.L. (1977). Motherese: The speech of mothers to young children. In N. Castellan, D. Pisoni, & G. Potts (Eds.), *Cognitive theory, Vol. 2* (pp. 177–217). Hillsdale, NJ: Lawrence Erlbaum Associates Inc.

Nielsen, L. (1991). Spatial relationships in congenitally blind infants: A study. *Journal of Visual Impairment and Blindness, 85,* 11–16.

Ninio, A., & Snow, C. (1996). *Pragmatic development.* Boulder, CD: Westview.

Nordin, V., & Gillberg, C. (1996). Autism spectrum disorders in children with physical or mental disability or both: I. Clinical and epidemiological aspects. *Developmental Medicine and Child Neurology, 38,* 297–313.

Norgate, S. (1996). *Research methods for studying the language of blind children.* Milton Keynes: The Open University.

Norgate, S., Lewis, V., & Collis, G. (1997, September). Developing the capacity to refer: How the study of blind infants informs theoretical frameworks of lexical development. Paper presented to the 7th European conference on developmental psychology. Rennes, France.

Norris, M., Spaulding, P.J., & Brodie, F.H. (1957). *Blindness in children.* Chicago: University of Chicago Press.

Ochaita, E. (1984). Una aplicación de la teoría piagetiana al estudio del conocimiento espacial en niños ciegos [An application of the Piagetian theory to the study of spatial knowledge in blind children]. *Infancia y Aprendizaje, 25,* 81–104.

Ochaita, E. (1993). Ceguera y desarrollo psicológico. In A. Rosa & E. Ochaita (Eds.), *Psicología de la ceguera* (pp. 111–202). Madrid, Spain: Alianza Editorial.

Ochaita, E., & Huertas, J.A. (1993). Spatial representation by persons who are blind: A study of the effects of learning and development. *Journal of Visual Impairment and Blindness, 87,* 37–41.

Ochaita, E., Huertas, J.A., & Espinosa, A. (1991). Representación espacial en los niños ciegos: una investigación sobre las principales variables que la determinan y los procedimientos de objetivación mas adecuados [Spatial representation in blind children]. *Infancia y Aprendizaje, 54,* 53–79.

Ochaita, E., Rosa, A., Pozo, J.I., & Fernández, E. (1985). Clasificaciones y seriaciones: un importante desfase en el desarrollo cognitivo de los ciegos. *Revista de Psicología General y Aplicada, 40,* 395–419.

Odom, S.L., Peck, C.A., Hanson, M., Beckman, P.J., Kaiser, A.P., Lieber, J., Brown, W.H., Horn, E.M., & Schwartz, I.S. (1996). Inclusion at the preschool level: An ecological systems analysis. *Social Policy Reports SRCD, 10*(2–3), 18–30.

Olson, M. (1987). Early intervention for children with visual impairments. In M.J. Guralnick & F.C. Bennett (Eds.), *The effectiveness of early intervention for at risk and handicapped children* (pp. 297–324). Orlando, FL: Academic Press.

Oshima-Takane, Y. (1992). Analysis of pronominal errors: A case study. *Journal of Child Language, 15,* 95–108.

Oshima-Takane, Y., & Benaroya, S. (1989). An alternative view of pronominal errors in autistic children. *Journal of Autism and Developmental Disorders, 19,* 73–85.

Palacios, J. (1987). Contenidos, estructuras y determinantes de las ideas de los padres: Una investigacion empirica. *Infancia y Aprendizaje, 39/40,* 113–136.

Palacios, J. (1990). Parent's ideas about the development and education of their children: Answers to some questions. *International Journal of Behavioral Development, 13,* 137–155.

Parsons, S. (1986a). Function of play in low vision children: Pt. 1. A review of the research and literature. *Journal of Visual Impairment and Blindness, 80,* 627–630.

Parsons, S. (1986b). Function of play in low vision children: Pt. 2. Emerging patterns of behaviour. *Journal of Visual Impairment and Blindness, 80,* 777–784.

Passini, R., & Proulx, G. (1988). Wayfinding without vision: An experiment with congenitally totally blind people. *Environment and Behavior, 20,* 227–252.

Peraita, H., Elosúa, R., & Linares, P. (1992). *Representación de categorías naturales en niños ciegos.* [Representation of natural categories by blind children]. Madrid, Spain: Trotta.

Pérez-Pereira, M. (1989). The acquisition of morphemes: some evidence from Spanish. *Journal of Psycholinguistic Research, 18,* 289–312.

Pérez-Pereira, M. (1991). Algunos rasgos del lenguaje del niño ciego [Some features of the language of the blind child]. *Anales de Psicología, 7,* 197–223.

Pérez-Pereira, M. (1994). Imitations, repetitions, routines, and the child's analysis of language: Insights from the blind. *Journal of Child Language, 21,* 317–337.

Pérez-Pereira, M. (1998). Desarrollo y educación familiar en niños ciegos. [Development and family education of blind children]. In M.J. Rodrigo & J. Palacios (Eds.), *Familia y desarrollo humano* (pp. 483–500). Madrid, Spain: Alianza Editorial.

Pérez-Pereira, M. (1999). Deixis, personal reference, and the use of pronouns by blind children. *Journal of Child Language, 26.*

Pérez-Pereira, M., & Castro, J. (1992). Pragmatic functions of blind and sighted children's language: a twin case study. *First Language, 12,* 17–37.

Pérez-Pereira, M., & Castro, J. (1994). *El desarrollo psicológico de los niños ciegos en la primera infancia* [Psychological development of blind children in the early years]. Barcelona, Spain: Paidós.

Pérez-Pereira, M., & Castro, J. (1995). Repercusiones evolutivas de las formas de interacción y comunicación en el niño ciego [Developmental consequences of interaction and communication in the blind child]. *Substratum, 7,* 103–124.

Pérez-Pereira, M., & Castro, J. (1997). Language acquisition and the compensation of visual deficit: New comparative data on a controversial topic. *British Journal of Developmental Psychology, 15,* 439–459.

Pérez-Pereira, M., & Castro, J. (in press). Syntactic development of Spanish blind children. *Journal of Speech Language and Hearing Research.*

Pérez-Pereira, M., & Conti-Ramsden, G. (submitted). The role of directives in verbal interactions between blind children and their mothers. *Journal of Visual Impairment and Blindness.*

Pérez-Pereira, M., Forján, T., & García, S. (1996). *A comparison of the acquisition of Galician and Spanish forms of possession in bilingual children.* Paper presented at the 7th international congress for the study of child language. Istanbul, Turkey.

Perner, J. (1991). *Understanding the representational mind.* Harvard, MA: The MIT Press.

Perris, E.E., & Clifton, R.K. (1988). Reaching in the dark toward sound as a measure of auditory localization in infants. *Infant Behavior and Development, 11,* 473–491.

Peters, A.M. (1977). Language learning strategies: does the whole equal the sum of the parts? *Language, 53,* 560–573.

Peters, A.M. (1983). *The units of language acquisition.* Cambridge: Cambridge University Press.

Peters, A.M. (1987). The role of imitation in the developing syntax of a blind child. *Text, 7,* 289–311.

Peters, A.M. (1994). The interdependence of social, cognitive, and linguistic development: Evidence from a visually impaired child. In H. Tager-Flusberg (Ed.), *Constraints on language acquisition: Studies of atypical children* (pp. 195–220). Hillsdale, NJ: Lawrence Erlbaum Associates Inc.

Peters, A.M. (1995). Strategies in the acquisition of syntax. In P. Fletcher & B. MacWhinney (Eds.), *The handbook of child language* (pp. 462–482). Oxford, UK: Blackwell.

Peters, A.M., & Menn, L. (1993). False starts and filler syllables: Ways to learn grammatical morphemes. *Language, 69,* 743–777.

Peterson, C.C., & Siegal, M. (1995). Deafness, conversation and theory of mind. *Journal of Child Psychology and Psychiatry, 36,* 459–474.

Piaget, J. (1937). *La construction du réel chez l'enfant.* Neuchâtel, Switzerland: Delachaux et Niestlé.

Piaget, J. (1959). *La formation du symbole chez l'enfant. Imitation, jeu et reve. Image et representation.* Neuchâtel, Switzerland: Delachaux et Niestlé. (Spanish version: *La formación del símbolo en el niño.* México: Fondo de Cultura Económica, 1961.)

Piaget, J. (1971). El lenguaje y el pensamiento desde el punto de vista genético. In J. Piaget, *Seis estudios de Psicología* (pp. 111–124). Barcelona, Spain: Barral Editores. (Original work published 1964 in French: *Six études de Psychologie.* Genéve, France: Editions Gonthier.

Piaget, J., & Inhelder, B. (1948). *La représentation de l'espace chez l'enfant.* Paris: Presses Universitaires de France.

Pine, J. (1992). Maternal style at the early one-word stage: re-evaluating the stereotype of the directive mother. *First Language, 12,* 169–186.

Pine, J. (1994). The language of primary caregivers. In C. Gallaway & B.J. Richards (Eds.), *Input and interaction in language acquisition* (pp. 15–37). Cambridge, UK: Cambridge University Press.

Pine, J., & Lieven, E.V.M. (1993). Reanalysing rote-learned phrases: individual differences in the transition to multi-word speech. *Journal of Child Language, 20,* 551–571.

Pine, J.M., Lieven, E.V.M., & Rowland, C.F. (1997). Stylistic variation at the "single-word" stage: relations between maternal speech characteristics and children's vocabulary composition and usage. *Child Development, 64,* 807–819.

Povinelli, D.J., & Eddy, T.J. (1996). What young chimpanzees know about seeing. *Monographs of the Society for Research in Child Development, 61,* 3.

Pozo, J.I., Carretero, M., Rosa, A., & Ochaita, E. (1985). El desarrollo del pensamiento formal en adolescentes invidentes: Datos para una polémica. *Revista de Psicología General y Aplicada, 40,* 369–394.

Preisler, G.M. (1991). Early patterns of interaction between blind infants and their sighted mothers. *Child: Care, Health and Development, 17,* 65–90.

Preisler, G.M. (1995). The development of communication in blind and in deaf infants—similarities and differences. *Child: Care, Health and Development, 21,* 79–110.

Preisler, G.M. (1997). Social and emotional development in blind children: A longitudinal study. In V. Lewis & G. Collis (Eds.), *Blindness and psychological development in young children*. Leicester, UK: British Psychological Society Books.

Premack, D., & Woodruff, G. (1978). Does the chimpanzee have a theory of mind? *Behavioral and Brain Sciences, 1,* 515–526.

Pring, L. (1988). The "reverse generation" effect: A comparison of memory performance between blind and sighted children. *British Journal of Psychology, 79,* 387–400.

Prizant, B.M. (1983). Language acquisition and communicative behavior in autism: toward an understanding of the "whole" of it. *Journal of Speech and Hearing Disorders, 48,* 296–307.

Rattray, J. (1997). What can we learn about communication from visually impaired infants? Paper presented at the 7th European conference on developmental psychology. Rennes, France.

Réger, Z. (1986). The functions of imitation in child language. *Applied Psycholinguistics, 7,* 323–352.

Rescorla, L. (1980). Overextension in early language development. *Journal of Child Language, 7,* 321–335.

Reynell, J. (1978). Developmental patterns of visually handicapped children. *Child: Care, Health and Development, 4,* 291–303.

Reynell, J. (1979). *Manual for the Reynell–Zinkin scales: Developmental scales for young visually handicapped children*. Windsor, UK: NFER Publishing Company.

Rieser, J.J., Hill, E.W., Talor, C.R., Bradfield, A., & Rosen, J. (1992). Visual experience, visual field size, and the development of nonvisual sensitivity to the spatial structure of outdoor neighbourhoods explored by walking. *Journal of Experimental Psychology: General, 121,* 210–221.

Rivière, A., Belinchón, M., Pfeiffer, A., & Sarriá, E. (1988). *Evaluación y alteraciones de las funciones psicológicas en autismo infantil*. Madrid, Spain: CIDE.

Rivière, A., & Coll, C. (1987). Individuation et interaction avec le sensoriomoteur: Notes sur la construction génetique du sujet et de l'object social. In M. Siguán (Ed.), *Comportament, cognition, conscience: La psychologie à la recherche de son object* (pp. 64–87). Paris: Presses Universitaires de France.

Rogers, S.J., & Puchalski, C.B. (1984). Development of symbolic play in visually impaired young children. *Topics in Early Childhood Special Education, 3,* 57–60.

Rogers, S.J., & Puchalski, C.B. (1988). Development of object permanence in visually impaired infants. *Journal of Visual Impairment and Blindness, 82,* 137–142.

Rogow, S.M. (1981a). Developing play skills and communicative competence in multiply handicapped young people. *Journal of Visual Impairment and Blindness, 75,* 197–202.

Rogow, S.M. (1981b). The appreciation of riddles by blind and visually handicapped children. *Education of the Visually Handicapped, 13,* 4–10.

Rosa, A. (1980). Las operaciones de conservación y seriación en los sujetos privados de visión. *Revista de Psicología General y Aplicada, 35,* 1007–1021.

Rosa, A. (1981). Imagenes mentales y desarrollo cognitivo en niños ciegos de nacimiento. *Estudios de Psicología, 4,* 24–67.

Rosa, A. (1993). Caracterización de la ceguera y las deficiencias visuales. In A. Rosa & E. Ochaita (Eds.), *Psicología de la ceguera* (pp. 19–49). Madrid, Spain: Alianza Editorial.

Rosa, A., & Ochaita, E. (1988). ¿Qué aportan a la psicología cognitiva los datos de la investigación evolutiva en sujetos ciegos? *Infancia y Aprendizaje, 41,* 95–102.

Rosa, A., & Ochaita, E. (eds.). (1993). *Psicología de la ceguera*. Madrid, Spain: Alianza Editorial.

Rosch, E. (1973). On the internal structure of perceptual and semantic categories. In T.E. Moore (Ed.), *Cognitive development and the acquisition of language* (pp. 111–144). New York: Academic Press.

Rosch, E. (1978). Principles of categorization. In E. Rosch & B.B. Lloyd (Eds.), *Cognition and categorization* (pp. 27–48). Hillsdale, NJ: Lawrence Erlbaum Associates Inc.

Ross, S., & Tobin, M.J. (1997). Object permanence, reaching, and locomotion in infants who are blind. *Journal of Visual Impairment and Blindness, 91,* 25–32.

Rowland, C. (1983). Patterns of interaction between three blind infants and their mothers. In A.E. Mills (Ed.), *Language acquisition in the blind child: Normal and deficient* (pp. 114–132). Kent, UK: Croom Helm.

Rowland, C. (1984). Preverbal communication of blind infants and their mothers. *Journal of Visual Impairment and Blindness, 78,* 297–302.

Sarriá, E., & Rivière, A. (1991). Desarrollo cognitivo y comunicación intencional preverbal: Un estudio multivariado. *Estudios de Psicología, 46,* 35–52.

Scaife, M., & Bruner, J.S. (1975). The capacity for joint visual attention in the infant. *Nature, 253,* 265–266.

Schaffer, H.R. (1984). *The child's entry into the social world.* New York: Academic Press.

Schaffer, H.R. (1996). *Social development.* Oxford, UK: Blackwell.

Schlesinger, H.S. (1987). Effects of powerlessness on dialogue and development: Disability, poverty, and the human condition. In B. Heller, L. Flohr, & L.S. Zegans (Eds.), *Psychosocial intervention with sensorially disabled persons* (pp. 1–27). London: Grune & Stratton.

Searle, J. (1969). *Speech acts: An essay on the philosophy of language.* Cambridge, UK: Cambridge University Press.

Secadas, F. (1988). *Escala observacional del desarrollo* [Observational scales of development]. Madrid, Spain: TEA Ediciones.

Seelye, W. (1983). Physical fitness of blind and visually impaired Detroit public school children. *Journal of Visual Impairment and Blindness, 77,* 117–118.

Shatz, M. (1978). Children's comprehension of their mother's question-directives. *Journal of Child Language, 5,* 39–46.

Shum, G., Conde, A., & Díaz, C. (1992). Pautas de adquisición y uso del pronombre personal en la lengua española: Un estudio longitudinal. *Estudios de Psicología, 48,* 67–86.

Slobin, D.I. (1973). Cognitive prerequisites for the development of grammar. In C.A. Ferguson & D.I. Slobin (Eds.), *Studies of child language development* (pp. 175–208). New York: Holt, Rinehart & Winston.

Slobin, D.I., Gerhardt, J., Kyratizis, A., & Guo, J. (1996). *Social interaction, social context and language.* Hillsdale, NJ: Lawrence Erlbaum Associates Inc.

Slossen, R.L. (1984). *Slossen Intelligence Scale.* Aurora, NY: Slossen Educational Publications.

Smith, N.V. (1973). *The acquisition of phonology: A case study.* Cambridge, UK: Cambridge University Press.

Snow, C. (1983). Saying it again: The role of expanded and deferred imitations in language acquisition. In K.E. Nelson (Ed.), *Children's Language, Vol. IV* (pp. 29–58). Hillsdale, NJ: Lawrence Erlbaum Associates Inc.

Snow, C.E. (1994). Beginning from baby talk: Twenty years of research on input in interaction. In C. Gallaway & B.J. Richards (Eds.), *Input and interaction in language acquisition* (pp. 1–12). Cambridge, UK: Cambridge University Press.

Snow, C.E., Perlmann, R., & Nathan, D. (1987). Why routines are different? Towards a multiple-factors model of the relationship between input and language acquisition. In K.E. Nelson & A. Van Kleeck (Eds.), *Children's language, Vol. VI* (pp. 65–98). Hillsdale, NJ: Lawrence Erlbaum Associates Inc.

Sorce, J.F., Emde, R.N., Campos, J.J., & Klinnert, M.D. (1985). Maternal emotional signaling: Its effects on the visual cliff behavior of 1-year-olds. *Developmental Psychology, 21,* 195–200.

Sostek, A.M. (1991). Development of the blind child: Implications for assessment and intervention. In D. Keating & H. Rosen (Eds.), *Constructivist perspectives in developmental psychopathology and atypical development* (pp. 193–201). Hillsdale, NJ: Lawrence Erlbaum Associates Inc.

Speidel, G.E. (1989). Imitation: A bootstrap for learning to speak? In G.E. Speidel & K.E. Nelson (Eds.), *The many faces of imitation in language learning* (pp. 151–179). Berlin, Germany: Springer-Verlag.

Speidel G.E., & Nelson, K.E. (1989). A fresh look at imitation in language learning. In G.E. Speidel & K.E. Nelson (eds.), *The many faces of imitation in language learning* (pp. 1–21). Berlin, Germany: Springer-Verlag.

Spelke, E.S., & Cortelyou, A. (1981). Perceptual aspects of social knowing: Looking and listening in infancy. In M.E. Lamb & L.R. Sherrod (Eds.), *Infant social cognition: Empirical and theoretical considerations* (pp. 61–83). Hillsdale, NJ: Lawrence Erlbaum Associates Inc.

Stern, D.N. (1985). *The interpersonal world of the infant: A view from psychoanalysis and developmental psychology*. New York: Basic Books.

Stine, E.L., & Bohannon, J.L. (1983). Imitations, interactions and language acquisition. *Journal of Child Language, 10,* 589–603.

Stone, W., Lemaneck, K., Fishel, P., Fernandez, M., & Attmeier, W. (1990). Play and imitation skills in the diagnosis of autism in young children. *Pediatrics, 86,* 267–272.

Streri, A. (1993). *Seeing, reaching, touching: The relations between vision and touch in infancy* (T. Pownall & S. Kingerlee, Trans.). Cambridge, MA: MIT Press. (Original work published 1991)

Sugarman, S. (1984). The development of preverbal communication. In R. L. Schieffelbusch & J. Pickar (Eds.), *The acquisition of communicative competence* (pp. 23–67). Baltimore: University Park Press.

Tager-Flusberg, H. (Ed.) (1994a). *Constraints on language acquisition: Studies of atypical children.* Hillsdale, NJ: Lawrence Erlbaum Associates Inc.

Tager-Flusberg, H. (1994b). Dissociations in form and function in the acquisition of language by autistic children. In H. Tager-Flusberg (Ed.), *Constraints on language acquisition: Studies of atypical children* (pp. 175–194). Hillsdale, NJ: Lawrence Erlbaum Associates Inc.

Tager-Flusberg, H., & Calkins, S. (1990). Does imitation facilitate the acquisition of grammar? Evidence from a study of autistic, Down's syndrome and normal children. *Journal of Child Language, 17,* 591–606.

Tillman, M.H. (1967). The performance of blind and sighted children on the Weschsler Intelligence Scale for children: Study II. *International Journal for the Education of the Blind, 4,* 106–112.

Tillman, M.H. (1973). Intelligence scales for the blind: A review and implications for research. *Journal of School Psychology, 11,* 80–87.

Tobin, M. (1972). Conservation of substance in the blind and partially sighted children. *British Journal of Educational Psychology, 42,* 192–197.

Tobin, M. (1994). *Assessing visually handicapped people: An introduction to test procedures.* London: David Fulton Publishers.

Tomasello, M. (1995). Joint attention as social cognition. In C. Moore & P.J. Dunham (Eds.), *Joint attention: Its origins and role in development* (pp. 103–130). Hillsdale, NJ: Lawrence Erlbaum Associates Inc.

Tomasello, M. (1999). *The cultural origins of human cognition.* Cambridge, MA: Harvard University Press.

Tomasello, M., & Call, J. (1997). *Primate cognition.* Oxford, UK: Blackwell.

Tomasello, M., Kruger, A.C., & Ratner, H.H. (1993). Cultural learning. *Behavioral and Brain Sciences, 16,* 495–552.

Trevarthen, C. (1980). The foundations of intersubjectivity: Development of interpersonal and cooperative understanding in infancy. In D. Olson (Ed.), *The social foundations of language and thought: Essays in honor of J.S. Bruner* (pp. 316–342). New York: Norton.

Trevarthen, C., & Hubley, P. (1978). Secondary intersubjectivity: Confidence, confiding and acts of meaning in the first year. In A. Lock (Ed.), *Action, gesture and symbol: The emergence of language* (pp. 183–229). NY: Academic Press.

Triana, B. (1991). Las concepciones de los padres sobre el desarrollo: Teorías personales o teorías culturales. *Infancia y Aprendizaje, 54,* 19–39.

Tronick, E., Als, H., Adamson, L., Wise, S., & Brazelton, T.B. (1978). The infant's response to entrapment between contradictory messages in face-to-face interaction. *Journal of the American Academy of Child Psychiatry, 17,* 1–13.

Tronick, E., Als, H., & Brazelton, T.B. (1977). Mutuality in mother–infant interaction. *Journal of Communication, 27,* 74–79.

Tröster, H., & Brambring, M. (1994). The play behavior and play materials of blind and sighted infants and preschoolers. *Journal of Visual Impairment and Blindness, 88,* 421–432.

Ungar, S., Blades, M., & Spencer, C. (1995). Visually impaired children's strategies for memorising a map. *British Journal of Visual Impairment, 13,* 27–32.

Ungar, S., Blades, M., & Spencer, C. (1996).The ability of visually impaired children to locate themselves on a tactile map. *Journal of Visual Impairment and Blindness, 90,* 526–535.

Ungar, S., Blades, M., & Spencer, C. (1997). Teaching visually impaired children to make distance judgements from a tactile map. *Journal of Visual Impairment and Blindness, 91,* 163–174.

Urwin, C. (1978). The development of communication between blind infants and their mothers. In A. Lock (Ed.), *Action, gesture, and symbol: The emergence of language* (pp. 79–108). London: Academic Press.

Urwin, C. (1979). Preverbal communication and early language development in blind children. *Papers and Reports on Child Language Development, 17,* 119–127.

Urwin, C. (1983). Dialogue and cognitive functioning in the early language development of three blind children. In A.E. Mills (Ed.), *Language acquisition in the blind: Normal and deficient* (pp. 142–161). London: Croom Helm.

Urwin, C. (1984a). Communication in infancy and the emergence of language in blind children. In R.L. Schieffelbusch & J. Pickar (Eds.), *The acquisition of communicative competence* (pp. 479–524). Baltimore: University Park Press.

Urwin, C. (1984b). Language for absent things: Learning from visually handicapped children. *Topics in Language Disorders, 4,* 24–37.

Vihman, M. (1996). *Phonological development: The origins of language in the child.* Oxford, UK: Blackwell.

Von Tetzchner, S., & Martinsen, H. (1981). A psycholinguistic study of the language of the blind: I. Verbalism. *International Journal of Psycholinguistics, 7–3*(19), 49–61.

Vygotsky, L.S. (1978). *Mind in society: The development of higher psychological processes.* Cambridge, MA: Harvard University Press.

Vygotsky, L.S. (1986). *Thought and language.* Cambridge, MA: MIT Press.

Walker, E., Tobin, M., & McKennell, A. (1992). *Blind and partially sighted children in Britain: The RNIB survey, Vol. 2.* London: HMSO.

Warren, D.H. (1984). *Blindness and early childhood development.* New York: American Foundation for the Blind.

Warren, D.H. (1994). *Blindness and children. An individual differences approach.* New York: Cambridge University Press.

Watson, J.S. (1985). Contingency perception in early social development. In T.M. Field & N.A. Fox (Eds.), *Social perception in infants* (pp. 157–176). Norwood, NJ: Ablex.

Webster, A., & Roe, J. (1998). *Children with visual impairments: Social interaction, language and learning.* London: Routledge.

Weist, R.M. (1991). Spatial and temporal location in child language. *First Language, 11,* 253–267.

Wellman, H.M., & Estes, D. (1986). Early understanding of mental entities: A reexamination of childhood realism. *Child Development, 57,* 910–923.

Wellman, H.M., & Woolley, J.D. (1990). From simple desires to ordinary beliefs: The early development of everyday psychology. *Cognition, 35,* 245–275.

White, K.R., Taylor, M.J., & Moss, V.D. (1992). Does research support claims about the benefits of involving parents in early intervention programs? *Review of Educational Research, 62,* 91–125.

Wills, D.M. (1979). Early speech development in blind children. *The Psychoanalytic Study of the Child, 34,* 85–117.

Wilson, B., & Peters, A.M. (1988). What are you cookin' on a hot?: Movement constraints in the speech of a three-year-old blind child. *Language, 64,* 249–273.

Wilson, J., & Halverson, H.M. (1947). Development of a young blind child. *Journal of Genetic Psychology, 71,* 155–175.

Wimmer, H., & Perner, J. (1983). Beliefs about beliefs: representation and constraining function of wrong beliefs in young children's understanding of deception. *Cognition, 13,* 103–128.

Wishart, U.G., Bower, T.G.R., & Dunkeld, J. (1978). Reaching in the dark. *Perception, 7,* 382–387.

Wyatt, L., & Ng, G.Y. (1997). The effect of visual impairment on the strength of children's hip and knee extensors. *Journal of Visual Impairment and Blindness, 91,* 40–46.

Zazzó, R. (1948). Images du corps et conscience de soi. *Enfance, 1,* 29–43.

Zazzó, R. (1969). *Les débilités mentales.* Paris: Librairie Armand Colin.

Author index

Subject index